To Katharine and Steve

Reading's Abbey Quarter

An Illustrated History

John Mullaney

[signature: John Mull...]

Christmas 2014

© John Mullaney 2014

All rights reserved

No part of this book may be reproduced in any form
by photocopying or by any electronic or mechanical means,
including information storage or retrieval systems,
without permission in writing from the copyright
owners and publishers of this book.

ISBN 978-0-9572772-7-4

Published by Scallop Shell Press

29 Derby Road,

Caversham,

Reading.

RG4 5HE

FOREWORD

The Abbey Quarter in Reading is rich in history; it is also one of the most attractive parts of the town. Beneath its soil lie undiscovered treasures which may one day tell us more about its past.

Within the Abbey Quarter there are buildings by some of England's greatest architects. Moreover from the middle ages to the twenty-first century the area has been a seat of learning. Once it housed a magnificent library and just over one hundred years ago Reading University began its life here. Today it is the cultural heart of the town.

In this book I have traced the evolution of the story of the buildings which surround the open space we call the 'Forbury'. Where possible I have used illustrations, photographs and maps to show how and when the changes took place. In the 19th century the Abbey Ruins themselves were, at one point, in danger of being totally removed to make way for a housing estate. At another time the Inner Gateway, an icon of Reading's heritage, collapsed. There were suggestions it should be demolished. Fortunately it was rebuilt.

And so this a story of beginnings, of change, of degeneration and regeneration. History has no end and the story of Reading is still being written. How that story unfolds depends on an almost incalculable array of factors. However the decisions that we, the people of Reading, take today will be among the most telling of those influences.

John Mullaney, October 2014.

READING'S ABBEY QUARTER

CONTENTS

PART 1   AN HISTORIC OVERVIEW

Chapter 1.   The Abbey Quarter under the Tudors   1

Beginnings; Dissolution of the Monasteries; The Execution of Abbot Hugh, 1539; The Route of Abbot Hugh's Execution; The Abbey Lands and Property after the Dissolution; The Forbury after the Dissolution; The Abbey under Edward VI and Mary Tudor, 1547-1558; Elizabeth 1 1558-1603 and the Charter of 1560.

Chapter 2.   The Abbey Quarter in the 17th and 18th Centuries   9

Civil War, 1642-1645 and the Siege of Reading, 15-25 April, 1643; Sir Arthur Aston and the Forbury; The Commonwealth and the 1650 Survey; The Restoration of the Monarchy 1660; Clarges-Dalby –Blagrave-Vansittart; The 18th century – Illustrations of the Abbey Ruins; Sir Henry Englefield and the Beginnings of Scientific Archaeology; Sir Henry Englefield's Plan of the Abbey Ruins 1779.

Introduction to Part 2   20

PART 2   FROM ABBEY RUINS TO TODAY'S BUILDINGS

Chapter 1.   The Monks' Private Buildings;   21

The Cloisters and the Refectory; The Chapter House; South Transept, Passageway and Treasury; The Domestic Buildings in Modern Times.

Chapter 2.   The Abbey Church   27

The Nave and North Transept; Early 19th Century Excavations; The Abbey Church; The Abbey and the Great Ditch; The Lady Chapel; The Lady Chapel Site and the Prison; The County Gaol and Bridewell or House of Correction; 18th Century Changes; The New County House of Correction 1786; The Town Bridewell-Greyfriars; Other Prisons and Lockups; The Compter Gateway and the Hole; The Shades.

Chapter 3.   The Forbury County Gaol 1786-1844   42

Plan of the County Gaol and house of Correction 1828; Living Conditions; Punishment; The Guard Room; The Female Wards, 1824; The Garden and Orchard, 1826-1834, The Bakehouse and other outbuildings 1826; Debtors Ward, 1827; The Male Juvenile Section, 1831

Chapter 4.   Reading Gaol 1844-2014   47

Planning the New Prison; The Basement Area; Plan of Reading Gaol 1844; The New Prison in Use; Staffing; 19th Century Developments, (Flour Mills, Stone Breaking, Prisoners' Photographs, Executions, Other Structural Changes, The End of Capital Punishment, Oscar Wilde). The 20th Century; (1914-918 War, The Interwar Period 1920 –1939, War 1939 –1945, 1945-1969, 1969 –1978); Closure of the Prison, 2013.

Chapter 5.   St James' Church and School   63

St James' Church and the Site of the North Transept and High Altar of the Ancient Abbey. 1830-1840; Saving the Ruins; The Building of St James' Church; The Opening of the Church; The Pugin Design of St James' Church; The School Buildings; The Changing Face of the Abbey Ruins and St James' in Plans and in Pictures.

Chapter 6.   Abbots Walk. The Abbey Inner Gateway. The Abbey Mill   77

Abbots Walk; The Abbey Inner Gateway; 18th Century Views from the South; 18th Century Views from the North; The Abbey Gateway in the 19th Century (The Question of Ownership, The Restoration of 1861); The Abbey Mill; The Excavations of the Abbey Mill, 1964-1967; The Mill after 1960;

Introduction to Part 3   98

PART 3   THE SOUTH SIDE OF THE FORBURY

Chapter 1.   The Assize Courts and the Shire Hall   99

The Assize Courts and the Central Police Station; The Shire Hall

Chapter 2.	Between Shire Hall and St Lawrence's Church	103

Historical background: The Abbey Garden -The Open Space: Sutton's Royal Seed Establishment: The Prudential Building and Forbury Square: Pageant House, No 22 The Forbury.

PART 4   THE WESTERN EDGE OF THE ABBEY QUARTER

Chapter 1.	St Lawrence's Church and the Compter Gate	115

The Founding of St Lawrence's Church: The Compter Gate: The West End: The Three Faces of No 1 Friar St: The East End.

Chapter 2.	The Hospitium and the Municipal Buildings	124

The Hospitium of St John: The Parts of the Hospitium (1. The Residence, or Almshouse, 2. The Refectory, 3. The Dormitory): The First Reforms: The Hospitium 1539 –1786: Reading Grammar School: Victorian Developments: The Municipal Buildings 1870-1939: The Heart of Education in Reading: The British Dairy Institute: Reading Police Station and Magistrates' Court.

PART 5   THE FORBURY GARDENS

Chapter 1.	The War Years 1793 –1815	142

The Forbury and the Military:

Chapter 2.	The Forbury: 1815 to 1840	147

The Lay-out of the Forbury: The Open Space: The Hill: The Green: Some More Events in the Western Forbury 1800–1840.

Chapter 3.	The Creation of the Forbury Gardens 1840 –1860	156

The Coming of the Railway: The Eastern Forbury –

The Pleasure Gardens 1854–1860: The Abbey Ruins South of the Chapter House:

Chapter 4.	The Creation of the Forbury Gardens 1860 –1919	166

The Two Forburys: The Maiwand Lion: The Bandstand:

READING'S ABBEY QUARTER

Memorials to Henry I (The Forbury Cross, The Chapter House Commemorative Tablets

The Two Forburys; The Maiwand Lion; The Bandstand; Memorials to Henry I, (The Forbury Cross, The Chapter House Commemorative Tablets); The Victoria Gate.

PART 6   PLANS AND DEVELOPMENTS 1919 – 2000

Chapter I   Plans and Developments 1919 – 1939   175

The War Memorial; Proposals for Developing the Forbury; The Abbey Wall.

Chapter 2   The War Years 1939 –1945   179

Chapter 3   Plans and Developments 1945 – 2000   180

The Abbey Wall Area; The Forbury Road; The Abbey Mill; The Abbey Stables and Reading Library; The 1971–1973 Excavations of Reading Abbey; Reading Library 2014.

POSTSCRIPT   186

Trooper Potts

CONCLUSION   188

APPENDICES

Appendix A   Reading Abbey's Wealth at the Dissolution, 1539.   189

Appendix B   Inscriptions on St. James' Font, The Reading Abbey Stone.   189

Appendix C   The Discovery of the Reading Abbey Stone by James Wheble   189

Appendix D   Roger Amyce.   190

Appendix E   Record of Marriages and Burials at Reading Abbey   191

SOURCES AND FURTHER READING   193

NOTES   194

INDEX   207

ACKNOWLEDGMENTS   215

READING'S ABBEY QUARTER

Model of the Abbey in Reading Museum.
Details from the model appear on pages 104 and 124

Copyright Reading Museum (Reading Borough Council).
All rights reserved.

PART 1 AN HISTORIC OVERVIEW

CHAPTER 1   THE ABBEY QUARTER UNDER THE TUDORS

Beginnings

One of the great pleasures of travelling through England is discovering a cathedral and the green space in front of it: the cathedral close. It is often the last haven of calm in a busy commercial centre.

Reading may have lost its Abbey but it still has its green.

This book is an account of how, despite the destruction of the Abbey, despite becoming a major fortification in the Civil War, despite plans by private and public owners alike to build over it, despite being neglected, used as a rubbish tip and as a cattle market, despite all this, Reading managed to retain its green: the Forbury. It is also the story of what happened to the Abbey buildings: how some were destroyed and replaced, whilst others were adapted and are in use to this day.

The picture opposite shows what the area may have looked like just before the Dissolution of the Abbey in 1539. In the centre is the great west end of the Abbey Church. Immediately in front of this is the Inner Gateway, one of the few buildings still standing today.

Several tracks radiate out from the Gateway and to its left a broad pathway leads to the West or Compter Gate which abuts St Lawrence's Church.[1] The Compter Gate has now gone but the church still stands. Immediately north of the church are the buildings, including the guest dormitory and refectory of the Hospitium, which welcomed medieval pilgrims to Reading. Beyond are various outbuildings, probably used as workshops, and the North Gate. Along the north edge is the Plummery Brook, so called after the lead workings so essential to building the Abbey and its maintenance.

Within this ancient area, laid out over 900 years ago, lies the space which today we call the Abbey Quarter.

The Dissolution of the Monasteries

To discover why Reading still has this unique historic site, it is necessary to look back five hundred years to the Abbey and its destruction. Reading Abbey once not only dominated the town and regulated its trade and governance, but owned the land that today we call the Abbey Quarter. Our survey starts with the political and religious turmoil which began in the reign of Henry VIII, culminating in the Protestant Reformation under Elizabeth I.

The Reformation of the Catholic Church in England was justified, both at the time and later, by the need to cleanse a corrupt institution. The Dissolution of the Monasteries was one step in this process. Whether this was a mere cloak used by Henry VIII to cover his real purpose is a matter disputed over the centuries. Opinion often depends on which side in the great religious divide, Catholic or Protestant, one stands.

Did Henry break with Rome over a sincere belief that his marriage to Catherine of Aragon was a 'mortal sin'? As a staunch supporter of traditional Catholicism, as *defensor fidei*, did he believe the church needed internal reform?[2] Did he believe that the acquisition of Abbey lands and their wealth was a justifiable way of defending the realm against foreign influence and even invasion? Alternatively, was Henry's real purpose to fill his empty coffers and at the same time bolster his own power and underpin this by seizing the wealth of the monasteries, keeping much to himself but also distributing it to buy support? For some idea of the wealth this generated see Appendix A.

What is incontestable is that the claim by the Crown to own these church lands, and their income, brought about one of the greatest changes in property ownership in the history of England.

A Royal Commission, under the directorship of Thomas Cromwell, was appointed to enquire into the morals of all the monasteries, convents and priories in the kingdom. In 1539 the Commission came to Reading. Interestingly no fault could be found with the spiritual or temporal practices at Reading. The Commissioner, John London, writing to Cromwell, stated that *they have a gudde lecture in Scripture dayly in their Chapiter House both in Inglisch and Laten, to which is gudde resort, & the Abbot ys at yt himself.*[3] It was concluded that the financial affairs of Reading were also in good order. In spite of this, Henry claimed that the Abbot, Hugh Cook of Faringdon, by maintaining the rights of the Papacy over monastic land, had committed treason. Confiscation of the Abbey and its wealth and the trial of the Abbot were the consequences.

The Execution of Abbot Hugh Faringdon, 1539

The beautiful peaceful space outside the Abbey now became a place of brutal tragedy. Along with John Eynon and John Rugge, two of his fellow monks, Abbot Hugh was imprisoned in the Tower of London and finally brought to Reading to be tried. At the trial, where he was allowed no defence, he was accused of denying the supremacy of Henry VIII as Head of the Church of England. The jury consisted of local gentry whom the Abbot must have known well, many of them being long-standing tenants of the Abbey.[4]

It is likely that the trial was held in the manorial court over the Inner Gateway to the Abbey, next to the Abbot's house. The record of Abbot Hugh's last day shows that on the 14th or 15th of November, having been condemned to death,

PART 1. CHAPTER 1. THE ABBEY QUARTER UNDER THE TUDORS

he was stretched out and tied to a hurdle, then dragged through the streets of Reading.

It was reported that crowds gathered all along the way. Many spat at the Abbot and threw excrement. We know that he was dragged from the Abbey Gateway past the three main churches of the town: St Lawrence's, St Mary's and St Giles', and so back to the Forbury where some accounts say a 40ft gibbet had been erected. The likely spot was outside the great west door, opposite his own Abbot's lodgings. Here on the green, in front of the great abbey church, it is said that over a thousand of the townspeople gathered to witness the execution.

His sentence was to be put to death by hanging, drawing and quartering. In this form of punishment the prisoner was hanged but in such a way as to leave him conscious. The spinal cord was not broken, so allowing the disembowelling and burning of his entrails to be done whilst the prisoner was still alive. The limbs were then cut off: quartered. We have just seen that Abbot Hugh was first tied to a hurdle and dragged, or drawn, around the town. This is the origin of the phrase 'hanged, drawn and quartered' and it should read as 'drawn, hanged and quartered'. It was reserved as the punishment for treason and used sparingly before Elizabeth I's reign. However, either because the executioner was incompetent or because he took pity on the Abbot, Hugh died when he was hanged. John Rugge and John Eynon, sometimes spelt 'Onions', were also subsequently executed Eynon had been the priest in charge of St Giles' church.

The Inner Gateway to the Abbey

READING'S ABBEY QUARTER

The Route of Abbot Hugh's Execution

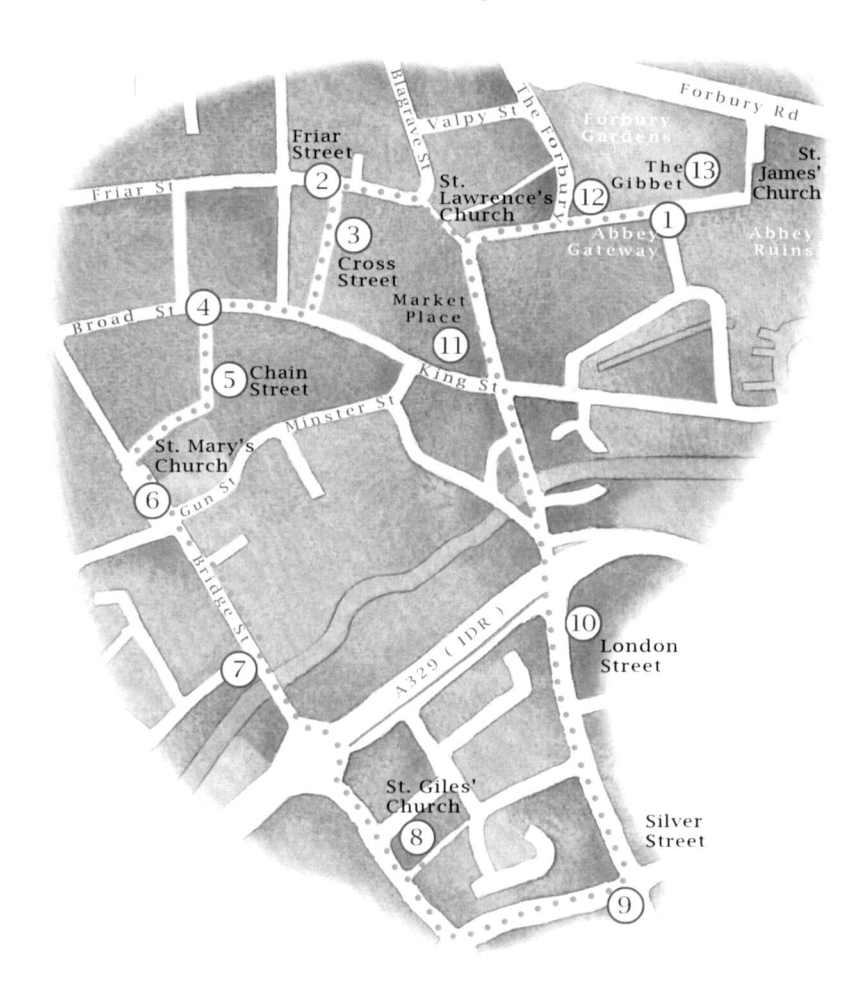

THE ROUTE OF ABBOT HUGH'S MARTYRDOM

1: The Abbey Gateway   2: New Strete (Friar St)   3: Gutter Lane (Cross St)
4: Broad St   5: Chayne Lane (Chain St)   6: Old Strete (The Butts)
7: Seaven Bridges (Bridge St)   8: St Giles Strete (Southampton St)   9: Siever Strete (Silver St)   10: London St   11: Shomakers Row (Market Place)   12: The Forbury
13: The Gibbet – (most probably in front of the Abbey Gateway)

PART 1. CHAPTER 1.   THE ABBEY QUARTER UNDER THE TUDORS

The Abbey Lands and Property after the Dissolution

Prior to these dramatic and vicious events, Thomas Cromwell had appointed Sir Thomas Vachell of Coley to make an inventory of the Abbey's goods and on the 17th of September many of its treasures had been removed. These included jewels and relics from the shrines, valuable sacred vessels and vestments.[4] Around the same time the monks and lay-servants were ejected from the monastery.

Vachell was put in charge of portable wealth whilst an outsider to Reading, Sir William Penison, thought to be of Italian origin, was responsible for the buildings. With Cromwell's fall from grace in 1540, Henry VIII appointed Penison as chief steward of the Borough. Under a new charter, granted by Henry, the burgesses of the town now had the right to chose their own mayor.[6] In 1541 Vachell became mayor of the town.

The Forbury after the Dissolution

All the Abbey property now passed to the Crown. Consequently Henry ordered that royal accommodation should be provided and the Abbot's old lodging was chosen for this purpose. New royal stables were established in the dormitory of the old Hospitium. It was at this time that we learn that Henry granted the profits of the two annual fairs to Penison.

Soon, in the reign of Edward VI, two extra fairs were created with their profits going to Edward Seymour, the Lord Protector. These were to be held in *le utter* (the outer) *courte in Reading called le Forbury.*[7]

It is not surprising that we encounter one of the few early references to the Forbury in connection with its financial worth. Just as there are detailed accounts relating the value of the Abbey property as it was sold off, so the value of the Forbury was measured by the income it could generate.

The Monks of Reading Abbey

Some fifteen years after the Dissolution, when the Catholic monarch Mary was on the throne, some of the monks were given pensions and annuities. By putting names to these faceless men, who merely go down in history as the *monks of Reading Abbey*, we can be touched by the more human element that lay behind those tragic and momentous events in the history of Reading.

Below are the names of some of these monks, companions of Abbot Hugh, who doubtless were numbered among those who had attended *gudde lecture in Scripture dayly in their Chapter House* and suffered at the hands of Henry VIII.

*John Jennys, John Fycas, John Wright:
John Harper, John Mylles, Elias Burgess,
John Turner, Philip Mathewe,
Luke Whitehorn, Thomas Taylor,
Robert Raynes, John Southe,
Richard Purser, Richard Butts.*
(Their first names in the original document are in Latin.)

Above – the Seal of the Abbey shows Henry 1 holding his Abbey and flanked by Saints Peter and Paul

The Abbey under Edward VI and Mary Tudor. 1547–1558

The fact that we hear little about the Forbury through the reigns of Edward VI and Mary Tudor helps to explain why this area was untouched and why it remained so for about a century. There was no attempt to build over it or divide it up into smaller plots. It was left unscathed, probably because its value lay in remaining as an open space for the fairs.

Under Edward VI, the King's uncle, Edward Seymour, the Duke of Somerset, along with Sir Richard Sackville, Chancellor of the Court of Augmentation, set about the systematic degradation of the Abbey. The Court of Augmentation had been created by Henry VIII to take control of, and manage, the accounts of the dissolved monasteries.

The Court appointed George Hynde to oversee the work. Hynde has left us detailed records of the disposal of the Abbey's assets, primarily the precious lead, but also stone and other materials from the Abbey. The result was that by 1549 most of the buildings had been gutted and stood roofless, open to the elements. Somerset was eventually found guilty of profiteering to his own personal advantage from the sale of monastic property. With his execution in 1552 the Abbey area reverted once again to the Crown. In fact King Edward made a Royal visit to Reading and stayed in *Kynges place,* namely the Royal apartments.

However it is only under his successor, Mary Tudor, that we again have mention of the Forbury. Mary retained Royal possession of the Abbey lands and appointed Sir Francis Englefield as its keeper. Englefield effectively became the governor of Reading.

A significant change to the use of the Forbury took place during Mary's reign. In 1556 the burial arrangements for parishioners of St Lawrence's were altered. The bodies of parishioners had previously been interred in an area outside the north wall of the Abbey church. A section of the Forbury alongside St Lawrence's was now allocated for this purpose. Small though this change may appear it would have considerable consequences for the layout of the Forbury and its relationship with St Lawrence's, and indeed the town, in later years.

Elizabeth I. 1558–1603 and the Charter of 1560

Within two years of her accession Elizabeth had granted Reading a new Charter.[8] Dated the 23rd of September, 1560, it formed the basis of the Corporation of Reading's civic status, its rights and its duties, many of which last to modern times.

With the return of a Protestant monarch, Englefield, a staunch Catholic, chose voluntary exile. His lands and property were confiscated and the Abbey once more came directly under the control of the Crown. In addition Englefield's

PART 1. CHAPTER 1. THE ABBEY QUARTER UNDER THE TUDORS

powers as governor of the town were mainly transferred to the Corporation, thereby strengthening its authority.

We learn much about the status of Reading from this Charter. Its 62 clauses cover all aspects of the town and its governance. For the first time the Charter granted the Corporation rights over sections of the old Abbey site, especially around St Lawrence's Church and the Hospitium.

For example, the school, which had been founded by Henry VII in the old Hospitium building, was given over to the town. The Charter granted the mayor and burgesses *our house and tenement or messuage with the appurtenances called the Scholhouse in Redinge aforesaid.*

Also included in the Charter were areas of the Forbury, including the North Gate, the Compter Gate and other various small properties such as two tenements near the *cage* or prison which stood alongside the south side of St Lawrence's Church.

It should be noted also at this point that the Blagrave family had begun to buy up leases on former Crown lands in this part of the former Abbey property. The west side of the Forbury also contained the vicarage for St Lawrence's and other smaller properties. Consequently the Corporation became the largest landholder in the area.

With regard to the open part of the Forbury, the Charter confirmed the right to hold the two extra fairs first granted to Seymour, making a total of four in all. These new fairs were to be held in February, (Candlemas), and September, (Michaelmas), and were to last three days. Having mentioned that the value of the Forbury lay in the income it could generate from fairs it is worth drawing attention to the importance contemporaries placed on specifying the area for this purpose, leaving no room for doubt about their location. It was stated that they *were to be holden and kept yearly in a certain place called the Forbury within the limits of the same Borough.*

Through this Charter the Corporation, and so the people of Reading, now had a legal right of entry to, and specified certain rights over, the area known as the Forbury. The story of the Forbury, and indeed of the whole Abbey Quarter, over the following three hundred years, is about how the town managed to maintain its *liberties* or rights over this area.

Land rights often entail the need for clear maps. The earliest known map of Reading was drawn by John Speed. This was part of his much larger work covering much of the country. Between 1608 and 1610 Speed published a series of fifty-four 'Maps of England and Wales'. His work had begun under Queen Elizabeth and continued through the reign of James I.[9] Although not designed for the purpose of delineating the Forbury, Speed's map most certainly would have helped in this respect.

READING'S ABBEY QUARTER

Speed's map of Reading shows the main features of the Abbey Quarter, many of which are recognisable today, although there are some clear inaccuracies.

Below is a detail taken from this map.

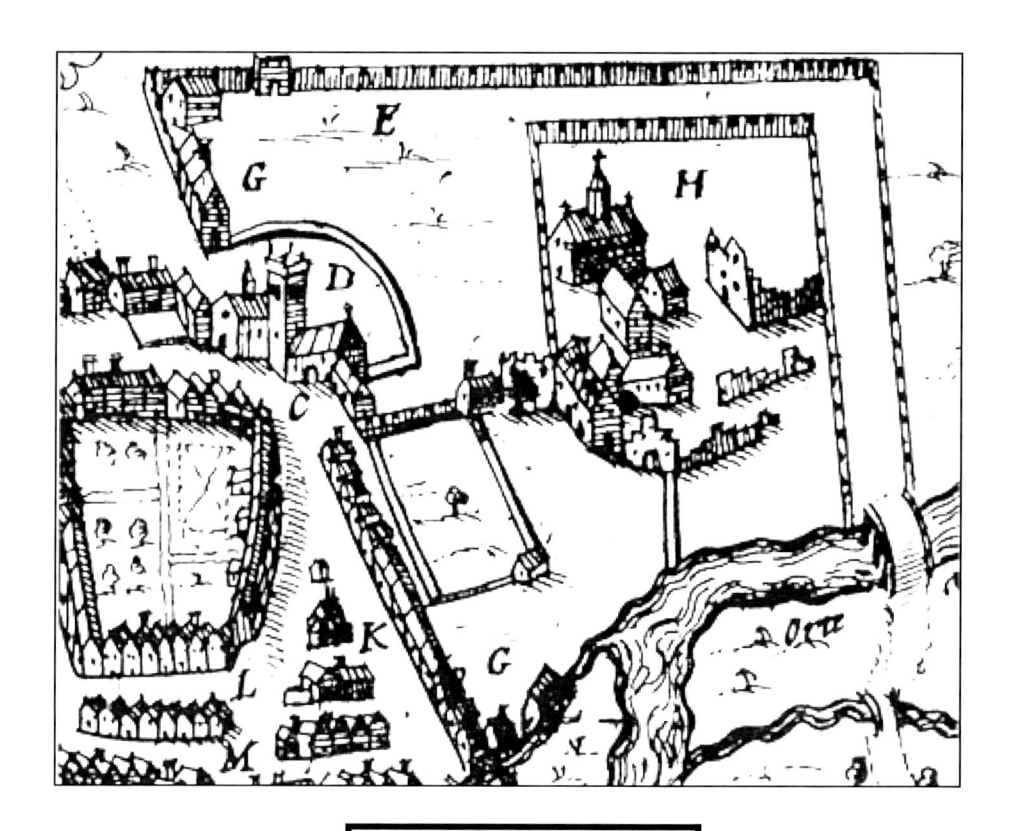

Detail from John Speed's
Atlas of Great Britain
1610-11

.Key adapted from the original

C	The Free School
D	St Laurence
E	The Forbury
G	Stables
H	The Abbey
K	Schomakers Row

CHAPTER 2

THE ABBEY QUARTER IN THE 17TH AND 18TH CENTURIES

The Civil War, 1642-1645, and the Siege of Reading, 15-25 April, 1643

The early years of the 17th century saw little change in the status of the area. In 1625 Charles I is reported to have stayed in the Royal residence, but to a great extent the town was left alone to carry on its trade and administer its own affairs. However, with the outbreak of Civil War in 1642, Reading found itself at the centre of the conflict which was to change the face of the town and of the Abbey Quarter.[1]

Henry Marten had been appointed to oversee the Parliamentarian defences of Reading. However, on receiving news of the King's advance along the Thames Valley, he withdrew to London.[2] Sir Arthur Aston was appointed Royalist Governor of Reading. He constructed a line of defences both by utilising the natural features of the town, namely its many waterways and marshy approaches, and by creating a formidable array of ramparts. Before the war Charles I did not wish to be seen to be allying himself too closely with the Catholic cause. Consequently Aston, a Catholic, had been dismissed from the King's service in 1641. Nevertheless, with the outbreak of the Civil War, Charles needed all the experienced generals he could muster and Prince Rupert persuaded the King to appoint Aston as Colonel General of the Dragoons. There can be no doubting Aston's abilities as a soldier. He distinguished himself at Edgehill and successfully commanded the defences in Reading, Oxford and finally Drogheda, where he met his end in 1649.

Competent as he was as a soldier, he was also overbearing and severe even by the standards of his day. It was reported that he hanged at least two people in Reading, more as an example to those who would challenge his authority than as a punishment following proof of guilt. He was resented by both his own troops and by the people of the town. This was equally true when he became governor of Oxford in 1643. Here he attacked the Mayor of Oxford and was relieved of his command by Charles. However he successfully built up Reading's defences and held out against much superior Parliamentarian forces under the Earl of Essex. The above map shows the defences before Aston constructed the 'great ditch' through the Forbury. This was a continuation of the ramparts which surrounded Reading, as seen on the complete map reproduced on the next page.

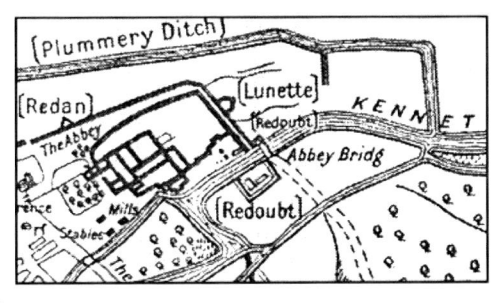

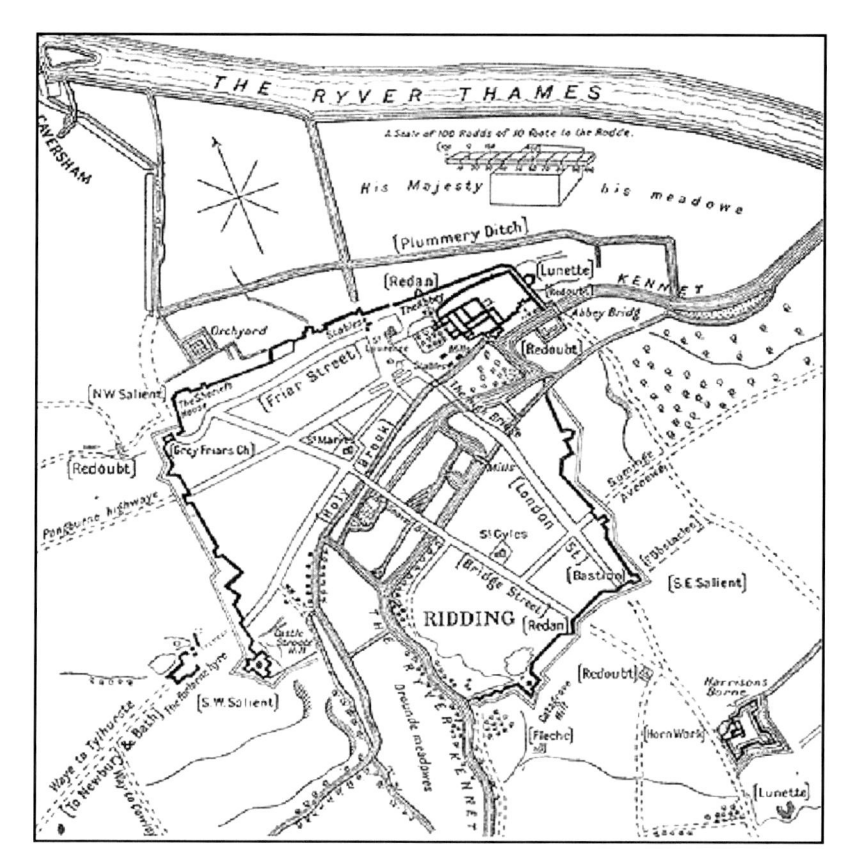

Civil War map held in the Bodleian library. This map was drawn before the Great Ditch was dug from the Cloisters through the Nave and across the Forbury as far as the Hill.[3] The dark heavy line marks the ditch and rampart which almost totally encircled Reading. The only sections not so defended were where the River Kennet and The Holy Brook, along with their associated marshy ground, gave the defenders a natural advantage.

Sir Arthur Aston and the Forbury

To strengthen the eastern approaches to the town Aston required a more secure position than that offered when he took over command. An examination of the map above shows how vulnerable to attack Reading was along the eastern approaches of the Thames and Kennet valleys. The Forbury offered the only naturally defensible position, surrounded as it was by two rivers and various 'ditches'. It was also situated on high ground, dominating the approaches to the town from the east.

The problem lay with what remained of the Abbey church, especially the great

PART 1. CHAPTER 2. THE ABBEY QUARTER IN THE 17TH AND 18TH CENTURIES

tower and northern transept. It may seem ironic that a Catholic general should be the one to finish off the work of the destruction of the great church. But, as we have seen, sentiment was not one of Aston's attributes. During the winter the town walls had been strengthened with stone obtained from Reading Abbey and the town's defences were further reinforced by a system of ditches, earthworks and forts. Even today visitors can see, next to St. James' church, two huge blocks of ruins that lie at an angle where they came crashing down. One theory is that Aston set a mine under the northern part of the old Abbey Church to give a clear line of fire for the cannon set upon the Hill.[4] He had raised the height of the latter and from it he constructed a defensive ditch and rampart which ran across the Forbury towards the Abbey cloisters, cutting through what remained of the nave and so down to the River Kennet.

There is another explanation of the mine, namely that it was ordered by Charles in 1644, after the Royalists had retaken the town but decided it was not worth retaining. In this case the mine was part of the slighting of the defences before surrendering Reading to the Parliamentarian forces for the final time.

Whichever account, if indeed either, is accurate the events of this period had long term consequences for the Forbury.

The appearance of that section of the Forbury Gardens, which partially covers the area once occupied by the Abbey church nave, dates to this period. The differences in today's terrain between the flat western section and the contoured eastern part of the Forbury Gardens may also be dated to this period in the town's history.

The two fallen blocks beside St James' Church.

Notice the slanting angle of the flints. This is the result of the walls and towers of the Abbey church having fallen some considerable distance, possibly after being blown up by a mine.

Also visible are some of the larger stone blocks embedded in the flint. These may be parts of the ashlar lining which covered the flint core.

READING'S ABBEY QUARTER

The Commonwealth and the 1650 Survey

Parliament's victory entailed the transfer of all former Royal property to the state.

Parliament commissioned a survey in 1650 which gives invaluable information about Reading and former Abbey property.

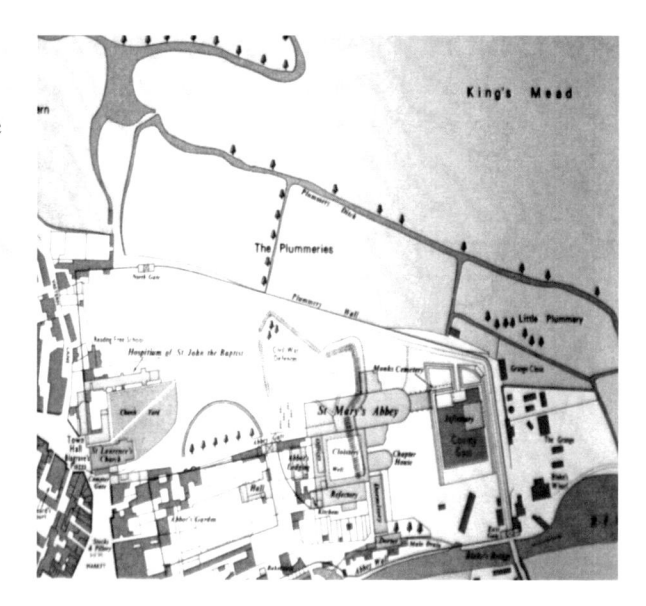

Map: *Historic Towns*, CF Slade

We have seen that there is some dispute as to whether the Abbey towers were blown up by Aston or later. We do know that Parliament considered that the *town is so full of inlets ... that it is almost impossible to make it tenable unless it is fortified as formerly ... In the meantime we intend to fortify the abbey and to make two forts.* This appears to be the limit of work carried out by Parliament in Reading for the remainder of the war and as we shall see it is possible that the 'two forts' were either not built or never completed.

The Survey of 1650 gives us a unique insight into the state of Reading after the vicissitudes of war. It was undertaken to ascertain the extent of the ex-crown property that was now under Parliamentary jurisdiction.

Crown land in Reading had been concentrated around the Abbey so the Survey provides invaluable detail concerning the Abbey Quarter at that time. It reports for example about:

1 The old Stable Block – by the Holy Brook with its yard and garden.

2 The Mill – described as a granary

3 The Porters Lodge by the west gate, near St Lawrence's church, which had cellars, a hall, buttery, three chambers and three garrets with a small yard and garden.

4 The former royal residence occupied by Richard Knollys, which had *two cellars, two butteries a hall a parlour a dining room ten chambers a garret, two*

PART 1. CHAPTER 2. THE ABBEY QUARTER IN THE 17TH AND 18TH CENTURIES

courtyards and a large gatehouse with several rooms adjoining to the said house and a small garden with an old small house built with stone.

We also learn that there was a stable, a dove house and a small garden measuring two acres. This latter was most probably the private garden pertaining to the abbot's lodgings.

But most important to our researches about the Forbury is the following statement: *There is, belonging to the said abbey, one court walled round called by the name of Forbury ... In which the towne doeth yearly keep foure fairs, and doth now lye common, and through which there are several waies, as passages, into and out of the kings' mead into the great barne and lodgings there.*

In other words Parliament recognised the Corporation's right to hold these fairs and to control access to the Forbury. So confident was the Corporation that, if challenged, it was ready to stand up for these rights or *liberties*. When a Colonel Hammond attempted to erect a gate and styles to restrict access, the Corporation claimed jurisdiction by saying only *so as he do in no measure prejudice the liberties of the town. For if he do the Town will endeavour to defend their liberties.*

Not only was the town now taking its rights over the Forbury to another level but it was also accepting its duties and obligations in caring for the area. An important example of this came in 1652. The Corporation took on the responsibility of restoring the Forbury by levelling the defensive ditch *whereby fairs may be kept and the inhabitants of the town enjoy their privilege as formerly.*

If one considers that the *great ditch* was reported to be 15 feet wide, with ramparts which some Parliamentarian accounts had put at the height of a house, then this was no slight undertaking. Yet records indicate that the levelling process was completed quickly since in 1653 it was stated that *the next cattle fair within this borough on St James' day next shall be kept in the Forbury and nowhere else.*

The Restoration of the Monarchy, 1660

With the restoration of the Monarchy, in 1660, former Crown lands were restored to Charles II. However the King showed little interest in his property in Reading. Unlike many of his predecessors he never stayed in the town and a year after the Restoration he leased the Abbey site to Sir Thomas Clarges for 40 shillings a year. The Royal Stables were, however, retained by the crown and expenditure made on their maintenance.

A dispute arose between Clarges and the Crown over the terms of his lease. During the 1650s several houses had been built in the Forbury. Clarges contended that these were included in his lease and that rent was therefore due to him from the Crown. Judgement was made in his favour and in 1667, by way of compensation, his lease was extended to 50 years and he received £160 back-rent for the properties mentioned. The important feature of this dispute was that, although Clarges established his rental rights against the Crown, he was forced to concede that his rights vis-à-vis Reading Corporation in the Forbury were very limited.

The Corporation was determined to keep the Forbury open for the *four fairs throughout the Forbury as granted by their Charter and that Sir Thomas Clarges be spoken with to remove all incroachments there.* A new era had begun. Individuals could now claim certain rights according to their leases. However Reading Corporation retained overall control of the Forbury and at times it was ready to enter into legal dispute with the tenants, leaseholders and 'landowners' of both the Abbey Ruins and the Forbury to *defend their liberties.*

Clarges—Dalby –Blagrave –Vansittart

The story of the Forbury and the Abbey Ruins, over the next century or so, is intimately connected with these four families. It must be remembered that this 'ownership' was, on the whole, in the form of leases. Reading Corporation owned some areas granted to them by the Crown. The terms of the leases mainly concerned *users' rights,* especially in the Forbury.

In 1723 Clarge's grandson sold his lease to John Dalby and Anthony Blagrave. The Blagrave family, as we saw on page 7, had already begun to acquire an interest in the Forbury.

John Dalby, steward of Reading to 1760, was in debt so that on his death his son Thomas and his widow sold their lease to Henry Vansittart. In 1780 the Crown lease to Blagrave and Vansittart was extended by 21 years but at an increased cost. So it was that the major part of the Abbey ruins and the Forbury passed to these two families.

View across the Forbury to Caversham Bridge and St Peter's Church. 1791.[5]

PART 1. CHAPTER 2. THE ABBEY QUARTER IN THE 17TH AND 18TH CENTURIES

There were other minor holdings but as a general guide the eastern section of the Forbury, following a north-south line bisecting the Gateway, belonged to Vansittart, whilst the area west of this belonged to Blagrave.

Let us look at how the various areas of the Abbey Quarter fared through the 18th century

The 18th century – Illustrations of the Abbey Ruins

Apart from building other houses amongst the old ruins and against the remaining walls, no effort was made to maintain them. In fact they were regarded more as a useful quarry or dumping ground rather than as possessing any intrinsic value.

For instance, in 1754, General Conway used *several massive pieces of wall which could not easily have been reduced* for building a bridge at Wargrave. This was construed at the time as a great work of philanthropy, but in hindsight much valuable archaeological information must have been lost.

It is during the 18th century that for the first time we come across sketches and plans of the Ruins and the Abbey Gateway. Many of them are inaccurate, fanciful representations. As the century progresses the influence of the *Picturesque* movement becomes evident. Nevertheless when viewed together they help build a picture of the area before the population explosion of the 19th century. Incidentally very often it is the dress and the activities of the people shown in the background which gives these illustrations even greater interest.

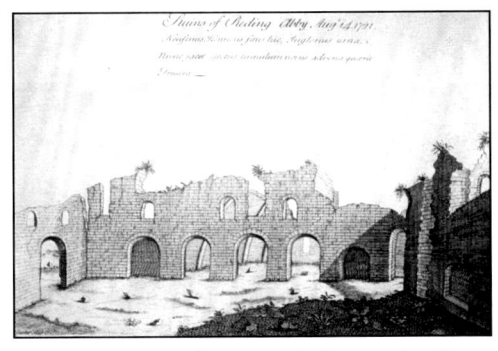

William Stukeleys' drawings of 1721 are among the first, if not the first, of the Abbey. View from the west of the Chapter House from the Cloisters. (See plan on page 21). [6]

A more 'picturesque' version of Stukeley's drawing. [7]

1773. Godfrey / Renoldson. View from the south. The Refectory wall is to the fore, in front of the openings leading to the Chapter House. [8]

1786. Page-Boswell. View from the north of the two fallen blocks, looking through to the entrance to the Cloisters. [9]

1791. Tomkins. View from the east of the south transept, St Lawrence's church just visible, through a large window arch, in the background. [10]

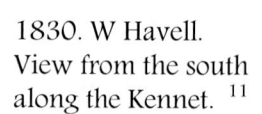

1830. W Havell. View from the south along the Kennet. [11]

PART 1. CHAPTER 2. THE ABBEY QUARTER IN THE 17TH AND 18TH CENTURIES

Sir Henry Englefield and the Beginnings of Scientific Archaeology

If the *Picturesque* movement appealed to late 18th and early 19th century ideas of Romanticism and fanciful representation, this was countered by the rationalism of the Age of Enlightenment which also characterised the 18th century. Sir Henry was a man of his times: a man both of the sciences and of the arts.

Sir Henry was a descendent of Sir Francis Englefield.[12] He owned the Whiteknights estate and, like his ancestor, he was a staunch Catholic. He was an important figure in Reading and his achievements have left their mark to the present. In 1778 he was elected a Fellow of the Royal Society, and in the following year Fellow of the Society of Antiquaries, eventually becoming its vice president, then president. However, because of his Catholicism, he was subsequently replaced by the Earl of Aberdeen. Under his direction the Society produced a series of engravings of English cathedrals. He also carried on research in chemistry, mathematics, astronomy, and geology. His *Discovery of a Lake from Madder*, a treatise on textile dyes, won for him the gold medal of the Society of Arts.

An association with the family lives on today in the shape of the Earley Charity. As its website says: *this has assumed the role of one of the major local charities in central southern England which it has done in two ways. First, it built a beautifully appointed high-quality residential care home for local elderly people, Liberty of Earley House, which it continues to run, and secondly, it has developed a wide-ranging and innovative programme of grant-making both to individuals and to organisations in the neighbourhood of Earley.* It was money from the Englefield bequest that allowed this charity to be established and to flourish.[13]

As a Catholic he also helped his co-religionists in Reading as the laws proscribing Catholic practice were repealed during the latter part of the 18th century. Thanks to his generosity the small Catholic community in Reading received church furnishings and vestments when their first chapel was opened in Finch's Buildings in 1792. These gifts were transferred to the purpose-built, 'Chapel of the Resurrection', when it was opened in 1811. The church of St James in the Abbey Ruins has its origins in this early community and the founder of the Chapel of the Resurrection is buried in front of the altar, just as the founder of Reading Abbey, Henry I had been buried in front of its own high altar.[14]

But Englefield's most visible monument must be the Ruins themselves. As the 19th century expansion of Reading put pressure on the value of land for industrial development and housing, the Ruins offered a tempting space for expansion. Gradually the people of Reading and the Corporation came to value their ancient heritage but it was no foregone conclusion that the Ruins would survive. Englefield was one of the first of many whose work helped save the Abbey and its surrounding land from destruction. Later we shall see how the Ruins and the Forbury were rescued and meet some of the people who followed in Englefield's footsteps and worked for their preservation.

Arguably more than any other individual, therefore, Englefield began the process of scientific archaeological study which helped raise public awareness of the importance of the Abbey Ruins to Reading. As a scientist and a Catholic, he was doubly fascinated by the Ruins. Much of our knowledge and, it needs to be said, many of our popular assumptions, date to Sir Henry's excavations and his interpretation of them. Subsequent archaeological work has confirmed rather than questioned Englefield's findings. Indeed as Cecil Slade says, *his is a sober, factual survey and the starting point for modern studies.*[15]

Sir Henry Englefield's Plan and Key of the Abbey Ruins 1779

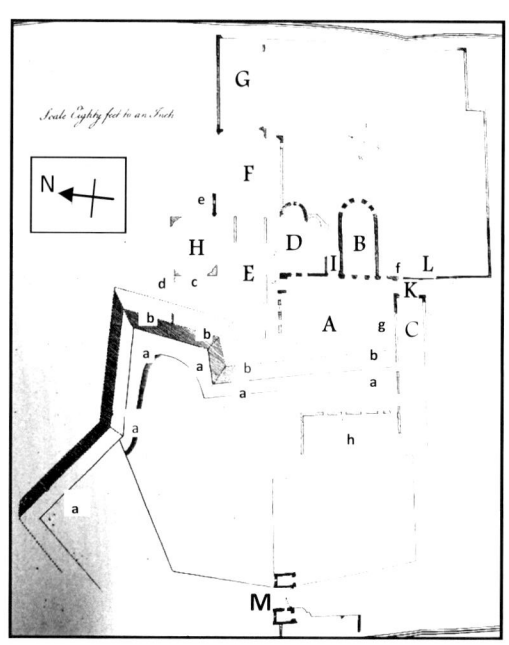

KEY

A The Cloister court — 148 ft sqr
B The Chapter House — 78 by 42
C The Refectory — 72 by 38
D The South Transept of the church
E The Nave of the church
F The Choir of the church
G The eastern chapel of the church (the Lady Chapel)
H The North transept of the church
I A passage vaulted two stories (sic)
K A passage vaulted
L A wall once enclosing two rooms
M The great gate (the Abbey Gateway)

a The top of the rampart thrown up in the civil wars, which crosses the cloister.
b The ditch of the rampart.
c The spot where the mine was sprung.
d The leaning masses of wall.
e A small house built by the late Lord Fane.
f The remains of a stair-case.
g The lavatory.
h Probable situation of the dormitory.

Note that the plan's orientation is such that North is to the left. To help locate the position of the buildings shown and of the earthworks, St James' Church is immediately to the left of the area marked H. The d, below and to the left of the H, described as the leaning masses of wall, lies just to the south of St James' south wall.

PART 1. CHAPTER 2. THE ABBEY QUARTER IN THE 17TH AND 18TH CENTURIES

Overlay map showing St. James' Church and related buildings and outline of the Ancient Abbey, based on Englefield's survey.

The overlay plan uses Englefield's Survey and shows the relationship between the Abbey buildings, the modern Forbury and St James' church.

We have seen Cecil Slade's comments on the importance of Englefield's work. He also notes that Englefield *produced the first modern survey* (of the Abbey) *accompanied by accurate plans and elevations.*[16]

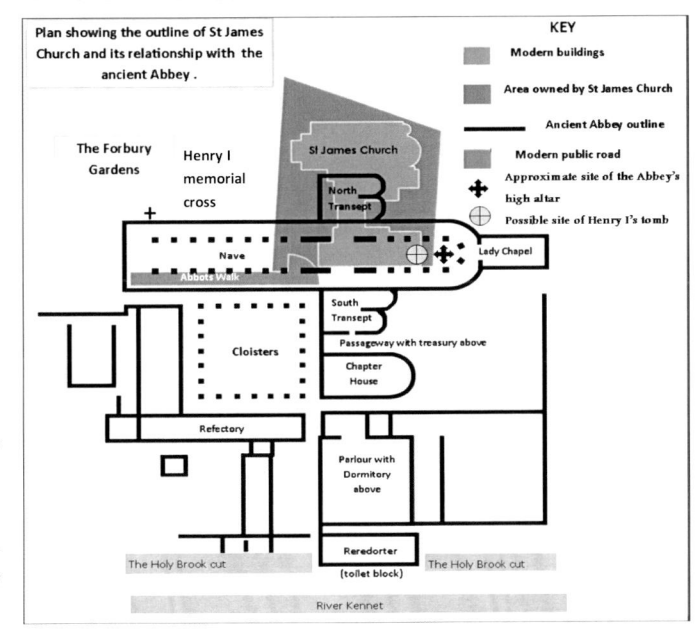

With the benefit of modern aerial photography it is possible to overlay Englefield's plan with that of an absolutely accurate digital image. Where the existing ruins remain, the two coincide in remarkable detail. It would be reasonable, therefore, to accept the accuracy of Englefield's other observations for parts of the Abbey that are no longer extant.

To corroborate this an examination was recently made of part of the ruins rarely looked at: those that remain within the precincts of St James' Church and associated buildings. If Englefield's drawings are accurate then there ought to be the remains of a pillar or respond as part of the third north aisle pillar.

The photograph above shows this is the case and that it is in exactly the correct location. The exposed flint remains, with the base of a respond, are situated exactly as predicted by Englefield. The brick wall to the rear is the modern school building.

READING'S ABBEY QUARTER

Introduction to Part 2

In Part 2 we shall look at the various sections of the ancient Abbey, starting with the Cloisters and working our way to the Inner Gateway and the Abbey Mill. We shall see how these buildings have fared over time and, where relevant, what has replaced them. In the process we shall see some of their history and, where available, trace their evolution, since the Dissolution, through illustrations and photographs.

The Cloisters and the Refectory

The illustration below shows the Cloisters in the centre. The Refectory building is the long pitched roof building. The Chapter House, with its conical east end, is to the right.

PART 2   FROM ABBEY RUINS TO TODAY'S BUILDINGS
CHAPTER 1 THE MONKS' PRIVATE BUILDINGS

The Cloisters and the Refectory

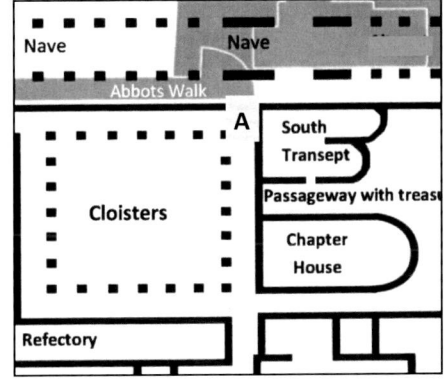

The Cloisters lay immediately to the south of the south aisle of the Abbey Church, just north of the Refectory and to the west of the Chapter House. It was here the monks would both rest and walk in meditation following their meals. They would also solemnly process from the Church, following the chanting of the Divine Office, through the Cloisters to the Refectory or the Chapter House.

The word 'cloister', *claustrum* in Latin, literally mean 'closed off' or 'enclosure' and was a private space for the monks. The term could also be applied to the whole monastery, as the word 'kloster' is used in modern German. The Cloisters' entrance from the church was at the point marked with an **A** on the diagram, through the arched doorway shown in the following illustrations. In many ways the cloisters were the hub of the monastery as they gave access to all the other main buildings of the 'enclosed' area and to the church.

Left: View from the south. This photograph was taken in 1893 and shows two young girls in front of the doorway 'A'. Through the arch the west gable of St James' church can be made out. The wall to the right is part of what remains of the west wall of the south transept. [1]

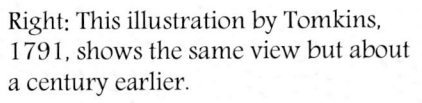

Right: This illustration by Tomkins, 1791, shows the same view but about a century earlier.

The archway has been blocked off and a small wooden door inserted. [2]

The observant viewer may spot the lack of the stonework above and to the left of the opening in the 18th century illustration. The fact that they are clearly shown in the 1786 Boswell drawing on page 16 and the late 19th century photograph above, shows the care one must take in interpreting such sources.

Today there are no remains above ground of the cloister. There are some illustrations dating to the end of the 18th and early 19th centuries which give indications of what the original building may have been like. We have seen that Englefield's survey is the first reliable archaeological study. In the 1830s James Wheble, having bought the Cloisters, intended to excavate them and we know he did uncover some artefacts. In the chapter about St James' church we shall look in greater detail at Wheble's work and his main discovery: the Reading Abbey Stone. However when he died, unexpectedly, in 1840 his son James Joseph evidently did not wish to carry on his father's work and he sold the plot. In a later chapter we shall see how the boundary between the Cloisters and the south aisle of the ancient abbey church was developed.

As for the Cloisters themselves, much of the area was incorporated into the Abbots Walk buildings and their gardens. However, between 1964 and 1967, the area was extensively and professionally excavated.[3]

The Refectory, or dining area, is immediately to the south of the Cloisters. It was here that the monks ate their meals, usually in silence, with one of the community reading from the Scriptures or other suitable writings. The Abbot and senior monks, such as the prior and sub-prior, would have eaten at a high table. Parliament met at Reading on several occasions, having left London on account of the plague. It is said that the Lords met in the Refectory.[4]

Today the area between Abbots Walk and the Refectory wall is laid out as a public space reminiscent of a cloister. Only a section of the south wall remains. The north wall, which features in Stukeley's 1721 drawing, page 15, has disappeared.

The sculpture, 'Robed Figure', by Elizabeth Frink, was placed in the 'cloister garden' in 1988.

PART 2. CHAPTER 1. THE MONKS' PRIVATE BUILDINGS

The Chapter House

Leading off the Cloisters to the east was the Chapter House. In a Benedictine medieval monastery this was the main meeting place for the monks. It was where the community would have met daily and read out a chapter of the Rule of St Benedict, the Bible or some other spiritual text. We should recall that at the time of the Dissolution it was reported that the monks had *a gudde lecture in Scripture dayly in their Chapiter House both in Inglisch and Laten.*

When required the assembled monks would discuss the business of the day and take any decisions deemed necessary concerning the running of the monastery.

The Chapter House also acted as the Great Hall, or *aula magna*, where the monarchs would have held audience on their visits to Reading. We have just seen that when Parliament sat at the Abbey the Lords met in the Refectory. It has been claimed that the Commons met in the Chapter House.

One of the earliest images we have of the Chapter House, was drawn by William Stukeley and published in 1721, as seen on page 15. The view is from the west, looking from where the Cloisters would have stood, into the Chapter House. The barrel vaulting can be made out through the three main arches. On either side of the three open arches are two blocked-off doorways. The arch to the right led to the monks' private quarters, including their dormitory. The one to the left led to a passageway, between the Chapter House and the South Transept, which may have served as a vestry. There are signs that there was an upper floor which may have been the Treasury. The arch to the far left is the entrance from the Cloisters into the south aisle of the church that we saw on the previous page. The wall to the far right was the north wall of the Refectory which no longer stands.

The illustration to the left was drawn by Charles Tomkins in 1791. The view is from the reverse angle to that of Stukeley, as it is looking west, through the arches back towards the Cloisters. It will be noted that all the lower arches in this drawing are blocked off. The barrel vaulting is clearly discernible and there is a thatched wooden lean-to against the south wall.[5]

23

The South Transept, the Passageway and the Chapter House

The South Transept features two rounded apsidal bays. These were a hallmark of Cluniac abbey buildings. Immediately to the left of the Transept is the pitched roof of the passageway between it and the Chapter House. Several suggestions have been proffered as to the purpose of this passageway, the most common being that there was a vestry on the ground floor and a treasury above.

PART 2. CHAPTER 1. THE MONKS' PRIVATE BUILDINGS

Between Englefield's excavations and the 1830s any digging was haphazard and poorly recorded. If anything the romantic ideals of the Picturesque movement prevailed. A ruinous state was considered a charm in its own right and little if anything was done to protect what was left of the ancient Abbey. In 1805 Tomkins made a note about the *several who dig* in the Chapter House. Following the building of the National School a road was constructed connecting it with the main road in the Forbury. This would have entailed some more disturbance as a certain amount of digging was required, but no records were kept of any finds.

Tomkins, c. 1791 [6]

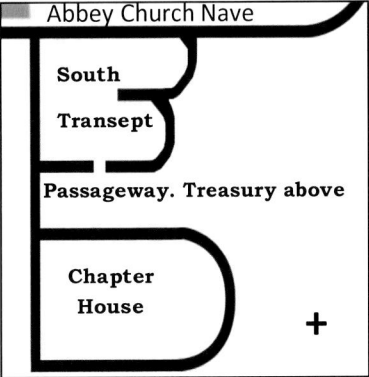

South Transept, Passageway and Treasury

We have seen several views of the Chapter House, the passageway and South Transept. Above right is another similar view from an illustration by Tomkins in 1791. The crosses (+) in the two diagrams indicate the approximate position of the people shown in the drawing.

These two pictures, along with the plan based on Englefield's survey, give an accurate idea of the location and state of the ruins at the turn of the 18th to 19th centuries. Today little remains of the South Transept and this was true when the first drawings were made 250 years ago.

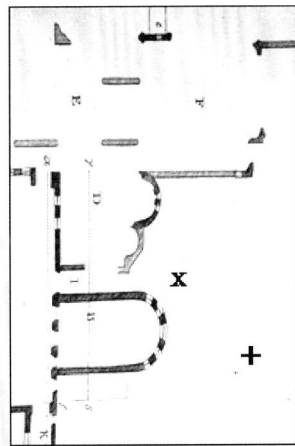

The photograph shows the more southerly chapel of the South Transept with the Passageway arch to the left. The end building of Abbots Walk is visible. An **X** on the diagram, marks the spot from which the photo was taken.

25

The Domestic Buildings in Monastic Times

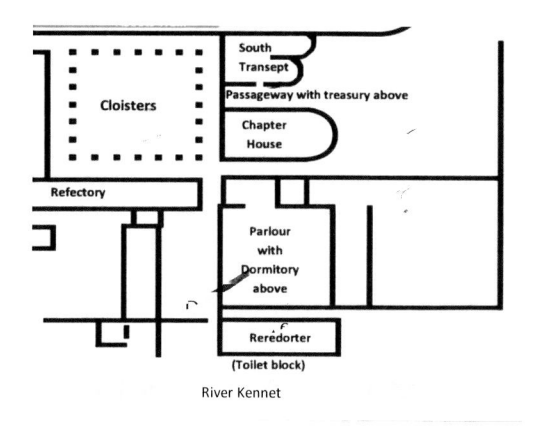

From the Cloisters a far doorway led into a passageway which itself led to a series of domestic buildings. There was a two storey structure which probably housed the monks on the upper floor. At ground level there would most likely have been the Parlour and Warming Room. Behind this was a *necessarium* or toilet block. Some of this survives today although considerably altered. The *necessarium*, also known as the *reredorter*, was served with a cut from the Holy Brook so that the waste from the latrines was flushed away and into the River Kennet. An alternative opinion about its location is discussed on page 91.

Immediately to the west of the Dormitory-Parlour wall was the Refectory.

Very few of the early illustrations show this area in any detail. Being near the Kennet it was used for activities connected with the river and canal. As we shall see in a later chapter, houses were built along the south wall of the Refectory, which itself was much changed over the years.[7] Below are two contemporary photographs of the south wall of the Refectory.

PART 2. CHAPTER 2.   THE ABBEY CHURCH

CHAPTER 2 THE ABBEY CHURCH

The Nave and the North Transept.

We saw how, at the time of the Reformation, the main body of the church was the first to suffer. The roof and leading were stripped off and the furnishings removed. This was in contrast with the Abbot's Lodging and Chapter House. The latter was used in differing ways over the centuries, culminating in the National School. We have seen both in written descriptions and in pictures that various buildings were erected within and around the Chapter House area.

The same sources also allude to similar constructions around the main body of the old Abbey church. Englefield specifically refers to the *small house built by the late Lord Fane*.[1] This is most likely the same as that shown on the 1786 illustration on page 18. Recent measurements would indicate that the ruins against which the house were built are the same remains that today lie within the grounds of St James' church, behind the presbytery. They are shown in the contemporary photograph alongside and marked with an **'e'** on the overlay diagram and copy of Englefield's plan above.

Above: Detail from Englefield's survey with original lettering.

This block, now behind St James' presbytery, is marked as an **e** on Englefield's plan and on the overlay diagram, See also page 16 for the illustration by Boswell showing the *small house*. The brick building is the north wall of the early 20th century school.

27

Early 19th Century Excavations

Following Englefield's survey, later excavations, when they did occur, tended to be in connection with clearing the ground for further building and were rarely undertaken for their own sake or involved making scientific records of any archaeological discoveries.

So we read in Coates' work that in 1793, whilst foundations for the new gaol were being dug in the area of the south transept, *several fragments of glazed tiles* were uncovered. On digging deeper, to about 6 or 7, feet more *fragments of glazed tiles* were uncovered as was p*art of a base of a clustered pillar and a piece of stone with zig-zag ornament of elegant pattern.*[2]

A more exciting find was made in 1815 when a stone sarcophagus was unearthed in the Nave of the old church.

Whether any archaeological digging occurred or finds were made in 1828, when staging was erected for the public to view the public hanging of three men, is not recorded. The three were Burnett, White and Field who had killed a gamekeeper whilst poaching. Reports at the time put the numbers attending the execution at between 16 to 20 thousand people. What impact this had on the grounds themselves we are not told. What it does show is how fast the population of Reading was increasing. It was this pressure in numbers that was to drive future developments and, in one particular case, a different attitude to the Abbey as a place of special significance to Reading.

Much of the eastern section of the old Abbey lands: the Nave, the Cloisters, across to the Abbey Gateway and north to the Forbury Hill, was owned by the Vansittart family. Nicholas Vansittart had been a leading member of several Tory governments. He retired from politics in 1823 and was raised to the peerage as Baron Bexley. By the late 1820s and early 1830s he let it be known that he was considering demolishing his section of the Abbey Ruins to make way for houses and a road to service them.

The 'Berkshire Chronicle' railed against these plans as *an idea worthy only of a Goth or a Vandal.*[3]

It would appear that finally public opinion was beginning to look upon the ancient Abbey Ruins as a civic asset and felt that the elected officers of the town should take some responsibility over their future.

Having looked at the state of the Chapter House and Cloister area we shall now turn our attention to the main body of the Church: its Nave, North Transept and Lady Chapel.

PART 2 . CHAPTER 2.   THE ABBEY CHURCH

The Abbey Church

Whereas the Chapter House and some other residential areas of the Abbey were retained for further use after the Reformation, the great church itself was less fortunate.

We have seen that, almost immediately following the Dissolution, the roof was stripped of its lead and various consignments of stone were used, both officially and unofficially, for buildings in and around Reading and even further afield. Consequently, even by the middle of the 17th century, little was left of the Abbey Church.

Detail from Reading Abbey seal | Detail from John Speed's Atlas of Great Britain, 1611

The earliest images which give us an idea of the look of the church are from the original medieval seals and Speed's Atlas of 1610 –11. Though somewhat stylised they do give us the impression of a church with a nave and a tower topped with a small spire. Neither image shows the existence of the transepts which archaeological evidence clearly indicates were present.

However we do have a 13th century image of Henry I holding his Abbey. Again this is a stylised portrait but it gives us a different view and one that suggests the existence of a transept and a much longer nave than indicated in the previous images. The fact that the east end under the towers and spires does not have the addition of the Lady Chapel is consistent with this having been built at a later date, in 1314.

Although the eastern section was in ruins by the end of the 18th century, at least there were sufficient remains to allow illustrators such as Tomkins and antiquarians such as Englefield to observe the outline of the ancient Abbey church. This was not the case with the Nave and the western end. Today, as then, there is no evidence of these above ground and little archaeology has been done in this area. The last known reference to the Nave as a standing structure was during the Civil War. So it is to this period we must turn to see why so little remains today.[4]

Henry I holding Reading Abbey church. Matthew Paris *Historia Anglorum*

READING'S ABBEY QUARTER

Below are two plans spanning the 150 years or so between the Civil War and Englefield's survey. The third and final image is Slade's composite map of the area. When combined the three maps give a good representation of how and why the area around the Abbey church changed. The 'Great Ditch' radically altered its appearance and destroyed much archaeological evidence.

The Abbey and the Great Ditch

Figure **a** is an extract from the Civil War map already shown on page 9.

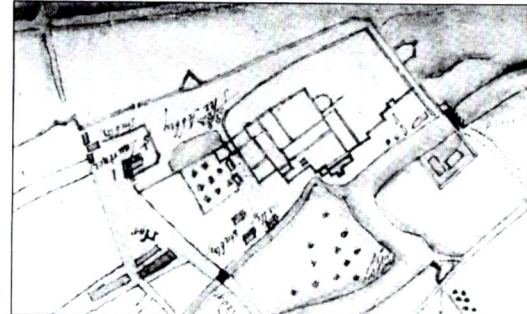

Fig a.

Figure **b** is Englefield's drawing outlining his excavations in 1779, showing his interpretation of the line of the Great Ditch.

A cross, **+**, has been inserted to show the position of the modern church of St James, opened in 1840.

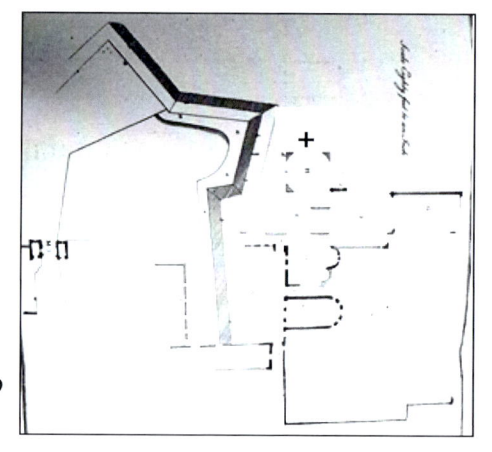

Fig b

Figure **c** is taken from Slade's *Historic Towns*.[5]

It shows in overlay the outline of the Abbey and the Great Ditch created by Aston during the Siege of Reading.

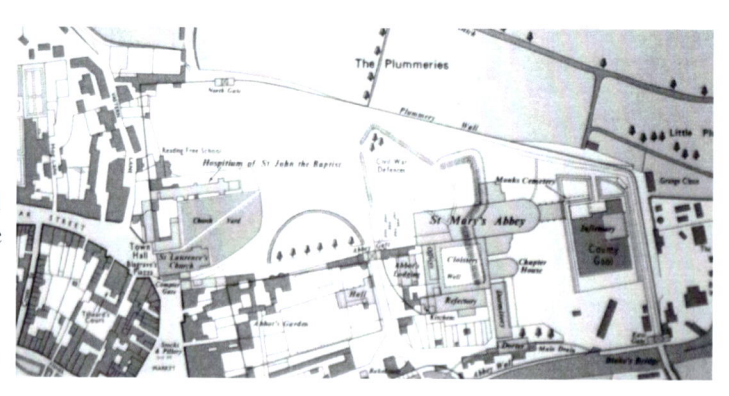

Fig c.

30

PART 2 . CHAPTER 2.   THE ABBEY CHURCH

It is clear that the construction of the 'Great Ditch' had a major impact on the site. It not only completed the destruction of the Nave of the Abbey church and the Cloisters but had profound effects on the future of the Abbey Quarter and any archaeology in the area. It is useful, therefore, to understand more about this Great Ditch. We can do this by looking in detail at Slade's and Englefield's studies of the Ditch.

Figures d^1 and d^2 combine the information given in figures **b** and **c** on page 30.

By inserting the outline of the Abbey as generally agreed, and as given by Slade, we can begin to see the relationship between the military Civil War map and the Abbey buildings.

The top sketch, d^1 shows Slade's findings, whereas the lower one, d^2 is based on Englefield's researches.

There is some slight difference between Englefield and Slade as to the exact line of the Great Ditch (the heavy dark line) but both agree that it ran through the nave and the cloisters.

It may be that the point on Englefield's plan, marked on d^2 with ‡, should coincide with the *redan,* slightly to the west.[6]

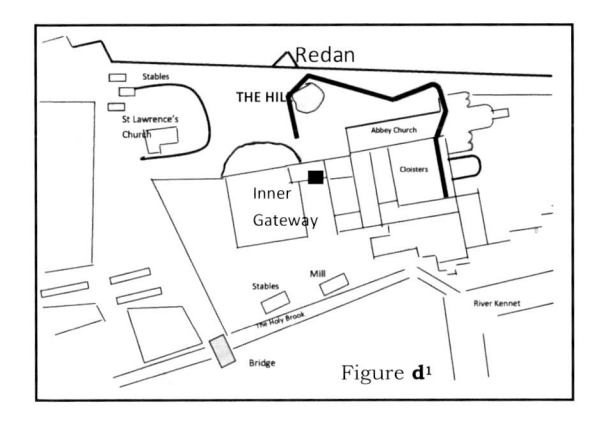

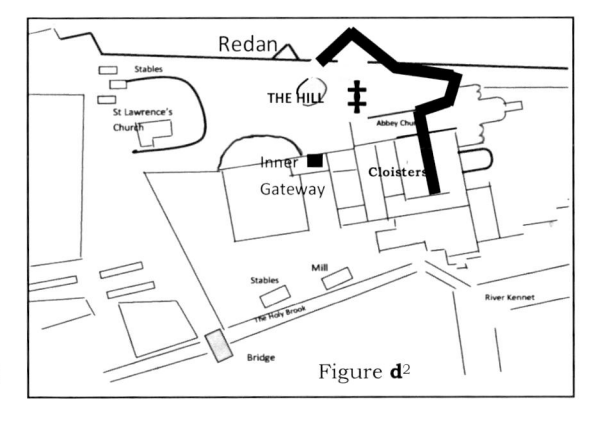

Figure d¹

Figure d²

Whichever plan is more accurate there is no questioning the consequences for what remained of the Nave of the church and the Cloisters. They were totally obliterated. We have also seen that in 1652 the defences were levelled and the ditch filled in. This no doubt not only completed the destruction of the Nave and associated areas to the west of the Transepts and the Chapter House but also caused incalculable damage to any remaining archaeology.

We shall next look at the site of the Lady Chapel. This latter was added in 1314 and was the final part of the ancient Abbey to be built.[7]

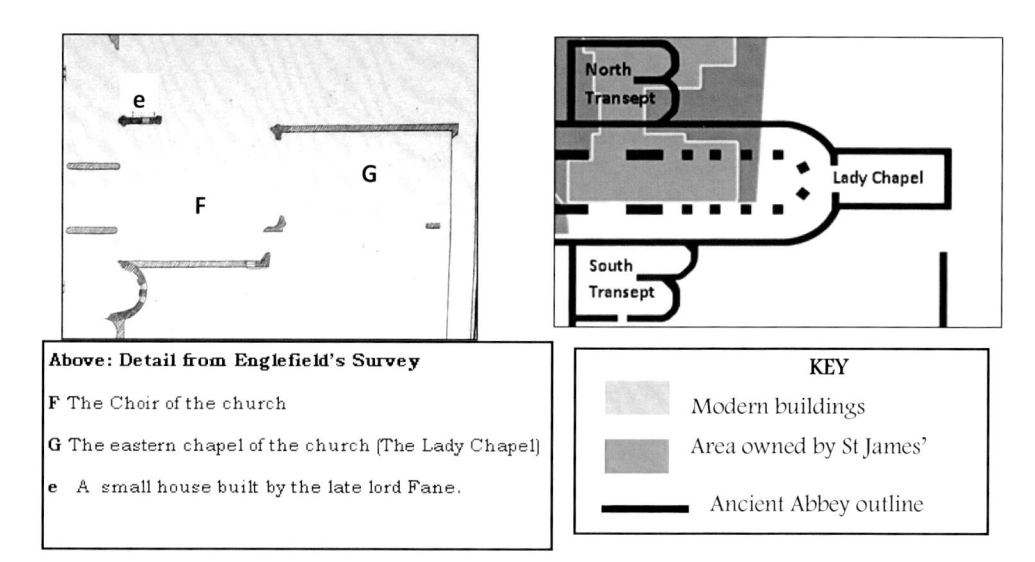

The Lady Chapel

Above: Detail from Englefield's Survey

F The Choir of the church
G The eastern chapel of the church (The Lady Chapel)
e A small house built by the late lord Fane.

KEY
Modern buildings
Area owned by St James'
Ancient Abbey outline

The eastern extension, or Lady Chapel, was added in 1314. It is logical to speculate that this would have been built in the Decorated style, similar to that of the window in St Lawrence's churchyard which has tracery typical of that period. It is more than reasonable to assume that a similar style would have been used in the Abbey's 14th century Lady Chapel. It has even been suggested that parts of this window, though from St Lawrence's, originated from the Lady Chapel itself. (See page 120)

Whereas there are many 18th and early 19th century illustrations of the southern part of the Abbey, there is very little pictorial evidence of the Nave and the Lady Chapel. The Page-Boswell drawing from the north, see page 16, is one of the very few from this angle.

To understand why so little remained by the late 18th century we have to remember that at the Dissolution, and shortly afterwards, this was the area that was most extensively plundered. The Civil War defences demanded yet more destruction so that little remained of the Nave, North Transept and Lady Chapel. Towards the end of the 18th century another development completed the process: the placing of a prison on this site.

Window in St Lawrence's churchyard

PART 2. CHAPTER 2. THE ABBEY CHURCH

The East end of the Abbey and the 14th Century Lady Chapel

The east end of the Chancel is depicted here with its apsidal chapels and rounded apse, constructed in Norman Romanesque style. The Lady Chapel, built in 1314, is in the Decorated style with its distinctive pointed arches, elaborate window tracery, buttresses and decorated pinnacles.

The Lady Chapel Site and the Prison

The site of the Lady Chapel is under part of the area that became Reading Gaol. In order to understand how this came about and discover the origins of the 19th century prison, made famous by Wilde in his poem, *The Ballad of Reading Gaol,* we need to look further back in time at the origins of Reading's prisons and how they evolved.

The County Gaol and Bridewell or House of Correction

There is some evidence that Reading's original gaol was founded in 1314, the same year as the building of the Lady Chapel.[8] The gaol was situated on Castle Street where St Mary's church, (not the Minster Church), now stands. It has been claimed that its original purpose was to hold prisoners who had previously been housed at Wallingford Castle Whether or not this is strictly accurate, we do know, through burial records of St Mary's (the Minster Church), that there was a prison here in the late 16th century. There are even records of births in the gaol. The building was small and designed for felons awaiting trial. The gaolers were unpaid and made their living by charging the inmates for necessities, including food and clothing. It would appear that later the same building was used as a House of Correction, also known as a Bridewell. This type of institution was named after a Royal Palace in the City of London, which was converted in 1553 into a 'house of correction' and an orphanage. The term became widely used for a place of short term punishment for minor offences and to house vagrants.

18th Century Changes

The above arrangements for those guilty of lesser criminal acts and debtors continued well into the 18th century. In 1731 a list of rules regarding the care of prisoners was drawn up by the County Assizes, stipulating the provision of drink and food and the prices to be charged. In 1767 an additional building, adjacent to the existing one in Castle Street, was purchased to create an extension to the prison. These newly acquired buildings were demolished and Collier, a local builder, was engaged to erect a purpose-built addition to the gaol. The improvements included separate rooms for sick male and female prisoners.

In 1779 John Howard, the great prison reformer, visited Reading and reported on its prisons. It was quite clear that the existing provision was insufficient for the town's needs. The pressure on finances, during and following the American War of Independence, further exacerbated the situation. Howard also noted that the buildings housed not merely *nine felons and nine debtors* but also nineteen men who had been taken or 'pressed' to serve in the Royal Navy.

PART 2. CHAPTER 2. THE ABBEY CHURCH

By 1784 the Berkshire Quarter Sessions came to the conclusion that the provision for prisoners in Reading and Wallingford was totally inadequate. The Sessions decided that a completely new, purpose built, House of Correction was needed for the County. The Court of Quarter Sessions also decided not to cooperate with the town, which had its own 'Bridewell' at Greyfriars, but to proceed with a building of their own. The site chosen was at the east end of the Forbury and the architect selected was Robert Furze Brettingham, who had recently designed the High Bridge over the Kennet, a structure that survives to this day.

The New County House of Correction 1786

In 1786 the 'Reading Mercury' reported on the opening of the new House of Correction: *The prison is built on the solitary principle recommended so repeatedly of keeping culprits to themselves; every prisoner having a separate cell and a distinct yard to walk in.*[9]

There was on ongoing debate between those who advocated *the solitary principle* and others who favoured a communal, but *silent*, regime. The controversy was to dominate the theory of prisons for much of the 19th century and, as we shall see, played a significant part in the design of the new Reading Gaol in the middle of the 19th century.

Almost immediately it became clear that, in addition to the need for a new Bridewell or House of Correction, the County Gaol itself in Castle Street, was 'unfit for purpose' and that there was no space for further expansion. However the cost of the new Bridewell had been covered through loans that had to be repaid from the County Rates, consequently it was not felt prudent to borrow yet more money for a new County Gaol. It was therefore decided to combine the two institutions on the same site. George Knight, Keeper of the County Gaol, was appointed at £25 per annum as keeper of both institutions. Collier was finally awarded the building contract at a cost of £3000. This firm was to became famous in Reading for its distinctive brick work, still much in evidence around the town. Once again Brettingham was selected as the architect.

Although convict labour was employed in unskilled heavy clearance work, Collier preferred his own recruited workforce for the main building operations. At first progress was good; the top layer of gravel presented few difficulties. However the workmen soon dug down to the foundations of the ancient Abbey with the remnants of its flint and stone walls. When rebuilding was undertaken in 1972 these again presented a considerable challenge, even with the use of modern powered excavating equipment.

The 18th century builders also encountered human remains as they came across the burial ground of the Abbey. The 'Monks' Cemetery' is marked on the early

18th century historic map of the area as lying immediately to the north east of the Lady Chapel. Whilst work was in progress the 'Gentleman's Magazine' of January 1786 reported that, while digging the foundations of the House of Correction, workmen had uncovered, in a vault, a leaden coffin inside which was a poorly conserved skeleton. It was presumed that the richness of the coffin suggested that this had been a royal burial, but no further evidence was found to corroborate the theory. The plan below shows the siting of the new House of Correction and Gaol according to Slade's map.

Plan showing the ancient Abbey outline, the site of the early 19th century prison and of St James' church.

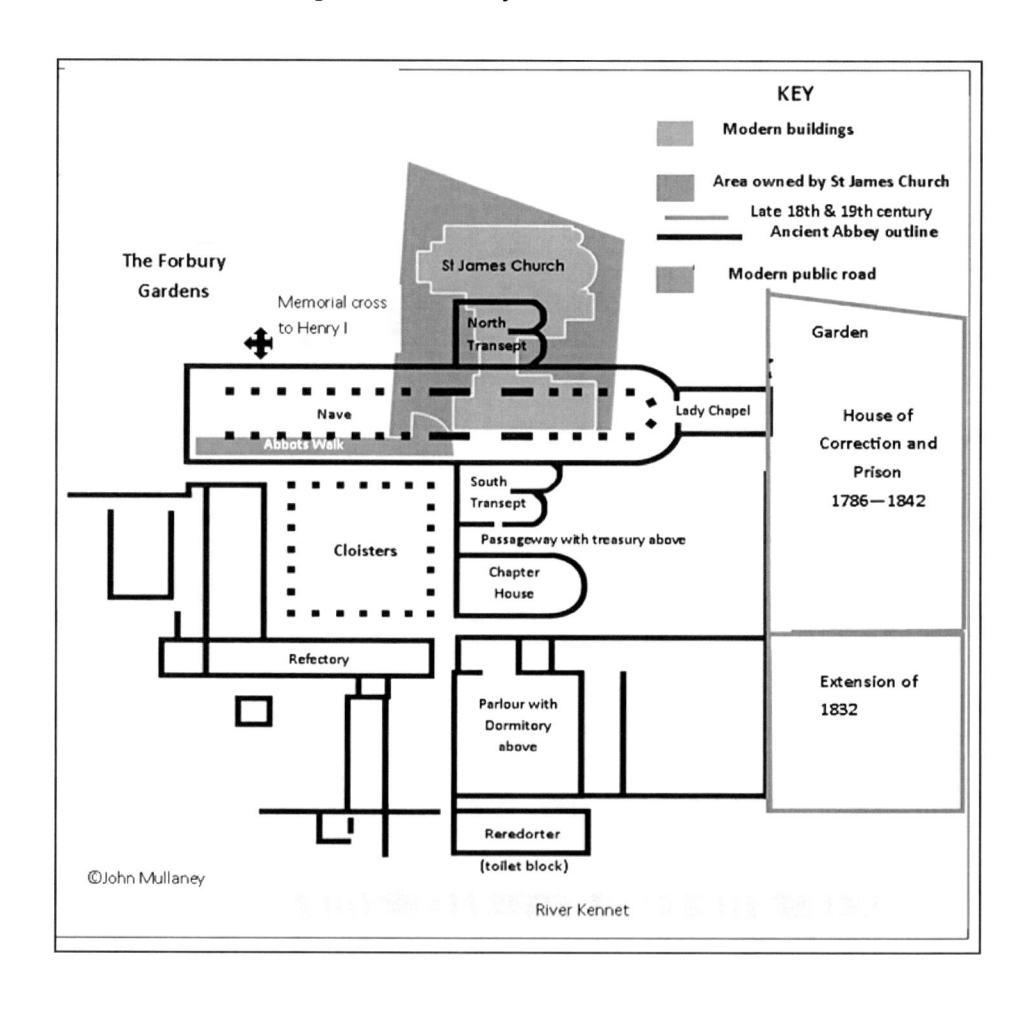

PART 2. CHAPTER 2. THE ABBEY CHURCH

In Chapter 3 we shall take a closer look at the new County Gaol. Before doing this it is necessary to understand that the town had its own places of detention into which the Corporation was empowered to commit offenders, vagrants and even those who could no longer care for themselves financially. Unlike felons who had been committed by the County Assize, those found guilty and given a custodial sentence by local magistrates were imprisoned in the town or borough prison often known as the Bridewell.

The Town Bridewell – Greyfriars

In addition to the County Gaol, Reading had a Borough *Bridewell* which was situated in the ruins of Greyfriars Church.

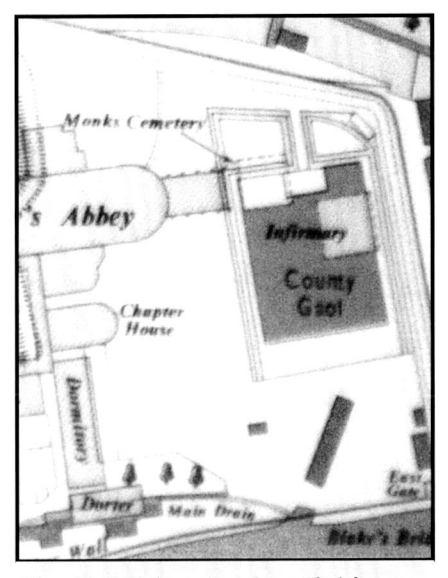

The siting of the prison from Slade's map.

How this came into existence is the story in microcosm of how England dealt with the poor, the vulnerable and the criminal after the Dissolution of the Monasteries.

Before the Reformation Greyfriars had been a Franciscan friary. As part of Henry VIII's reforms this was dissolved in 1538. Within the next few years its ownership was divided between the town and a certain Robert Stanshaw. The town Corporation intended to convert its part into a guildhall. The town claimed the *body and syde Iles of the Church* whilst Stanshaw took possession of the *choir, cloister, burial ground orchards, gardens ditches, lands, tenements...*[10]

By 1578, however, the building was being used as a workhouse, called a 'Hospital', for Reading's three parishes. The change in use was partly because the Corporation felt that the building was unsuitable as a meeting hall and partly due to the passing of the 1576 Act which required every town to provide work for the unemployed. We shall see that the Corporation moved to the upper floor of the old Hospitium, above the School House, (page 130). It is possible that the Corporation was spurred on by the Act to look for new premises, thereby presenting the town with a building, the old friary, that they could use to comply with the new law. The Act required that raw materials, such as wool and hemp, should be provided for the poor who supplied the labour, thereby fulfilling the legal obligation *to provide work for the unemployed.* It would appear that Greyfriars acted mainly as a place for the elderly and children as the earliest accounts record that there were 14 old people and 12 children in the Hospital.

In 1601 the 'Act for the Relief of the Poor' was passed. This Act aimed at consolidating the piecemeal legislation regarding the poor, the vulnerable (the elderly and children), the unemployed and even the criminal, that had been passed since the Dissolution of the Monasteries. This was arguably one of the greatest achievements of the Elizabethan period. It was certainly one of the longest lasting, being left virtually unchanged until 1834. Some its provisions and ideas persisted until the foundation of the Welfare State in the 1940s.

This Law made each parish responsible for supporting the legitimately needy in its community and taxed wealthier citizens to provided basic shelter, food and clothing. At least one commentator has argued that its establishment prevented the worst excesses of starvation and discontent that were witnessed over Europe during times of famine and economic stringency over the next 300 years. 'La Grande Peur' of 1789, immediately prior to the French Revolution, is amongst the most notorious of these waves of discontent.[11]

The 1601 Act had concentrated on the poor and the vulnerable. Criminals were a separate problem and another Act in 1607 enabled the creation of Houses of Correction. Whereas the Poor Houses, or Hospitals, were not intended as places of punishment, the opposite was true of the Houses of Correction. Work was compulsory and detention was mandatory. The inmates of a House of Correction had to be committed by a Justice of the Peace or the Mayor. There were strict rules as to who could be detained. Children under 12, adults over 60, pregnant women, anyone with sickness or disease or lacking a hand, could not be sent to the House of Correction. It was a place for the able bodied to work and be punished for a specific crime or crimes. They were literally 'workhouses'. Raw materials and implements were to be provided and the inmates were required to produce goods which were sold to pay for their upkeep. The rules regarding punishments were likewise explicit. An offender could be whipped as part of the punishment, but this could occur only once. If the offender showed remorse then the whipping could be commuted. At Reading the whipping post was in front of St Lawrence's church. This punishment was only administered on Friday afternoons and in the presence of at least two appointed persons from a list which included the Vicar of St Lawrence's, specified officers, constables and bailiffs.[12]

Although the Act establishing Houses of Correction was passed in 1607 it was not until 1614 that part of the Hospital was converted into a House of Correction for the town. As we saw above, the town did of course have the prison on Castle Street, but the inmates of this institution were committed by the Assizes or County Court. After 1614 Greyfriars operated both as a Hospital and as a House of Correction.[13] The same person appointed to be in charge of one institution was also responsible for the other. Although we might recognise some of the offences as meriting punishment, such as *poaching* or those who

PART 2. CHAPTER 2. THE ABBEY CHURCH

beat or ill use constables in the execution of their duty, today we would find it hard to understand why those *who sit drinking at the time of divine service* or *fathers of illegitimate children* should be punished by committal to a House of Correction.

The start of the Civil War in 1642, saw a change in the use of Greyfriars. Initially Reading was held by the Parliamentarians under Sir Henry Marten. However he retreated to London and the town was occupied by the Royalists under the governorship of Sir Arthur Aston. It would appear that under both Parliament and King, the House of Correction section of Greyfriars was occupied by the military.[14]

The Bridewell c.1810: today's Greyfriars Church

However there is evidence that the Hospital continued. There are records dating from 1642 to 1644 detailing requests by Henry Tubb, who was in charge of the Hospital, for payments due for the upkeep two female Hospital inmates: Ann Bennet and Goody Bayly.

By 1644 Tubb and William Woodde, as joint keepers of the Hospital and House of Correction, were petitioning the Corporation for the repair and re-opening of the House of Correction. They also petitioned the County for the money that had not been paid during and for some time prior to the war. The County of Berkshire had being paying the Reading House of Correction a sum to cover the costs of inmates sent there by the County Sessions. The lack of records of any money for the Hospital is a strong indication that it was around this time that Greyfriars lost its Hospital/Poor House element and became solely a House of Correction or Bridewell.

Over the next two centuries it also served as a prison for the County, in addition to the County Gaol. John Howard, on his visit to the town in 1779, commented on its deplorable conditions: the dearth of fresh water supply, the mingling of the sexes and of different categories of inmates and the lack of an exercise yard. In 1810 the roof of the nave, being in danger of collapse, was removed. John Man recorded this event and that a wall had been built to separate the male and female sleeping quarters.[15] Cells had been incorporated into the remnants of the side aisles of the old church. Those without private means to pay for food, bedding and clothing had to rely upon the little support offered by the Elizabethan Poor Law. At least the removal of the roof allowed for fresh air, but little else seems to have improved. In 1837 the Inspector of Prisons condemned the Bridewell for its overcrowding, commenting on the fact that there were only three habitable cells and that there were six people confined in just one of these small spaces. This occurred despite the fact that in 1831 it had been agreed that the Borough Justices could confine their excess of prisoners in the County Gaol. It should be remembered that this was a period of increasing civil unrest and even fear of armed uprising. The agricultural riots of the 1830s, made famous by the Swing riots and the case of the Tolpuddle Martyrs, had resulted in a sudden increase in the prison population.

In 1844, as we shall see, a new County Gaol was built and in 1850 the Borough came to an agreement with the County authorities that, at a charge of £6 per head, they could house their prisoners in the new gaol. Despite the decision finally to close the Greyfriars Bridewell it was still available to take back two female prisoners in 1842 whilst the new prison was being built on the Forbury Road site.[16]

The Greyfriars Bridwell finally ceased to function when the building was acquired in 1863 by The Rev. Phelps who established Greyfriars Church.

Other Prisons and Lockups

We have seen that Castle Street and Greyfriars prisons were the main places of detention in Reading. However there were other sites that were used as places of internment and punishment. We shall look at these before returning to the new Forbury County Gaol and House of Correction.

The Compter Gateway and the Hole

Situated alongside the southern aisle of St Lawrence's Church, the Compter Gateway had housed the Abbot's prison for offending monks and town miscreants. It consisted of three small rooms above the archway, with the Compter House adjoining. In the 17th century it was mainly used to house debtors and civil offenders. However by the 18th century the Corporation had lost its right to enforce payment of small debts so the prison fell into disuse. The picture above shows St Lawrence's around 1850. A single cell was situated at its eastern end. It was dubbed the

St Lawrence's Church c1850 [17]

PART 2. CHAPTER 2. THE ABBEY CHURCH

'Hole' by the locals and was behind the studded door at the end of the arcade. In a railed-off enclosure next to the 'Hole' there was a lock-up where the town stocks and ducking stool were stored. To the right of the illustration the round-cornered building is the Compter House, residence of the Head Constable who was responsible for the occupants of the 'Hole'. The Compter House was also the location of the Magistrates' Court until 1862, when a police station and courtroom were built at High Bridge House. It should be noted that the County Assizes were held in the Town Hall, situated in the old Hospitium building to the north of St Lawrence's church.

The Shades

During the 18th century another place for short term confinement, mainly for public order offences, was a lock-up behind 'The Shades' public house on the corner of Gun Street and Minster Street near to the Oracle. It is worth mentioning in passing that the Oracle had been founded by the Kendrick family and completed in 1628. It was designed as a complex covering about 2 acres, consisting of a workhouse with a range of workshops around a courtyard. It was a centre of the cloth industry, especially silk. The building continued in use until the closure of the Oracle in 1850.[18]

Site of The Shades and entrance to the Oracle, in 1850 [19]

The same site in 2014

READING'S ABBEY QUARTER

CHAPTER 3.   THE FORBURY COUNTY GAOL, 1786 – 1842

We saw how the new County Gaol and House of Correction came to be built on the site of the Abbey's Lady Chapel. We shall now examine how this institution was managed and what life was like for its inmates

Plan of the County Gaol and House of Correction in 1828

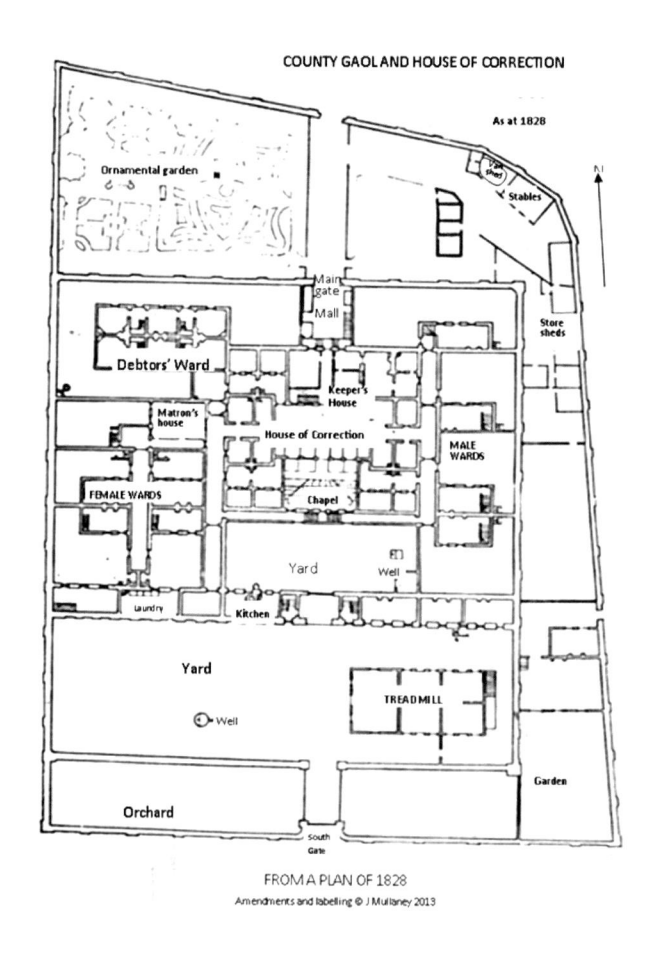

FROM A PLAN OF 1828
Amendments and labelling © J Mullaney 2013

TREADMILL   –   1817

FEMALE WARDS ADDED   –   1824

ORNAMENTAL GARDENS AND ORCHARD   –   1826 under Governor Eastaff

DEBTORS' WARD   –   1827

PART 2. CHAPTER 3. THE FORBURY COUNTY GAOL, 1786 – 1842

Living Conditions

The standard of the building work in this new gaol was far from satisfactory. The roof leaked, the privies in the cells were unusable and *offensive*. The iron plating fixed to the cell doors was so poorly attached that it was easily removed. Soft wood and other inferior material had been used throughout. Consequently the Justices withheld payment from Brettingham and banned him from working for the County again. In fact he went on to design prisons elsewhere in the country.

The privies were finally removed from the cells in 1828, though this appeared to be mainly from fear that the sewer system might be used as an escape route. John Man's account of the prison in his book of 1810, 'A Stranger in Reading', makes interesting reading. He describes the building in the following way:

At the Eastern end of the Forbury is the County Gaol and Bridewell, a modern brick building on Mr Howard's plan. In front is the keeper's house and at small distance behind is a very neat chapel... Behind the wards is a large courtyard surrounded by a high wall but open to the sun, here the prisoners occasionally walk. Round the outer wall is a garden enclosed by another wall but lower where some convicts are occasionally employed. The prisoners are dressed in party coloured clothes half blue, half yellow from head to foot except for shoes.[1]

Punishment

These were days of public executions and the keeper, George Knight, was consulted about the siting of the scaffold. Execution was by hanging. The 'drop', as the gallows were called, was placed on the roof at the west end of the prison with a viewing area for the public to have a good sight of the proceedings. This viewing area was approximately where St James' church now stands. It was reported that in 1833 a crowd of 5000 witnessed the execution of John Carter.[2] Although hanging was the most frequent form of implementing the death penalty other forms of capital punishment were, until the 1830s, theoretically still in place. These included 'gibbeting' and 'hanging in chains'.

There were well over 200 crimes for which the death penalty could be given. These included blackening one's face whilst committing a crime such as poaching. Even children as young as 7 could be condemned to death where there was *strong evidence of malice*. Reforming pressures however meant that fewer people were executed than the law at first sight would indicate.

Records show 26 executions took place at Reading between 1800 and 1844, but there were only 9 from 1844 to 1913. Just 7 of the 26 were for murder, the rest were for a variety of crimes, mainly robbery and theft but also forgery.[3]

William Cubitt is credited with inventing the 19th century version of the treadmill in 1817. Reading Gaol was the one of the first prisons to install his invention. It was designed as a productive feature, unlike the treadwheel, and it was used to produce flour. The power source came from the prisoners. The image below gives some idea of what it must have been like.

It was constructed by Messrs Penn at a cost of £1700 and required 32 prisoners to operate it. At one reckoning a working day of ten hours entailed the equivalent of climbing a staircase two and a half miles high.

Immediately on its introduction there was a revolt by the prisoners. Although some of their demands were met, chiefly the provision of appropriate footwear, the main consequence was the appointment of an extra prison officer, a 'turnkey', and the addition of bars and doors on the compartments to prevent revolt. Work was carried out in silence; the penalty for breaking this rule was three days solitary confinement on bread and water.

When the price of flour fell the prison authorities considered it more economical to buy in flour for the prison bakery rather than produce it themselves. In 1828 the Justices entered into a contract with Samuel Slaughter, a local miller and corn merchant. This ensured the mill's survival in the short term. By 1834 it was clear that the mill was operating at a loss and the new Governor, Edward Hackett RN, suggested converting the mill into a treadwheel. This would remove any pretence of its utilitarian function and it would become purely punitive. However, disconnecting the treadwheel from the mill resulted in mechanical problems which prevented it from working at all. It was consequently reinstated as a mill and remained operative until 1841 when it was dismantled as part of demolition in preparation for the new gaol.

The Guard Room

There was considerable civil unrest following the end of the Napoleonic wars in 1815. The causes of this are complex. They were linked with economic depression, fuelled in part by the introduction of the Corn Laws which kept the cost of bread artificially high, large scale unemployment exacerbated by the demobilisation of the armed forces, and fewer jobs as a consequence of industrialisation and mechanisation. Alongside these pressures the

PART 2. CHAPTER 3. THE FORBURY COUNTY GAOL, 1786 – 1842

unprecedented growth in the population of England, which characterised the 19th century, was well under way. The population was doubling every 50 years and Reading was no exception. In addition, the spread of revolutionary ideas such as the concept of 'democracy' added to the sense of unease throughout the country. Consequently it was considered necessary to maintain an active militia. Even their loyalty was open to doubt; so much so that the government ordered that their muskets and ammunition should be kept locked in the County Gaol. Hence the Berkshire Militia guard room became part of the gaol buildings.

The Female Wards, 1824

These were added to the west of the gaol in 1824. There was an increase in the number of females being convicted of offences meriting prison. This was partly caused by the deteriorating economic conditions in the country at large and the general increase in the population.

The Garden and Orchard, 1826 –1834

Governor Thomas Eastaff (1826-1834) was a keen horticulturalist. He laid out an ornamental garden to the west of the northern entrance to the gaol along the Forbury Road. This consisted of brick paths, herbaceous borders, flowering trees and shrubs. Its outline can be discerned in the 1828 plan (see page 42). By 1834 he had added an orchard of 69 apple trees, 10 pear trees, 7 peach trees, 5 grape vines, 200 red and white currant bushes and 3 asparagus beds. Little if any of this produce was used for the benefit of the inmates of the gaol.

The Bakehouse and other outbuildings, 1826

To the east of this northern entrance the 1828 plan shows a variety of outbuildings. These included the bakehouse and adjoining bread stores which were added in 1826, just two years before the new contract with Samuel Slaughter.

There is also a van house. This structure housed the vehicle used to transport prisoners from the gaol to the courts. There were also forges, workshops and storehouses along this easterly edge of the gaol.

The Debtors Ward, 1827

Perhaps it was a sign of the times that debt became an increasing problem. Together with the demographic and socio-economic pressures already alluded to, it is not surprising that it became necessary to provide more accommodation for debtors in an era when debt, until cleared, could result in imprisonment. Prior to the building of the new gaol, debtors had been housed in the Compter Gate and Greyfriars Bridewell.

The new block overlooked the prison matron's garden and house. Despite the strict rules of silence there are several reports of this being ignored by the male inmates of the debtors' block as they made contact with the female prisoners, who frequently used the matron's garden to hang up their washing.

The Male Juvenile Section 1832

The need for more space was identified by the Visiting Justices in 1830. There were over 140 inmates in a prison designed for 100. The problem became a crisis the following year when the number rose to 250 and the old Greyfriars Bridewell had to take the overflow. This rise in prisoners followed the rural unrest of 1831, known as the 'Swing Riots'.

Using a legacy of £1000 left by Augustus Schuts, a former Justice of the Peace, which he specified should be used for *the confinement of persons committed there for idleness or slight offences,* the authorities planned to build provision of an infirmary and a separate block for young male offenders. Although William Cubitt provided the first plans, the Justices chose a local man, Richard Billings, as the architect in charge. Cubitt had complained about the distance he would have to travel from his home in Lowestoft. The building contract was awarded to George Ball. Work was begun in 1832 and the prison area was extended from the south entrance and wall down towards the River Kennet.

CHAPTER 4   READING GAOL 1844 – 2014

Planning the New Prison

Despite all these improvements it became increasingly obvious that the facilities were inadequate. As noted the population increase in itself put extra strain on accommodation. This was exacerbated by continuing and increasing civil unrest as well as the growth in crime. In 1832 there were still only three turnkeys or warders, and they found it increasingly difficult to maintain discipline.

By 1841 the chaplain, the Reverend John Field, made a detailed report to the Quarter Sessions of Visiting Justices, listing the problems facing the prison authorities. Field was motivated by his concern for the spiritual welfare of the inmates and saw that this was affected by the physical conditions they faced. He made several recommendations, which included increasing the number of turnkeys and employing a teacher to raise the deplorable standards of literacy. He advocated the implementation of the 'separate system' of confinement to allow *the criminal time for his own reflection.*

In the same year the Inspector of Prisons, Colonel Jebb, and the Home Secretary, Sir James Graham, voiced their concerns to the County authorities about the state of the prison. They condemned the overcrowding which increased the risk of fever. Typhus, known by several names including prison fever, was spread through insanitary conditions which allowed the human body-louse to feed on infected persons and then pass this on to other inmates. In confined conditions, such as prevailed in Reading Gaol, the risk of infection was very high.

Their report also commented on the lack of refractory cells which allowed for the isolation of violent prisoners, the lack of chapel space and the grouping together of prisoners within different punishment categories. The committee which was subsequently set up quickly came to the conclusion that *the present construction…was such as to preclude any possibility of effectual improvement.* Col. Jebb concluded that for about £15,000 a new prison could be built capable of holding 150 prisoners. It was suggested that by re-using material from the existing structure the cost might be even less.

The debate between advocates of the benefits of either the 'silent' or the 'separate' systems continued. The proponents of the latter prevailed and in 1842, at Easter, the Justices agreed to commission a new prison building. Its design was to follow the New Model Prison of Pentonville.

Plans were invited and to prevent any accusation of undue favour or influence these were submitted under a *nom de plume.* From the seventeen or so entries two were selected. The preferred choice was submitted by George Gilbert Scott and William Bonython Moffat. The design of a local architect, John Berry Clacy, who was to become the County architect, was selected as reserve runner up and he was awarded £50.[1] Although Jebb had initially recommended a gaol for 150, the designs produced planned for 220 prisoners and 20 debtors. This was upheld by the Justices. The extra cost, it was thought, could be defrayed by retaining the north entrance instead of building a separate southern entrance which would entail a new, lengthy and so costly, driveway. In August 1842 the building contract was initially awarded to John Jay of London Wall at a cost of £24,000. However by the November of that year Jay had been declared bankrupt and the contract was awarded to Messrs Baker and Son of Stangate Wharf, Lambeth.

Building work was begun immediately and the problem arose of where to place the existing inmates. As no national scheme for the commitment of prisoners existed they had to be dispersed throughout the County. Fifty men and twenty women were sent to Abingdon, four men and two women to Windsor. Two women were sent back to the old Greyfriars Bridewell; fifty-two places were retained for prisoners who were committed for trial. Debtors stayed in the gaol.

The first section to be demolished was the 1832 Juvenile Extension (see map page 36). The foundations for the central hall and southern wing were excavated. However the declaration of bankruptcy of Jay's brought the building to an abrupt stop. Messrs Baker and Son, the builders, quickly stepped in so that, by the spring of 1843, of the old prison only the chapel and four nearby cells remained, accommodating thirteen debtors as well as two convicts, a man and a woman.

The Basement Area

Not shown in the diagram on page 50 are the basement areas under A, B and D wings. Their construction was facilitated by the sloping ground which fell away from west to east. Half of the basement under A wing was allocated to the Berkshire Militia as an armoury and equipment store. This had its own separate access via a covered passage to the guard room near the stable block, to the east of the building. The rest of the basement under A wing was used as kitchens. There were boilers which not only heated the coppers and steamers but also provided a heating and ventilation system for the prison. The basement under D wing was used as a reception area for newly arrived prisoners. Also in this area were the *dark cells*. These were for the detention of prisoners who were deemed in need of further punishment and committed to solitary confinement. The cells had no windows or artificial lighting and had double thickness doors to render them soundproof. New arrivals were shown these cells as a warning against breaking the prison rules. The warders' mess and store rooms were under the central hall whilst under B wing there were baths.

PART 2. CHAPTER 4. READING GAOL, 1844 – 2014

Costs escalated, partly owing to errors in calculations by Scott and partly owing to the need to replace, in its entirety, the outer wall. It had been assumed that parts of this could be retained. However it was soon discovered that the section near to the River Kennet was unstable.

In fact one of the points of controversy was the elaborate design of the outer wall. Scott himself claimed that this added only £350 to the overall cost. The figure was disputed and other estimates put it nearer to £3500. However, the result was a building which became an imposing Reading landmark where once had stood an equally grand building, the Abbey, five hundred years beforehand.

A visitor to Reading, whether arriving by train or by road from London, would see this large edifice, with its imposing 18 foot boundary wall of smooth brickwork, corner turrets and crenellations redolent of a late medieval castle. Its distinctive red Tilehurst brick and Bath quoin stonework were to be a feature of Reading for the next century and more.

The 'Illustrated London News' of the 17th February 1844 reported:

Standing as it does on the rising ground at the entrance of Reading,
and close to the site of the venerable abbey,
this new prison is from every side the most conspicuous building,
and, architecturally, by far the greatest ornament to the town.

The Illustrated London News, 17 February 1844.　　　Courtesy Reading Library

READING'S ABBEY QUARTER

Plan of Reading Gaol 1844

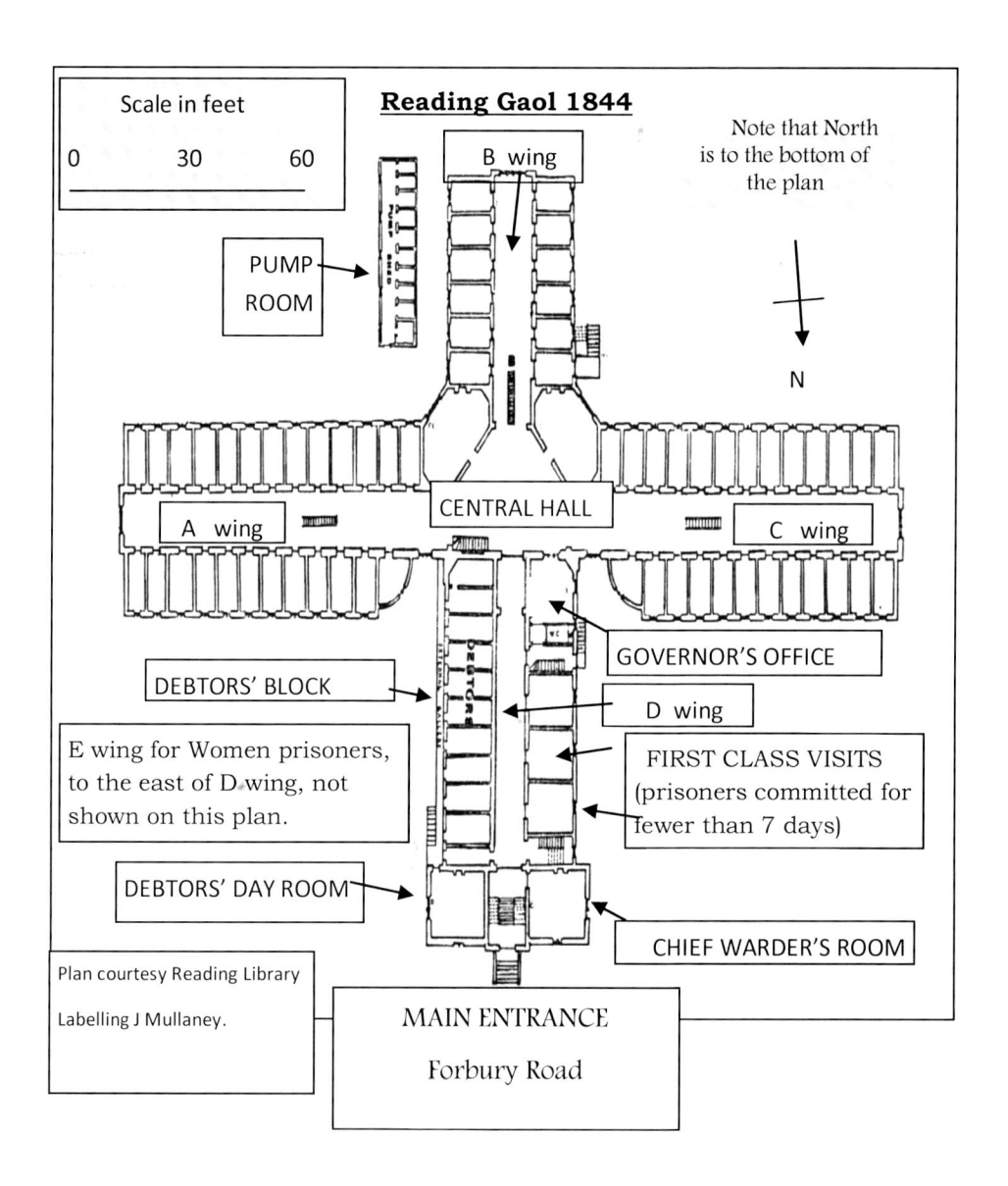

Reading Gaol 1844

Scale in feet: 0 — 30 — 60

Note that North is to the bottom of the plan

B wing

PUMP ROOM

N

CENTRAL HALL

A wing

C wing

GOVERNOR'S OFFICE

DEBTORS' BLOCK

D wing

E wing for Women prisoners, to the east of D wing, not shown on this plan.

FIRST CLASS VISITS (prisoners committed for fewer than 7 days)

DEBTORS' DAY ROOM

CHIEF WARDER'S ROOM

Plan courtesy Reading Library
Labelling J Mullaney.

MAIN ENTRANCE
Forbury Road

PART 2. CHAPTER 4. READING GAOL, 1844 – 2014

The following three photographs show the striking nature of the brick and stonework of George Gilbert Scott's design.

Reading Borstal, showing the Chaplain's and Governor's residences, 1966 [2]

The Governor's residence, 1910 [3]

North-west turret shortly before demolition, with St James' school in the background, 1972. [4]

The New Prison in Use

It would be a mistake to think that these apparently decorative elements were for show only. Pugin had laid down the principles of neo-gothic architecture and one of these was that no element should be incorporated into a design unless it fulfilled a practical function. George Gilbert Scott, an admirer of Pugin, certainly followed this advice at Reading.

These were uneasy times, socially and politically. Within four years of the prison's opening, in 1848, Europe would erupt into the Year of Revolutions. In England the Chartist movement, with its demands for greater democracy, was at its peak. In addition there was the Irish potato famine and the call for the repeal of the Corn Laws. All contributed to a fear of civil unrest, if not revolution.

The design of the prison in the form of a medieval castle was not therefore totally decorative. Indeed the Berkshire Militia had their military stores beneath the east wing. They had a separate entrance and this area was not under the jurisdiction of the prison authorities but of the military.

The heavily reinforced, iron-studded, north door was the only entrance to the prison. Those decorated turrets on either side of the door were in fact designed to withstand attack. The narrow loop-holed windows set at angles permitted enfilade fire: namely uninterrupted fire along the widest axis of the armaments. The flat roofs above the gateway and the turrets, as in the case of any castle, gave the defenders site and range advantage. And so the flat roof not only served as a place of public execution but was a reminder of the gaol's strategic military function.

A Cell in Reading Gaol

Prison life was based on the new Pentonville 'solitary', or 'separate', system. Each prisoner had a cell, 13' by 7', and 10' high, where he lived and worked. The floors were of red and black tiles, the walls whitewashed. Each cell had a wash basin and WC. Light and heating were provided through narrow apertures from the corridor. Until the introduction of a plank bed, the prisoner erected a hammock each night, the only other furnishings being a three legged stool, a fixed table and some shelves. Water was provided by pipe each morning and had to last the day. The door had an exterior lock only and a small trap door through which food and any other items could be passed.

PART 2. CHAPTER 4. READING GAOL, 1844 – 2014

By June of 1843 building work had reached the first floor level and by Michaelmas it was mainly completed and ready to receive prisoners. However the cost had risen to £40,000. It would appear that Scott had forgotten to include internal fittings and his own fees of £1250.

An 1844 report mentioned that the heating and ventilation systems were still not in place. By Easter the female accommodation was ready and by July the premises were handed over to the County. The first detainee committed to the Gaol was a certain Abraham Boswell of Waltham St Lawrence. He had been found guilty of indecent assault and attempted rape against a child of 2 years of age. His sentence was 6 months imprisonment with hard labour.

Staffing

In addition to the existing staff four assistant warders were appointed at £30 per annum.

The Interior of Reading Gaol [5]

There was also a resident engineer at £52, a cook: £30, a porter: £30 and a prison servant: £20. These all received a daily ration of 1lb bread, 1lb meat, ¾ oz. of coffee. 2oz. of sugar, ½ pint of milk plus, weekly, ½lb of butter and a *sufficient quantity of pepper, salt, mustard, vinegar and onions*. The reputation of the prison soon spread and in 1844 the Governor, Edward Hackett, was able to report that the prison was working smoothly: *We are justified in stating that at least a majority of those who have been a reasonable time under the discipline of Reading Gaol will leave it with the firm resolution to obtain henceforth an honest livelihood.*

Reading Prison Chapel, 1844 [6]

Religious instruction was central to the prison regime and its reformative ideology. Consequently the Chapel and the chaplain were important features of the prison. The Chapel was situated on the upper floor of D wing. Notice the separate boxed pews in the picture. Whereas it was not possible for any prisoner to see any other, the warders had a clear view of every boxed pew. Lincoln Castle, now a museum, has a similar chapel which may be visited today.

19th Century Developments

Flour Mills 1855

Those who favoured the solitary system, such as the chaplain, John Field, increasingly found themselves in the minority. In 1851 the Justices commented on the *relaxed state of muscular power and a diminution of physical energy amongst the convicts*. In other words they felt that the solitary system was not sufficiently physically rigorous. Moreover in 1854 the Government restricted the time for solitary confinement to nine months. The Justices in Reading settled upon the idea of installing six hand operated mills to produce flour. These were in full operation by the end of 1855.

Stone Breaking 1863

The 'airing yard' alongside E wing, for the use of women prisoners and laundry facilities, was converted into a stone breaking area. There was a heavy demand for broken stone and flint by road and house builders. This was a boom time for the building industry as population increased and towns expanded.

Prisoners' photographs 1870

This was a short lived experiment but one that involved the erection of a new building, a photographic studio, near the exercise yard. The concept had been pioneered at Winchester. At first the Justices were enthusiastic about it as a means of identifying criminals across the country, prisoners who used aliases and of course in identifying escapees. The Metropolitan Police were strong advocates but after six months, when there were no escapes and no record of impersonation, the Justices considered the venture a waste of resources.

Executions

The Capital Punishment Amendment Act of 1868 put an end to public executions. After this all executions had to take place within the walls of the prison in which the prisoner was being held. Their bodies were to be buried within the prison precincts.

We should recall that the last abbot of Reading had been cruelly executed only a few yards from the prison site. The sentence of hanging, drawing and quartering for treason was amended during the 18th and 19th centuries so that disembowelling was commonly commuted. Possibly the last occasion that the sentence was carried out in full was the execution for treason, at Southsea, of David Tyrie, in 1782. In 1814 the Treason Act formally removed the disembowelling part of the punishment and substituted normal hanging followed by post mortem decapitation. The Forfeiture Act of 1870 removed all reference to drawing and quartering from the Statute Book.

PART 2. CHAPTER 4. READING GAOL, 1844 – 2014

The photographic studio was converted into an execution chamber. Eight feet deep, and measuring 9' by 5', it had a lever operated trap door above which was a simple gallows consisting of a cross beam from which the rope was suspended, supported by two wooden upright posts.

The first of the new style executions were in March 1877 when the brothers Francis and Henry Tidbury were hanged for the murders of two police officers, Inspector Shorter and PC Drewitt. Over the next 36 years there were six more executions, the last, in 1913, being that of Eric James Sedgwick for murder.

In the early 1900s the First Class Debtors' cells in D wing were converted into specifically allocated 'condemned cells' with a passageway leading to a new 'drop' constructed alongside the main building.

Other Structural changes

The Prisons Act of 1877 brought Reading under the ownership and full control of the Crown. It was found that Reading Gaol was in good structural condition and efficiently managed, unlike many other prisons throughout the country. Minor changes were introduced such as the removal of the box pews in the chapel in 1879 and the conversion of the First Class Debtors' day room into a dedicated Catholic chapel.

The End of Capital Punishment

Following Sydney Silverman's bill of 1965, which resulted in an Act suspending capital punishment, the country moved in stages towards full abolition. At Reading the 'drop' was demolished in 1968 and the 'condemned cells' converted into offices.

As a postscript it is worth noting that the last remaining provisions for the death penalty were removed when section 21(5) of the Human Rights Act came into force in November 1998. In October 2003 the UK acceded to the 13th Protocol to the Convention for the Protection of Human Rights, which prohibited the death penalty under all circumstances. The UK Parliament may no longer legislate to restore the death penalty while it is subject to the Convention. It can only now be restored if the UK withdraws from the Council of Europe.

The
Ballad of Reading Gaol
By
C. 3. 3.

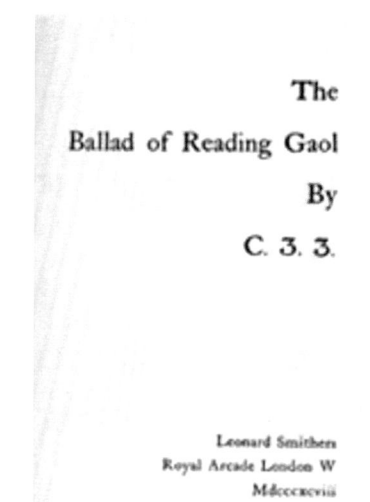

Leonard Smithers
Royal Arcade London W
Mdcccxcviii

One cannot write about Reading Gaol without mentioning its most famous detainee: Oscar Wilde. Convicted in 1895 of *gross indecency,* Wilde spent two years in Reading, in cell 3 on the third floor of C wing: C.3.3. Wilde was released in mid 1897 and wrote his famous poem in France where he spent the rest of his life, dying in 1900. *The Ballad of Reading Gaol,* originally published under the pen-name C.3.3, is a heartfelt commentary on capital punishment.

The first edition appeared in January 1898 without the author's name on the title page. It was published by Leonard Smithers at the Chiswick Press,

The 20th Century

War 1914–1918

The outbreak of war in 1914 brought about another change in the use of the gaol. With a sharp decline in prisoner numbers, by November 1915 there were only 71 inmates. It was proposed to disperse these elsewhere and use Reading as an internment camp for *male aliens* and those, even from neutral countries, suspected of being unsympathetic to the Allied cause. The men were not treated as convicted prisoners; they had committed no crime. Within the prison they had freedom of movement and communication, they could earn 14s a week and enjoyed a diet far better than most of the civilian and military population of the day.

This situation changed with the arrival in July 1916 of 37 Sinn Fein activists who had been involved in the Easter Rising and its aftermath in Ireland. The UK Government was unsure as to whether these men were to be treated as political detainees or criminals. They were housed separately in E wing and set about creating as much nuisance as they could but within the rules and regulations. In addition, air raids over London and elsewhere were causing concern. The glow from the prison central glass lantern was considered a risk so it was blacked out with a mix of oil and lampblack.

Following a mutiny at Lewes prison by Irish militants in 1918, some were sent to Reading. Despite the fear of further trouble there was none. When war ended the Irish were released and by the end of 1919 the remaining detainees had either been repatriated to their respective countries or given permission to stay in the UK. One notable detainee was William Cosgrave who later became the first President of the Executive Council of the Irish Free State from 1922 to 1932.

Interwar period 1920-1939

The prison remained empty and all plans to convert it into housing, a hotel or offices were rejected by the government. The 1920s saw an increase once again in civil unrest as the economic depression intensified and the fear of revolution spread. The 1917 Bolshevik Revolution in Russia, the General Strike of 1926 and the rise of Fascism all contributed to the sense of unease. It was considered prudent to retain the buildings in case of need. From 1935 various government departments began to use its facilities.

War 1939 –1945

Preparations were made to convert the premises into a detention centre similar to that of the time of the 1914-18 war. Borstal boys were employed to prepare it for this purpose. However by 1940 the buildings found a completely new set of occupants. The Canadian Army was given the facilities as a military detention centre for its own troops. Little is known about its use over this period, though it was reported by the few visitors who did gain access that guards patrolled the prison armed with machine guns!

There is some evidence that the 'basement area' was used as part of the decoding and sorting of military intelligence at this period. One lady, who died in the early 2000s, recounted how she would be taken from her home by military vehicle each morning and brought to the Gaol where, in an underground area, she worked on intelligence material connected with Bletchley Park.[7] There were indeed locations throughout the country known as Y Stations. The hub of this operation was Station X at Bletchley Park. Bletchley, as is now known, was at the centre of decoding enemy signals. It would appear that the Y Stations acted as listening posts and, because strict radio silence was kept at Bletchley, the information was passed to and from the Y Stations by courier. Whether Reading was in any way part of this network is still a matter of conjecture but this lady's testament indicates some covert operation was taking place. It is possible that the 'dungeons', as she called her workplace, were in fact the underground areas already mentioned and converted for this use. As the enemy would probably know, from their own intelligence sources, that Reading was a prison for Canadian troops, they would expect military style radio traffic here. In short, if this hypothesis is true, Reading gaol was used for covert military intelligence.

1945 — 1969

The premises were restored as a prison in 1945. Following the Criminal Justice Act of 1948 a new regime of Corrective Training was inaugurated. The system of remedial training for prisoners demanded some form of assessment so that only those suitable should be selected. Reading was chosen as this centre and the first detainees arrived in December 1949. However by 1951 it was decided to set up a Borstal Institution in the premises. Borstals were designed to give practical education to young offenders aged between 16 and 21, with the intention of reintegrating them into the community. The trainee would undergo a period of skill training then be released under the supervision of a probation officer. Reading, however, was used for boys who had not responded well in other Borstals. It was hoped that a regime of strict Correction would convince these offenders to mend their ways. The establishment was therefore designated as a Corrective and Recall Centre. Reading's reputation as a place to be feared and avoided spread amongst Borstal detainees throughout the country.

1969 — 1978

In early 1969 the Borstal was closed and the site once more became a prison. The buildings were to be completely modernised using prison labour. By February the first group of prisoners arrived and were housed in E Wing. One significant structural change was the demolition of the execution chamber adjacent to D Wing. The condemned cells were converted in offices. Although it had been the original intention to use outside professional contractors, the firm selected, Emery of High Wycombe, went into liquidation in 1972. So it was decided to use prison labour, calling upon those prisoners who had the necessary building skills and were capable of training others, a policy which helped in the rehabilitation of many ex-offenders.

Undoubtedly the most telling development for the people of Reading was the demolition of the19th century exterior wall. First to disappear were the two turrets and the houses flanking the main gate which had been the homes of the Governor and the chaplain. The old gateway stood for a short while longer. But it was too narrow to allow entry by large modern delivery vehicles and was also demolished. Within the prison precincts many alterations, both internal and external, took shape. Several old buildings were removed, new ones erected and alterations made to those left standing.

It was felt that this was an unprecedented opportunity to undertake a modern archaeological survey. There was even some hope expressed that the long lost tomb of Henry I, the Abbey's founder, might be discovered.

PART 2. CHAPTER 4. READING GAOL, 1844 –2014

What was unearthed was a previously unknown building which appeared to be a small chapel, 12' wide, with a semi-circular apse. Several more human remains were also discovered nearby but these were probably those that had been disturbed in the late 18th and mid 19th century digs.

Whilst the works were in progress the facility was designated as a Central Training Prison. This meant that those whose offences were deemed to put them at risk of attack by other prisoners were to be kept together in this one location. Such offenders included those convicted of sex crimes, especially against children, informers and those who had broken the prisoners' own code of conduct. Although there was concern that this could lead to problems with the local community and difficulties within the prison itself no such issues arose. Nevertheless it became clear that for the prisoners and their families, let alone their legal teams, the concentration of such prisoners in one location caused many difficulties in both time and money.

The Prison Gate 1966 [8]

Above is one of the last pictures of George Gilbert Scott's prison, showing the design of the main entrance before alterations either concealed or destroyed it.

Notice the Governors residence to the right and the chaplain's to the left. The main, and only entrance, to the prison was no longer serviceable. As we have seen it had been designed as a mini fortress built for ease of defence in case of civil unrest. However by the mid 20th century this was no longer necessary and other considerations, such as width of access for vehicles, needed to be accommodated.

Left, a 1910 photograph of the Governor's residence, also showing the ornate gardens in front of the prison which bordered the Forbury road.[9]

Right, a photograph taken in 1972. This shows the North West Turret shortly before its demolition. According to most archaeological assessments the High Altar of the Abbey is in this area. (p63)

St James' school is in the background.[10]

In 1973 Reading was designated a local prison. Alongside the need to rehouse detainees following the structural problems at Oxford prison, it was decided in 1978 that Reading should be designated as the County Gaol. In 1992 it also became a Remand Centre and Young Offender Institution (YOI).

Young Offender Institutions were created as a consequence of the 1988 Criminal Justice Act. The regime was much the same as that of an adult prison. However, there were some slight differences, notably the lower staff to offender ratio. Prisoners serving sentences at Young Offender Institutions were expected to take part in at least 25 hours of education per week, which was aimed at helping them to improve their behaviour, to develop practical skills for use in the outside world and to prepare them for lawful employment following their release. There were also opportunities for prisoners to undertake work in Community Service Volunteer programmes

PART 2. CHAPTER 4. READING GAOL, 1844 –2014

The Closure of the Prison, 2013

In September 2013 the Government announced the closure of the prison. A spokesman said the building was 'no longer fit for purpose'. This came as a surprise to many in the town and triggered a debate as to the use of the site and whether Sir George Gilbert Scott's building would be retained and if so in what form.

One certainty was that this part of the ancient Abbey quarter would undergo another phase in its thousand year history and its relationship with the town. With a short break during the inter-war years, there had been some form of prison on the site for over two hundred years. In fact we saw above that the earliest record of a possible prison in Reading was in 1314. This was the same year that the Lady Chapel was built at the east end of the Abbey church, the future site of Reading's last prison. The removal of the prison meant that, for the first time in about 700 years, Reading was without a prison.

The above illustration, entitled *South view of the supposed ruins of the castle.* is from Man's *History and Antiquities of the Borough of Reading*, c.1816. To the right it shows the southern wall of the House of Correction, with the Abbey Ruins in the background, the *supposed castle* being the nearer ruins. This could be one of the two forts, referred to on page 12, proposed by Parliament during the Civil War.[11]

READING'S ABBEY QUARTER

The Transepts, Chancel and Lady Chapel of the Ancient Abbey

This view shows the crossing of the Nave with the Transepts and Chancel. The tower has a spire typical of Cluniac abbeys, which was widely used in other later religious foundations. The Transepts each have two smaller towers in a similar design. These served as buttresses, with the towers providing downward thrust for extra strength and stability.

The Lady Chapel

1314

CHAPTER 5 ST JAMES' CHURCH AND SCHOOL

St James' Church and the Site of the North Transept and High Altar of the Ancient Abbey. 1830—1840

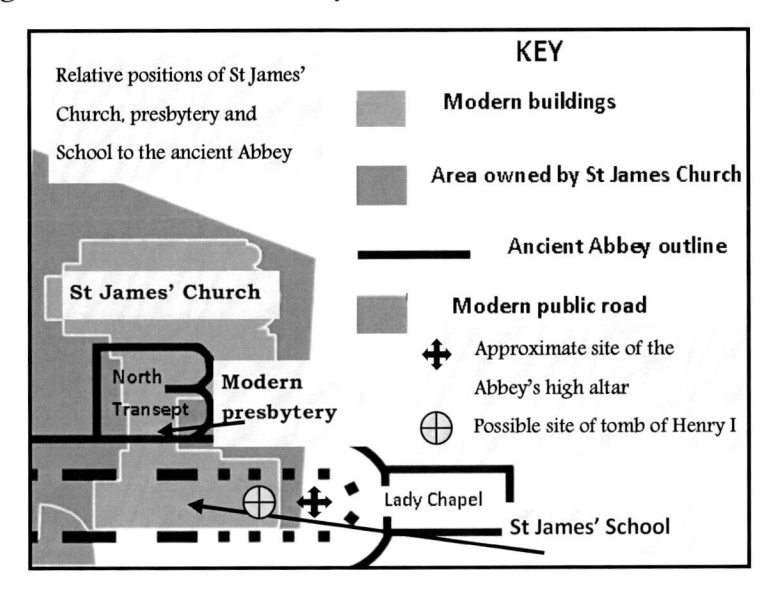

Relative positions of St James' Church, presbytery and School to the ancient Abbey

KEY
- Modern buildings
- Area owned by St James Church
- Ancient Abbey outline
- Modern public road
- Approximate site of the Abbey's high altar
- Possible site of tomb of Henry I

St James' Church — North Transept — Modern presbytery — Lady Chapel — St James' School

Saving the Ruins

On page 28 we left the story of the ruins and the various excavations with the comment that Lord Bexley was considering removing them in their entirety and replacing them with houses and a road. We also saw that 'The Berkshire Chronicle' opposed these plans as *an idea worthy only of a Goth or a Vandal.*

The sequence of events whereby the area eventually became public property is complicated by the fact that several landowners, in addition to Lord Bexley and James Wheble, were involved.

The greater part of the area was, however, originally in the hands of Lord Bexley. Following his stated intention to demolish the ruins in the early 1830s, there was a public subscription which raised the money he was asking to buy the half acre of so of land which comprised the main body of the ruins. By September 1833 this section had passed into the possession of a trust. It should be noted that Lord Bexley paid for the conveyancing. But the Trust was running short of funds and it became clear it could not afford to buy any more of the land. Indeed, even whilst negotiations were proceeding, several houses within the ruins had been demolished, as had some portions of the Abbey walls and some arches which stood at the end of the Refectory.

In 1834 James Wheble bypassed the protracted and stalled negotiations and bought the remaining section of the ruins directly from Lord Bexley. This included the eastern section of the Forbury, the land which is now Abbots Walk, the old Cloisters and Refectory behind the Cloisters and the area which is now owned by St James' church.

By 1835 the National School in the Chapter House had closed and its house had been demolished by 1837. The Trust was evidently conscious of the need to protect the area against vandalism and further deterioration of the site. However the Trustees had run out of money and decided they could do no more for the moment. Nevertheless they asked that the county of Berkshire, which owned the prison land, and James Wheble, who owned adjacent land, should fence this in. Their comments also noted that this would prevent *the encroachment* of workmen employed by speculative builders on neighbouring sites.

By 1839 the value of the area for public use was beginning to be realised. Reading Horticultural Society held its show in the ruins in May. Later in the year, on August the 8th, Reading Band gave a successful, well attended performance.

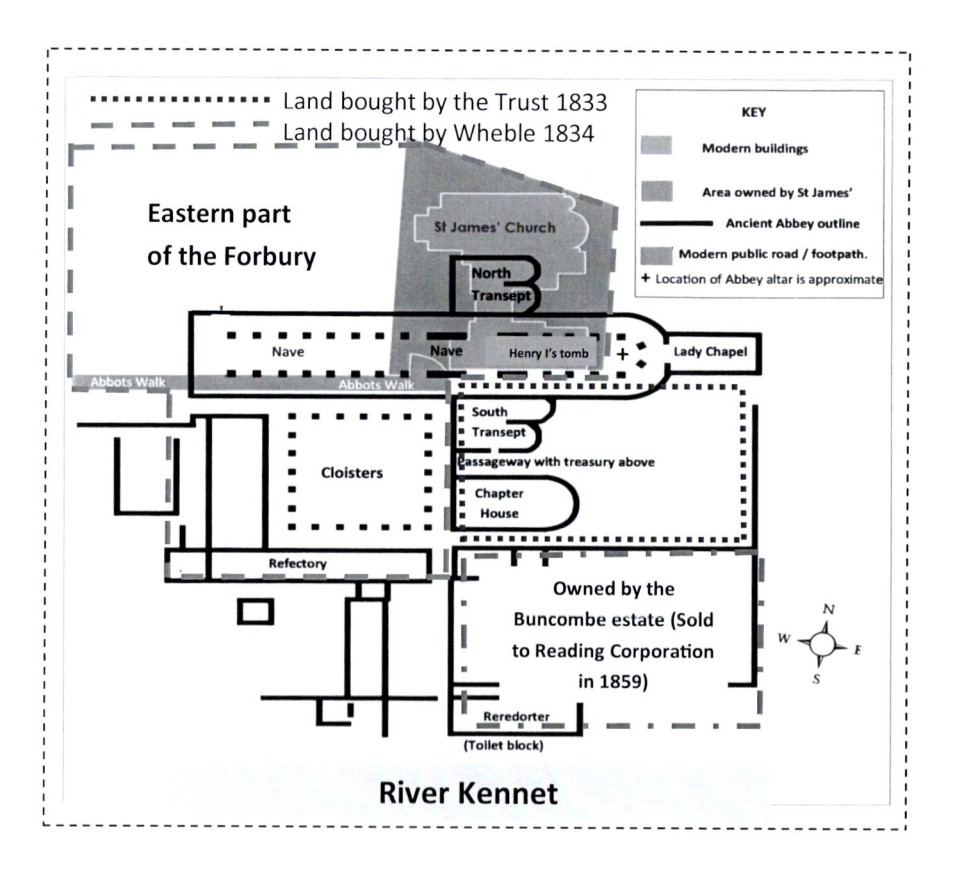

PART 2. CHAPTER 5. ST JAMES' CHURCH AND SCHOOL

The Building of St James' Church

Early in 1837 the Reverend Francis Bowland, the priest in charge of the Catholic Chapel of the Resurrection, in Vastern Street, sometimes known as Vastern Lane, received a letter. It informed him that the planned route of the *railroad* would involve the likely demolition of the Chapel and the house.

The exact location of the Chapel is debated and on-going research is attempting to solve the mystery. What is known is that in 1811 a French priest, François Longuet, built the first Catholic chapel in Reading since the Reformation in the Vastern Lane area. Longuet was murdered in 1817 and replaced in 1820 by Father Bowland. As the population of Reading grew and as the anti-Catholic laws were repealed, culminating in the Emancipation Act of 1829, so did the Catholic population of the area increase. For some time Father Bowland had been planning to enlarge the chapel or even build a new church.

It was at this point that the very wealthy local Catholic landowner, James Wheble, made an offer not only to provide the land for a new church but to fund the whole cost. In 1802 Wheble had inherited a vast fortune of at least £200,000, not including business interests and land in Kensington and probably elsewhere. He married a niece of the 14th Earl of Shrewsbury and bought Woodley Lodge, spending the next years adding to his estate. He was a staunch Catholic and philanthropist, also giving generously to various non-Catholic churches, and appears to have been well liked in the wider Berkshire community. In 1837 he became High Sheriff of Berkshire. He was also a keen amateur antiquarian with a special interest in the Catholic history of Reading, particularly the Abbey.

James Wheble 1779 –1840

The portrait shown here is most likely to be of him, rather than his father, also called James. The style of dress, the age of the person shown, the printing techniques and paper used all indicate that we are looking at the younger James Wheble. There is an outside possibility that it is of his father, who died in 1801 at the age of 72. However the portrait does not seem to be of a person in his late 60s or early 70s.

We have seen that Wheble had already bought a large portion of the ancient Abbey lands. According to contemporary records, such as the *Cowslade Manuscript*,[1] newspaper articles, his obituary and letters deposited in the Westminster Catholic archives, Wheble's initial intention was to excavate the ruins in order to discover more about the Abbey. Unfortunately he died, unexpectedly, in July 1840, just a few weeks before the church was due to be opened and so was unable to fulfil his intentions.

Wheble has left us with a detailed account of the excavations which unearthed the Abbey Stone on the January 24th 1835. It is made of oolitic limestone decorated with intricate carvings. Wheble had it converted into a baptismal font for the new church of St James, which was opened in 1840. There are similar pieces of stonework, though none quite as large, in Reading Museum.[2]

The Reading Abbey Stone excavated from the Abbey Ruins and converted into a baptismal font for St James' church.

Having acquired the land, Wheble was in a position to offer some of it for the new church, especially when it looked likely that the railway would mean the loss of the existing chapel. At what point he made the offer is not clear. It would appear that Wheble attempted to buy Greyfriars to convert it into a new Catholic church but this was turned down by the Corporation. As late as April 1837 Father Bowland was still collecting donations for the *new chapel*. Unfortunately we do not know if this was money that he was hoping to give to the church in the Forbury or if he had another site in mind.

For Wheble 1837 was one of the most significant years in his life. He became High Sheriff of Berkshire at the start of the year and was present to oversee the laying of the foundation stone of his new church in December. According to the 'Reading Mercury' report at the time, between three to four thousand people attended this event.[3] There was raked staging for the onlookers. Perhaps this was the same staging that had been used for the crowds who had come to witness the execution of John Carter in 1833.

Whatever the case, the foundation ceremony was a major event in the history of the town. Among those present was AWN Pugin. St James' was his very first church design.[4] Pugin was to become not only the leading Catholic architect of

PART 2. CHAPTER 5. ST JAMES' CHURCH AND SCHOOL

the first half of the 19th century but also a major British architect of international importance and renown. Under the overall supervision of Charles Barry, he was largely responsible for the Houses of Parliament and its clock tower, familiarly referred to as *Big Ben*. He was also one of the main judges at the Great Exhibition of 1851. St James' is therefore a building of considerable historical and architectural importance and as such merits closer consideration.

Above: St James Church in plate from "Reading Past and Present,"

Below: A page from "Reading Past and Present," by William Fletcher,

The first feature to note is its overall style. Pugin became famous as an uncompromising advocate of the neo-gothic, elaborate, pointed, style. St James', in contrast, is a minimalist Norman-Romanesque building. It has rounded arches and windows, its buttresses are plain and functional and it lacks superfluous decoration. We know from records in the 'Reading Mercury' and the Catholic magazine 'The Tablet' that this was deliberate: that Pugin and Wheble wanted a building that would reflect the style of the ancient Abbey. For some time it was thought that this was one of Pugin's minor works and it has often been underrated in learned commentaries. However a revision of this opinion is coming to the fore. Pugin himself, even at the height of his fame as a neo-Gothic architect, was beginning to revise his ideas, returning to a simpler style. The building retains all the integrity of Pugin's basic principals of architectural design as defined in his great work: *The True Principles of Christian or Pointed Architecture*. There was even some claim that Pugin disowned and turned his back of this church. Once again recent research has shown the passion Pugin retained for St James. In 1840, shortly after its official opening, he paid a visit to Reading after which he wrote a detailed letter listing all the work that still needed to be done and giving precise instructions as to how it should be completed. He even offered to pay for some of this out of his own pocket.[5] The letter was written in August 1840 by Pugin to the priest in charge of St James', Father Ringrose.

The illustration of the church on the previous page appears at first sight to be an early drawing of the completed building. In fact it appears in Fletcher's book, *Reading Past and Present,* published in the spring of 1838. This was only a few months after the laying of the foundation stone. It would not have been possible for the church to have been built within this time scale. It is quite clearly an artist's impression. There is still some doubt about the meaning of the wording in Fletcher's book. Is he saying that Wheble did the sketch or merely that he allowed Fletcher to draw it? The drawing is so accurate in many respects that one can but assume it came from the architect's plans. If so we are looking at something closely based on Pugin's first church drawing, if not the drawing itself. It should be noted however that on the drawing Fletcher has signed himself with the word *del,* indicating that he was the artist. We can only speculate as to the origins of the illustration.

In many ways it is very accurate but there are some 'errors' or differences from the completed work. Most noticeable is the most easterly buttress. In the drawing this has the same dimensions as the other five. In fact this buttress is much more robust. Whether at the time of building it was discovered that it needed to be much stronger, or whether this was always Pugin's plan we can not tell. It appears to have been built like this and not added at a later date. If this were the case it would have had to be done before 1844 when the illustration below was made and appeared in the 'Illustrated London News' on the 17th February 1844. There is no mention of any such problem in Pugin's letter mentioned above.

The new gaol and St James' Church [6]

Parts of the Abbey ruins: the wall of the North Transept and Nave, and beyond that the wall that divided the South Transept from the Nave, are visible between the church and the prison. Note that the north aisle and arcade of St James are not present in this depiction; these were added in the 20th century.

The siting of St James' is quite deliberate. It lies just to the north of the north transept of the old Abbey church. Wheble intended to carry out more excavations of the ruins, including areas that had not been previously looked at, most especially the Cloisters.

PART 2. CHAPTER 5. ST JAMES' CHURCH AND SCHOOL

The Opening of the Church

Wheble had planned to have the church officially opened on the 5th of August 1840. He even had special brasses fitted to the new font to mark the occasion. These brasses were attached before the ceremony and they record the finding of the font stone and the opening of the church.

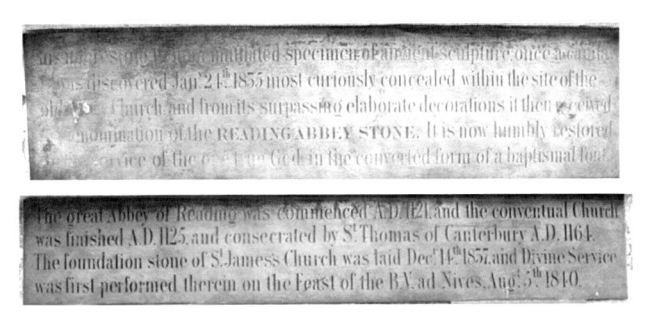

The first of the two brasses attached to the font records the discovery of the stone, whilst the lower brass commemorates the opening of the church on the 5th of August 1840. The full text of these inscriptions is in Appendix B.

Despite Wheble's untimely death, on the 20th of July, the ceremony went ahead so that his wishes should be respected, though without the pomp that had been planned. Nor was the building completely finished. Pugin visited the church shortly afterwards and wrote the letter mentioned above, cataloguing the work that was still required. Several questions remain unanswered as to the exact design of the whole complex. To date no plans have come to light so it is necessary to rely on contemporary descriptions and the few illustrations so far uncovered.

Apart from the drawings already mentioned there is another in Reading Library Local Studies section. This is in a book attributed to Marianna Frederica Cowslade and consists of a series of sketches.[7] Some of these are of people and others of places. It is dated 1833. The exact authorship of the sketches has not been established. Some may be by Marianna, but as she was born around 1827 it would not be possible for all the drawings to be by her. The one of St James' church must have been drawn after 1840, when the church was completed. Moreover, in the background there is a locomotive. The railway did not arrive in Reading until 1840.

The Pugin Design of St James' Church

Apart from its obvious interest as the earliest sketch we have of the church from this angle, the Cowslade drawing both raises further questions and possibly provides answers to some others. If we are looking at an approximately accurate representation of the buildings around 1840, then we have to ask whether Pugin also designed the priest's house. Tantalisingly we are only given a glimpse of the presbytery, nevertheless it does show its existence in 1840. This fits in with the transfer of ownership to the Catholic church, made by James Wheble, which mentions not only the church but also *associated buildings*. If the house was also designed by Pugin then we are looking at one of his early vernacular buildings.

The simplicity of Pugin's design is best expressed in the west door. The attention to detail, from the stone carvings to the wrought iron work and proportions of the archway, has resulted in a masterpiece of Norman Romanesque design. Several years later Pugin was to write his famous treatise: *The True Principles of Christian or pointed Architecture*. Despite St James' not being in the 'pointed style' it possesses all the elements advocated by Pugin.

So what do we know about the interior of the church and how do we know it? As noted, neither Pugin's plans nor any other drawings of the inside of the church have come to light. We do however have a detailed description of the opening of the church in 1840.

Top: St James' Church 2014 with the west door brought forward.

Left: The original west door before it was brought forward in 1926.

PART 2. CHAPTER 5. ST JAMES' CHURCH AND SCHOOL

This comes from 'The Tablet', the Catholic magazine which was founded in 1840. The interior of the church is described thus:

Immediately on passing the finely wrought–iron doors, the spectator's eye is carried to the eastern end, where, under the noble arch of the sanctuary, stands the altar, presenting at the first view a blaze of glory. Directly over it are three painted windows, of which the softened brilliancy of colouring produces the effect of clustered precious stones… At the western end is the choir, adorned also with two windows of singular beauty, and at the remote end of the choir is placed a powerful and richly toned organ. It is so placed as not to intercept the view of the central window.[8]

This account gives us a vivid picture of the inside of the church.

The photograph below shows the church as it would have looked at the time of its opening in 1840. Note the position of the font and *the noble arch* referred to above. The windows visible today are most probably those that so impressed the writer of the Tablet article.

The picture was taken before 1926 when an extra aisle was added to the south side and a porch was added. The reason given for this expansion was that *the need has been long felt not only for increased accommodation for the congregation but for a larger Sanctuary* and for Side Altars, Confessionals and a Baptistery, together with an improvement of the Sacristy arrangements.

Wilfred C. Mangan was the architect. The west end of the church, including Pugin's door and arch, was brought forward to create a porch. Mangan was careful to follow Pugin's Norman Romanesque style. A baptistery was incorporated to the south of the extension, into which the font was moved from its central position in the nave. A spiral octagonal staircase to the choir loft was added leading from the baptistery. The 'gallery' or choir loft, was *improved and extended*. The rear wall of the nave was moved to the position of the old exterior wall. It was at this time that the now distinctive feature of the sanctuary, the ambulatory, was added. A new Lady Chapel was built, partly using stones from the ancient Abbey.[9]

In 1962 a north aisle was added. This did not attempt to replicate the previous style. There have been several refurbishments of the church, the latest being in 2012 when the church was totally redecorated, the Lady Chapel was revamped and a shrine to St James of Compostela was created.

The School Buildings

Ellenor Cowslade, around 1840, wrote the following: *Catholic children can now go to their own Church or school without being hooted by a youthful rabble.*[10] We know from Slater's Berkshire Directory of 1850 that Mr and Mrs Dearlove ran a school in Vastern Street. Whether this was the building, previously the Chapel of the Resurrection and *adjoining house*, or elsewhere in the street is not known. The question is whether there was also a school attached to the church and presbytery from the very start or whether this occurred later. The Catholic

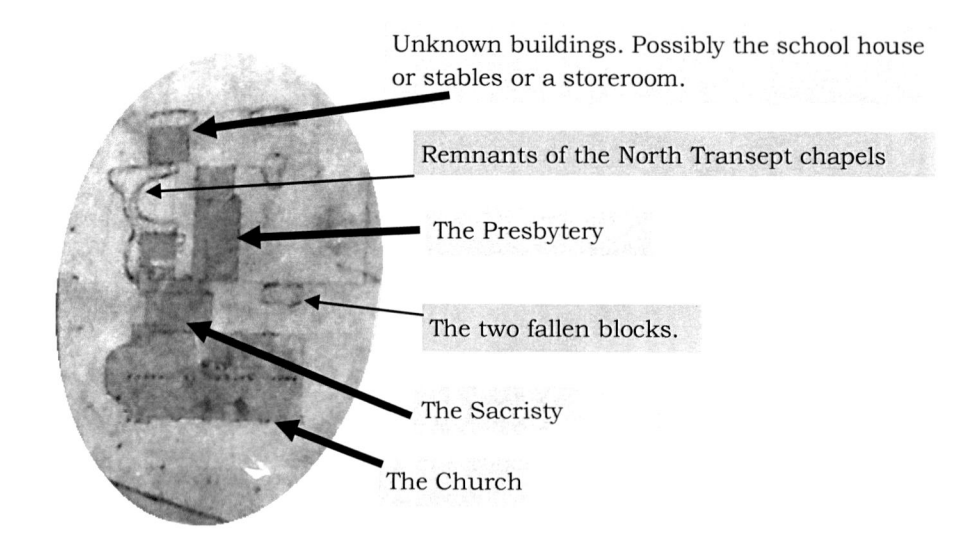

Unknown buildings. Possibly the school house or stables or a storeroom.

Remnants of the North Transept chapels

The Presbytery

The two fallen blocks.

The Sacristy

The Church

Above is an extract from the Board of Health Survey of 1853. The ruins are outlined, but not shaded and are indicated by arrows. The 19th century buildings are shaded in on the plan and indicated with heavy arrows.

PART 2. CHAPTER 5. ST JAMES' CHURCH AND SCHOOL

Poor School Committee records for 1853 show that £25 was given to Reading for its school.[11] Could it be there were two Catholic schools, one for poor children, the other for the children of wealthier parents? With regard to the buildings, the 1853 Survey shows an outbuilding, but its use remains unknown. By 1900, if the drawings are accurate, this had been altered. Photographs show that this building was a single storey structure under a pitched roof. The 1900 records say that it was occupied by the schoolmistress, Miss Darling, and her brother. The second school mistress, Miss Collins, lodged in the town.

The position of this building and its later replacements was alongside the dividing wall between the ancient north transept chapels and the sanctuary of the Abbey church.

The next image is catalogued by Reading Library as: *Forbury Gardens, Reading, from Forbury Hill, c.1880, looking downwards to the pond and garden. In the background are St. James's Roman Catholic Church, and Reading Gaol, with the ruins of the south transept of Reading Abbey Church in front of it.* Right 1880-1889: print with the caption, *View of gaol, Forbury, etc., Reading, from a photograph by Poulton.*[12] Only a detail of the photograph appears here. The church itself is not visible.

The original photograph, by Poulton, must have been taken before 1872, since that was the year the new school, with the flint frontage and bellcote which we see today, was built. It is nor present in this illustration. The architects were Morris and Stallwood.[13]

The photograph to the right, by Henry Taunt, is dated circa 1875 in the Reading Library catalogue.

There is no school building in this photo either, so we must assume that it was taken just before the school was built in 1872.

We do have a later photograph, by Frith, dated 1904, which shows the school

St James' and the Forbury c. 1870 [14]

with its distinctive bell tower. The image to the right is a detail from the full photograph which is shown below.

In 1912 Alexander Scoles was engaged to modernise the school building. In addition to other improvements he adapted the frontage to its existing appearance but retained the bellcote.[15]

PART 2. CHAPTER 5. ST JAMES' CHURCH AND SCHOOL

The Changing Face of the Abbey ruins and St James' in Plans and in Pictures

Because the church had been built alongside the Forbury Road, the view of the Abbey Ruins from the north was blocked so that it was no longer possible to have a clear sightline across to the remaining main body of the site.

The arrival of the railway likewise changed the character of the eastern approaches to Reading. The area was beginning to take the shape that we know today. The streams and meadows were covered over and replaced with roads, railways and shunting yards. The building of the new prison in the 1840s completed the transformation.[16]

Tomkins. 1791 [17]

Only 50 years separates these two illustrations. They are both from approximately the same viewpoint. In the first, 1791, drawing, the ruins are more or less as they had been since the Civil War.

By the time of the second illustration, around 1841, below, the arrival of the railway had completely altered the easterly approach to Reading.

We see the west tower of the new gaol, with St James' church to its right. The two great blocks of fallen masonry are now hidden by the church building.

The railway sheds and workshops are a major feature.

We know from contemporary reports that the noise and dirt from these caused many complaints from residents around the Forbury area.

The 1879 survey map shows the changes that had taken place since the 1853 Board of Health Survey. Both the presbytery and the school buildings had been extended, but the basic Pugin structure remained in place.[18]

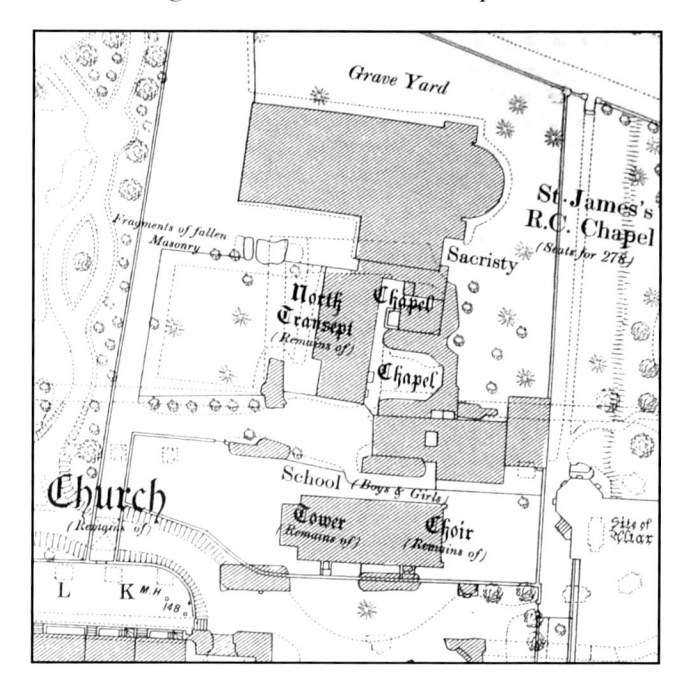

The photograph below, taken in 1904, clarifies the ground plan details. It shows the lean-to extension to the presbytery and the front of the school is just visible.[19]

CHAPTER 6. ABBOTS WALK. THE INNER GATEWAY. THE ABBEY MILL

Abbots Walk

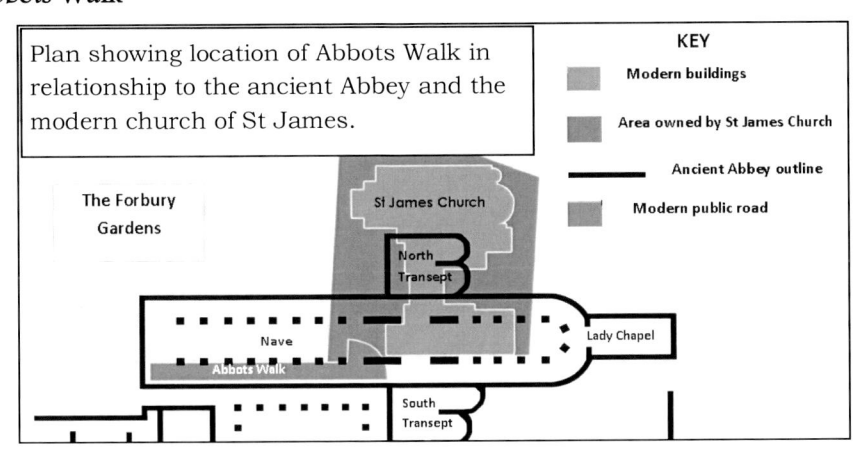

Plan showing location of Abbots Walk in relationship to the ancient Abbey and the modern church of St James.

KEY
Modern buildings
Area owned by St James Church
Ancient Abbey outline
Modern public road

As we have seen, James Wheble bought a significant portion of the Abbey ruins with the intention of carrying out further excavations, especially in the area of the former cloisters. Whether he originally planned it, or whether circumstances such as the arrival of the railway dictated events, he went on to build St James' church and presbytery on this land, and donated it, via his son James Joseph, to the Catholic church.

When James died prematurely in July 1840 his son James Joseph inherited his father's estate, including St James' and the Forbury area. It is clear that James Joseph did not wish to pursue his father's interest in archaeological excavation. In 1843 he sold the Cloister area to a builder for £730. In 1844 he also sold a strip of land, stretching from and including the eastern section of the Abbey Gateway as far as the Cloister arch, to a local solicitor, John Weedon. The latter bought the cloister area from the builder and constructed a new road, Abbots Walk. Over the next ten years or so twelve high quality houses were built along this new road. The 1851 census shows that members of the Cowslade family were in residence at number 12.

Contemporary photograph showing the Cloister arch and the end of Abbots Walk. Number 12 is the last house, adjacent to the ruins.

This overview of the Abbey offers an alternative concept of its appearance compared with that shown in the museum model opposite page 1.

PART 2. CHAPTER 6. ABBOTS WALK, THE INNER GATEWAY, THE ABBEY MILL

These two illustrations of Abbots Walk give a good impression of how the area became built up and the last remnants of the Abbey cloisters and other associated buildings were covered over during the second half of the 19th century.

Right: The Abbey Gateway 1902 [1]

The Abbey Inner Gateway

The Abbey Inner Gateway, popularly known as the Abbey Gateway, is one of the few of the Abbey buildings in Reading to have survived and to have been in more or less constant use since the Dissolution of the Abbey. Another is the Hospitium.

This famous illustration, by Tomkins, shows a somewhat bucolic, almost 'picturesque' view of the area. Through the ancient archway we are looking at the Forbury. There are sheep grazing and a cricket match is taking place. The Grammar School, under Dr Valpy, used the Forbury for games, sometimes coming into conflict with the townsfolk. Beyond we see the Plummery wall and the river Thames. In the centre, on the river, is a sailing barge. To the left are old Caversham Bridge and St Peter's Church. The far distance is framed with the Caversham hills and clouds cover the eastern sky.

Tomkins. View through the Inner Gateway [2]

This idealised vision nevertheless epitomises Reading's attachment to the area, one that it retains to this day. The Gateway has become an icon of Reading's past. Perhaps for this reason the town has, over the years, struggled to maintain it, even rebuilding it, almost from nothing, when it collapsed in the mid 19th century.

18th Century Views of the Gateway from the South

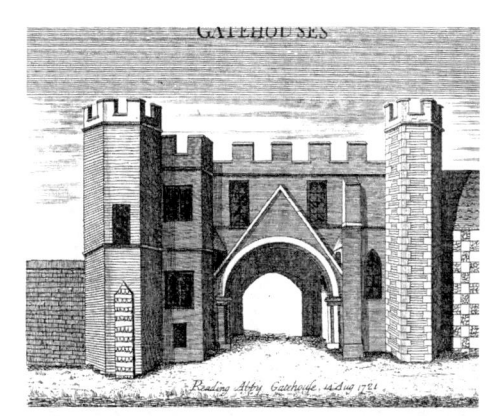

A. 1721 [3]

B Kearsley 1775 [4]

C. Ireland, 18th century [5]

The structure we see today only bears a passing resemblance to the original Gateway. By examining illustrations made over the last three hundred years we can trace part of its evolution.

The earliest illustration, A, was made in 1721. The Reading Library catalogue describes this as *The Inner Gateway, from the south. The top of the Gateway is crenellated. Print, entitled "Gatehouses. Reading Abby [sic] Gatehouse, 14 Aug. 1721. 18th century"*. Notice the crenellations and the chequered stone work reminiscent of St Mary's Minster in Reading.

Compare this with the three following views, likewise made in the 18th century.

The next, B, is attributed to Kearsley and dated 1775. The third, C, drawn by Ireland, also dates to the 18th century.

Both are views from the south looking towards the Thames and where the Forbury Gardens now stand.

The towers, window structures and walls, though different in all the pictures, nevertheless retain a certain consistency, the main difference being the lack of crenellations in the second and third pictures.

The Library gives no exact date for illustration C but it is similar to that by Tomkins, dated 1791, on the next page.

The houses are not visible in either C or D, so it would appear they had been demolished rather than merely hidden by the new wall.

PART 2. CHAPTER 6.. ABBOTS WALK, THE INNER GATEWAY, THE ABBEY MILL

The print on the right, D, is catalogued by Reading Library as *Reading Abbey. The Inner Gateway from the south. Print entitled "South Front of the Abbey Gate, Reading," drawn and engraved by Charles Tomkins, 1791.* The Gateway itself and the adjoining house to the right are possibly best know today as the home of Jane Austen's school. This however ceased to exist when it went bankrupt in 1796. The prints only give us tantalising glimpses of the building from its southern aspect.

D. Tomkins 1791 [6]

18th Century Views from the North

An illustration by Tomkins in 1791, this time from the north, shows a structure not dissimilar to that of Hooper, 1784. The nearer archway is pointed whereas the further arch leading to the south appears rounded.

Tomkins 1791 [7]

Hooper c. 1784 [8]

Close up of Tomkin's drawing of 1791

The windows, buttresses and towers are likewise fairly identical. In both drawings, just to the left, is the house that was part of the school mentioned above.

Note the wall to the left. As Slade comments this continued to divide the western and eastern Forbury and was there in the early 1860s.[9] It is clearly shown in the Tomkins and Hooper prints of the late 18th century.

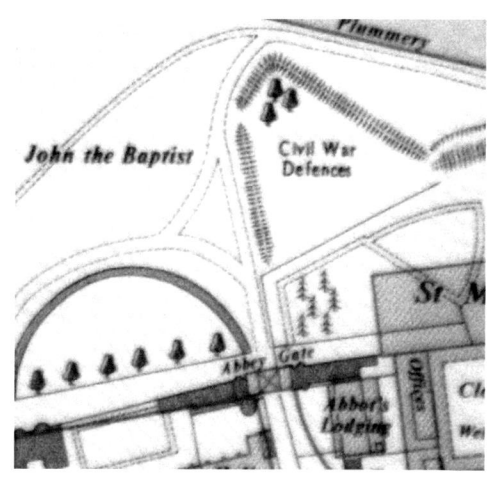

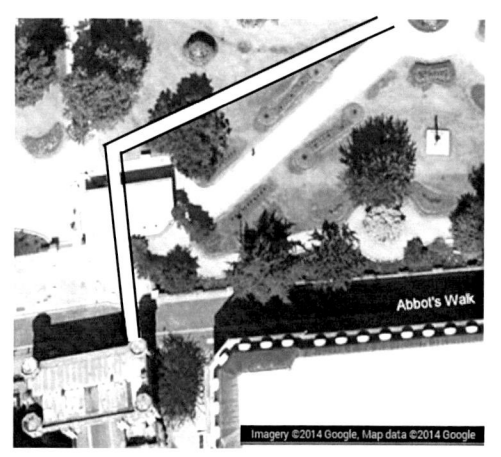

However the wall's exact line is unclear. If we look again at Slade's map we see that the wall turned eastward at a point almost in line with the north aisle of the Abbey church.

If Slade's drawing is accurate, then the wall ran where the white line within black borders is superimposed on the modern aerial photograph.

When was the wall erected? Did it date to the Civil War and the removal of the defences? The first section, to where it turns east, is apparently in line with the Civil War earthworks coming south from the Hill. However it does not feature in several prints dating even towards the end of the 18th century. This is not to say that it was not there. The angles of the prints just do not allow for its presence to be shown.

For example Kearsley's print of 1779 shows an easterly view from the north-eastern buttress of the Gateway. An interesting feature of this print is that it clearly shows a pointed arch on the outside of the gateway but a rounded one on an interior order.

Hence a view from the south would show a rounded arch frame to any view looking north from the south of the Gateway.

Kearsley 1779 [9]

PART 2. CHAPTER 6. ABBOTS WALK, THE INNER GATEWAY, THE ABBEY MILL

From a print dated 1800 –1809 [10]

Owen and Dace 1804 [11]

The lithograph, above left, is listed by Reading Library as the *Forbury Hill, Reading, looking southwards, c.1800.* We shall be looking at the Forbury, its Hill and other features in a later chapter. The right hand print appeared in a book of 1804 *The Beauties of England and Wales.* Here we see the wall in some detail: its size and a hint at its purpose. Behind it, in the left hand picture, are six fir trees. These exactly match those in Slade's drawing. These illustrations show that the wall portioned off a section of the eastern Forbury and that this 'shadowed' the line of the old Civil War defences.

The last picture, dating from 1790, once again gives a clear idea of the wall. Note the finials and gate which led to the house immediately to the east of the Gateway. As already mentioned this was Jane Austen's school. Whereas the boys' Grammar School used the open Forbury for sports it is likely that the young ladies of the Abbey Gateway school were restricted to the privacy of the walled area.

The Gateway 1790 [12]

The Abbey Gateway in the 19th Century

The Question of Ownership

The 19th century saw a period when, piece by piece, the Forbury, the Ruins and the Gateway were unified to become Reading's main green space for relaxation and entertainment. The Gateway was central to this process. We have seen how, just like the Forbury itself, the Gateway had been divided between two owners. The westerly part belonged to the Blagrave family whilst the eastern section was owned by the Vansittarts.

This changed when Wheble bought Vansittart's interest in 1834. We have seen (page 77) that in 1843 James Joseph Wheble sold the cloister area and his portion of the Gateway to a builder who, in turn, sold this on to a local solicitor, John Weedon. There were discussions between Weedon and the Corporation about maintaining the Gateway; the Corporation hoped to convert the eastern section into offices for the Board of Health. During these talks, and the consequent indecision as to its future, the building was not repaired or maintained. In fact it was rapidly deteriorating. By 1859 John Weedon's widow had agreed to sell the eastern section of the Gateway to the Corporation, who bought it for £50.

Likewise, after protracted negotiations, Blagrave agreed to sell his western section to the Corporation. By spring 1860 agreement was reached and, for £6,010, Colonel Blagrave sold not just his section of the Gateway but also the western area of the Forbury.

Above: 1830-1939 Fletcher. From the north [13]

1840 Fox Talbot. From the South [14]

These two illustrations, one of the northern aspect, the other of the southern, show the state of disrepair of the Gateway in the late 1830s and 1840s.

In 1821 the Gateway had been decorated for the celebrations to mark the coronation of George IV. One report noted that the *noble gateway was adorned with a large regal star.*

PART 2. CHAPTER 6. ABBOTS WALK, THE INNER GATEWAY, THE ABBEY MILL

The Restoration of 1861

Renshaw c.1850. From the north. [15]

1849 Cranstone and Fletcher. From the south. [16]

Photograph for 3D viewing. The Inner Gateway, from the north, c. 1860. There is an inscribed tablet on the tympanum above the arch. Double image for stereoscopic viewing. [17]

We have seen that by the late 1850s the whole of the Gateway had passed into the ownership of the Corporation. One plan was to convert it into a residence for the head gardener, known as the Superintendent, of the Pleasure Gardens. These had recently been created in the eastern section of the Forbury. We shall be looking at this topic in more detail in a later chapter.

By February 1859 the Corporation announced, through the Board of Health, that it would be making the requisite repairs and alterations to the Gateway. At about the same time, just alongside the Gateway, the construction of the new Assize Courts was underway. The contrast between the condition of the two buildings was plain to see. In fact the deterioration of the Gateway was so great there was a suggestion that it should be demolished, various tenders and proposals for refurbishment being considered too expensive or unsatisfactory.

George Gilbert Scott, designer of the Gaol and one of the leading architects of the 19th century, produced an estimate of £1000 to restore the Gateway. He reported to the Corporation that *the gateway is a work of architectural interest and value and is well deserving of the most careful restoration.* Despite some misgivings over the cost, it is to the credit of the Corporation that a subscription list was opened and the Board of Health agreed to pay half the sum required.[18]

The Gateway is such an important architectural feature, linking, as it does, medieval with modern Reading, that it is worth reproducing in full George Gilbert Scott's report to Reading Corporation, dated 30th March 1860.[19]

I have in compliance with your direction made a careful survey of the Abbey Gateway, in the first instance myself and subsequently by my experienced practical assistant, Mr Burlison. I find some parts to have suffered severely from structural failure and a greater portion to be very much affected by time and decay as well as by deliberate injury and alteration.
The parts which have structurally suffered are especially the Southern Arch with the Pier on its Western side (these will have to be in a considerable degree re-built) also the Pier at the North Western angle, which will demand some considerable and very substantial reparation. Next to these I will mention the base mouldings of the exterior, which have been cut away, almost through and must be renewed. The level of the ground has also been raised about one foot and nine inches, which I would recommend to be restored to its proper level. The next prominent deficiency is the entire loss of the Parapet both to the building generally and to its Turrets. This with the Cornice will have to be new. After these. The most marked deficiency is the removal or walling
up of several of the smaller windows, especially in the upper storey: these will have to be renewed or restored as the case may be.
Beyond what I have above enumerated, the principal external works required are of the nature of partial restorations, underpinning the general repairs. The Roof is covered with lead, which is not in good condition, and its timbers require to be, in many parts, renewed, its gutters re-modelled, etc. The Floor partitions, etc. will also demand considerable reparation. The Gateway is a work of great architectural interest and value and is deserving of the most careful restoration. It seems to date from about 1250 and is an excellent specimen of the style of the period. Many curious antiquarian questions suggest themselves in examining this ancient structure, but with these I will not at this time trouble you. It is not clearly apparent by what means the upper storey was originally approached, I imagine that it must have been by a staircase in the North Eastern portion and it might have been placed again in that position. The upper stories (sic) *would … become available for any purpose which might suggest itself. I am of the opinion that the cost of restoring the whole, as specified above, will approach closely to £1,000.*[20]

PART 2. CHAPTER 6. ABBOTS WALK, THE INNER GATEWAY, THE ABBEY MILL

It is worth drawing attention to several comments in Gilbert Scott's letter. First and foremost is his assertion that the Gateway was of great architectural interest and value and so merited great care in its preservation. The plans to demolish it were very quickly dismissed. The other is the fact that the ground level was significantly different from its original state. This is a factor often overlooked, even today. It makes sense, however, of one scheme which was to lower the passageway under the arch by two feet or so. When read in conjunction with Scott's letter this proposal is less bizarre than at first sight.

Consequently restoration began in late 1860. Old windows and doors were revealed and, in the process of clearing ruined portions, an ancient staircase was discovered. This may be the item Scott referred to towards the end of his letter.

There was still the issue of the overall cost. The builders, Messrs Wheeler, reduced their estimate to £1400 from £1800, once certain modifications were accepted. Despite some emergency remedial work the Gateway continued to deteriorate, so much so that by December 1860 it had to be shored up and the public were advised not to pass under the arch. Finally the road was closed to traffic and pedestrians. The precaution proved necessary as one of the southern buttresses collapsed *along with the pillar base of the arch itself.*

Matters came to a head when, in February 1861, a severe storm finally brought about a major collapse of the Gateway. The photograph on this page shows not only the extent of the damage but the remains of the wooden supports referred to above. Notice the gas light still in place to the right of the arch.

Despite a slow start, the building work by Wheeler, following Gilbert Scott's plans, was all but completed within six months. In August the Mayor, when opening the new Forbury Gardens, referred to the *handsome gateway before us.* The windows (frames and glass) were completed in January 1862 and by that summer plans were in place to let out the large room above the Gateway.[21]

As commented at the time Reading now possessed *one of the most beautiful specimens of the Norman architectural period ...in the south west of England.*[22]

The first illustration, A, shows the restored gateway. The Reading Library catalogue entry repeats the title on the print which reads, *The Inner Gateway, Reading Abbey, Restored* 1859. This is unlikely since, as we have seen, at that time the Gateway was a virtual ruin and the restoration only began in 1860.

A. Beecroft [23]

Illustration B, a modern photograph, is also of the north frontage. The accuracy of Beecroft's sketch, above, can be judged by comparing the two images.

The Abbey Gateway became a central feature of the area. It was used by many groups and societies over the years and has remained virtually unchanged from Gilbert Scott's time.

Today the Gateway is again facing a crisis. Its stonework has deteriorated and once more it is awaiting restoration.

B. Twentieth Century.

Sir George Gilbert Scott's words *The Gateway is a work of great architectural interest and value and is deserving of the most careful restoration* are as true today as they were over 150 years ago.

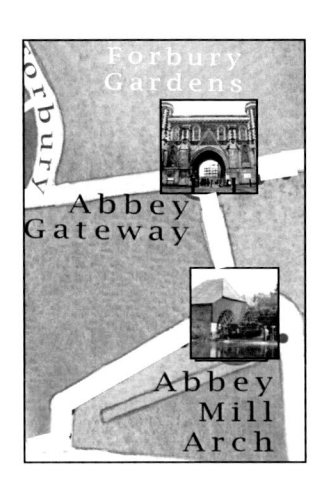

PART 2. CHAPTER 6. ABBOTS WALK, THE INNER GATEWAY, THE ABBEY MILL

The Abbey Mill

The Mill arch today. ©JR Mullaney

The Holy Brook leaves the River Kennet just south of Theale, some 6 miles to the west of Reading. It runs parallel to, and just north of, the Kennet river and canal until it reaches Reading. Today, once it enters the town, much of it is covered over by roads and buildings, making only brief appearances as at the northerly entrance to the Oracle shopping centre. Most modern opinion considers that the monks of Reading Abbey had widened and deepened the Holy Brook, probably by the use of sluices, so that in medieval times it ran at a higher level than the Kennet. This was to enable a greater head of water to build up to drive the undershot mills, such as those at Calcot and beside the Abbey, that lined the brook. It also allowed for the creation of fish ponds so that stocks of fish, one of the monks' staple foods, could be maintained. Certainly the evidence is that the last remaining vestiges of a mill, just south of the Gateway, show that the water level was sufficiently higher, some 5 feet, than the Kennet, to power this mill. Soon after passing the mill the level dropped as it re-joined the River Kennet just south of the Abbey buildings. This was also the location of the Abbey wharf which was so essential for provisions and trade. These two mills, at Calcot and to the south of the Gateway, were significant in being built of stone, demonstrating the importance the Abbey put on its ownership of these mills and the role they played.

There were also secondary channels leading away from the main Holy Brook stream. One, to the south, acted as a sluice in order to maintain water levels. Another appears to have been directed to the north to pass either under or near the reredorter (toilet block) to remove the human waste. Another diagram shows a channel which may have been designed to remove kitchen waste.

The Inner Gateway and the Mill

Different opinions have been offered as to where the Abbot's House lay. Some say it was the building to the right of the Gateway, others think that it was to its left alongside the spacious gardens shown to the top of the drawing. This latter was once thought to be the leper house but most modern opinion would not agree with this.

The Mill straddled the Holy Brook, its importance demonstrated by the fact that it was built of stone.

Rising from the Mill and Holy Brook towards the Gateway, the gardens would have been on a steep south-facing slope offering a magnificent setting for growing a variety of herbs, vegetables and fruit trees.

The Inner Gateway lies to the right of this illustration.
On the left is the Mill, straddling the Holy Brook

PART 2. CHAPTER 6. ABBOTS WALK, THE INNER GATEWAY, THE ABBEY MILL

In the 1980s Wessex Archaeology published the results of a survey of the waterfront. They reported that *excavations have shown that the first mill on the site dated to the late 12th century.* This is based on the evidence that the timber posts and planks that were uncovered are similar to those at the Abbey wharf. These timbers helped increase the speed of the water before the mill by narrowing its course, causing the 5ft. drop mentioned above. This mill may have replaced those mentioned by the Domesday Book in Reading. The construction of these would not of course have been connected with the Abbey, which was founded in 1121, though we cannot rule out subsequent developments.

Reading not only needed mills for milling grain for bread. By the late middle ages the town had become a centre for the cloth industry, which required water mills. The area where the Oracle shopping centre now stands, and which was the site of the original Oracle, became a manufacturing hub in the late 15th and 16th centuries.[24]

We have seen these two illustrations in earlier chapters. The first is by Dr Hurry and the second by Professor Slade. They both show the cut made to channel some of the Holy Brook water through the monastery and under the Reredorter.

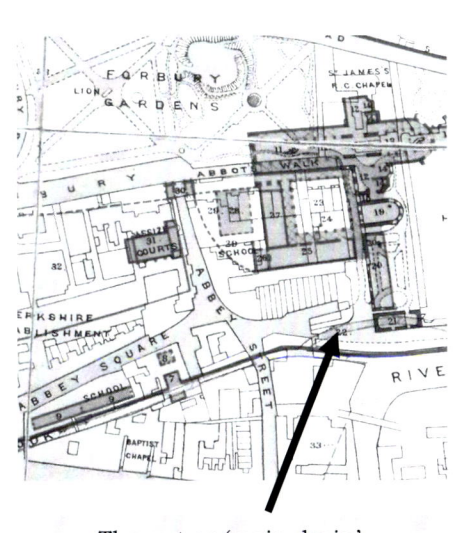

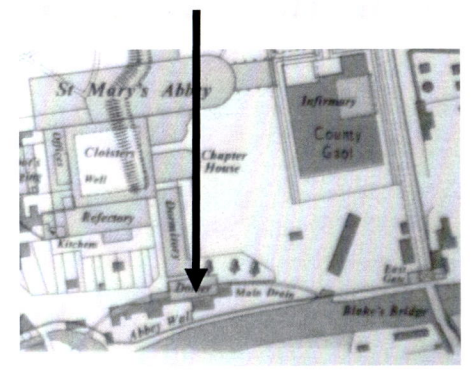

Neither map shows the existence of a possible southern overflow channel or the extra cut under the kitchens.

In 2014 an archaeologist from Wessex archaeology proposed an alternative theory, namely that the monastic toilet block was further to the west than originally thought. This would place it somewhere between the refectory and the dormitory. It was suggested that some masonry, indicating a substantial building, may have been part of a warehouse for a wharf serving boats coming from the Thames and the Kennet.

The cut or 'main drain'.

However these same buildings have also been attributed to the forts possibly constructed, at least in part, in the Civil War as part of the defences guarding the eastern approaches to Reading.[25]

If Reading's waterways were important to the Abbey, they continued to be vital for the town's industries, such as cloth making and tanning, after the Dissolution. They also played a significant part in its defences. The Civil War map shows the extent of Reading's waterway system and its strategic role in the defence of the town.

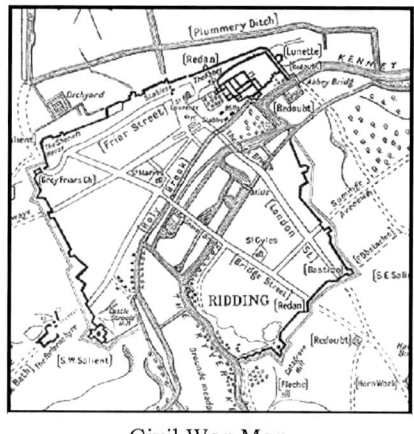

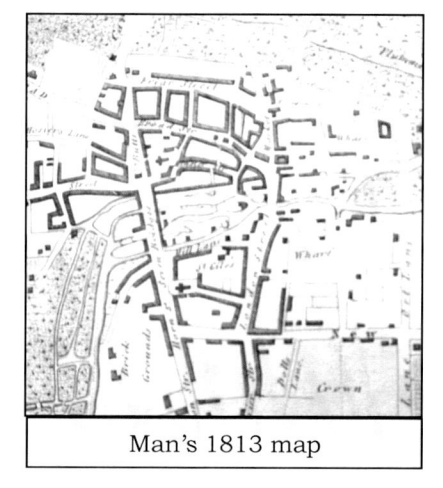

| Civil War Map | Man's 1813 map |

Not only does this map show the Kennet running along Reading's southern edge but the Holy Brook can be seen as the main waterway flowing through the centre of the town. The two are linked by channels which created an almost Venice-like townscape. If one considers that the map does not show all the lesser cuts, then the extent to which waterways played a significant role in the life of the town is clearly demonstrated. Man's map of 1813, shows a remarkably similar picture 160 years later.

It should be noted that, even as far back as the Domesday Survey, 1086, Reading had several mills. The 'burgh' of Reading, (and in all of Berkshire there were only two 'burghs', Wallingford and Reading), is recorded as having six mills. Four of the mills, and three fisheries, belonged to the King as part of his manor. Two more appertained to Battle Abbey. Land in Reading had been granted by William I to this abbey, near Hastings, which he had founded in thanksgiving for his victory against Harold in 1066. The area in Reading now known as 'Battle' marks the land once owned by Battle Abbey and it should be not be confused with the Abbey that Henry I founded in Reading in 1121.

However it is worth recalling that, in founding the new Abbey, Henry was developing his own manor and all its lands. Hence his endowment to the Abbey included not only the area where the Abbey was built but the whole town, its mills, all the produce of the lands and its markets. Domesday is painstaking in legitimising the Crown's ownership of Reading by proving that the 'burgh' had

PART 2. CHAPTER 6. ABBOTS WALK, THE INNER GATEWAY, THE ABBEY MILL

formerly belonged to King Edward (Edward the Confessor), from whom William claimed his title to the throne.

The Abbey Mill remained operational until 1959. There are few photographs of the mill before its demolition and nothing has come to light from earlier eras. The following photographs from Reading Library show its state of disrepair before the archway and the surrounding area were restored in the latter part of the 20th century.

Left: 1966. The view is towards the west, and there are steps to an upper floor behind the arch. [26]

Right: Abbey Mill, the middle and largest arch spanning the Holy Brook, looking west, c.1970. Behind the central arch, a building has been built over the brook on girders. [27]

Left: 1983 Excavation of the foundations of the stables in 1983, just west of the Mill Arch, before the new Central Library was built on the site, showing some old timbers from the Holy Brook edges. [28]

2013 Two photographs of the arch in 2013. Notice the difference between the central pointed arch and the rounded Norman archway style. Does this indicate, as some archaeologists believe, that there was a mill here before the mill recorded by Wessex Archaeology in 1966?

The excavations of the Abbey Mill: 1964-1967

In The Berkshire Archaeological Journal, Cecil Slade writes up the results of this extensive, and to the present, most comprehensive, archaeological survey of the Abbey area, concentrating as it did on the Cloister and Mill areas. Slade comments on the difficult conditions faced by the team. These included poor weather and excavation time being mainly restricted to weekends, owing to the fact that work had already begun on the new buildings.

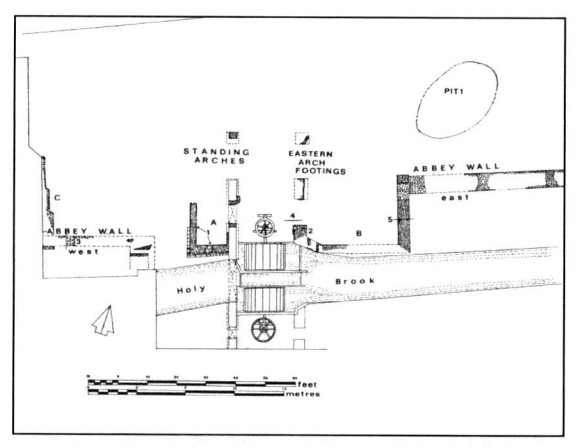

The Abbey Mill workings [29]

The overall conclusions were that the mill was built sometime just after 1121, the date of the founding of the Abbey, and that there had been several alterations over the next few centuries, hence the pointed arch, which itself had seen at least two alterations. It was thought that the round arch to the north

PART 2. CHAPTER 6. ABBOTS WALK, THE INNER GATEWAY, THE ABBEY MILL

may preserve the original concept. The arch piers however had *suffered no perceptible alteration.* Indeed the lower footings of flint in yellowish mortar are similar to those found elsewhere in the Abbey complex.

In 1860 the mill was rebuilt and became known as Soundy's Mill. This incorporated new roller-mill technology to produce the finer flour required by modern biscuit makers. A new four storey building was constructed over the Holy Brook and flanking it, (see photo on p96). However the core medieval structure was retained within the mill itself. This consisted of an area 54 by 20ft, bounded by the original walls, within which there was a space of 25 by 20ft within two internal walls, which housed the water wheels. J. Kenneth Major, writing in the Berkshire Archaeological Journal (see note 29), estimated that there were two Tudor undershot wheels dating from post Dissolution times with a maximum of two storeys immediately above for the grain and storage. Until the onset of the Industrial Revolution milling was done to order, known as 'toll milling', and so storage was not such an important consideration. However the requirements of speculative milling, 'trading milling', meant that more storage space was needed.

The Mill after 1860

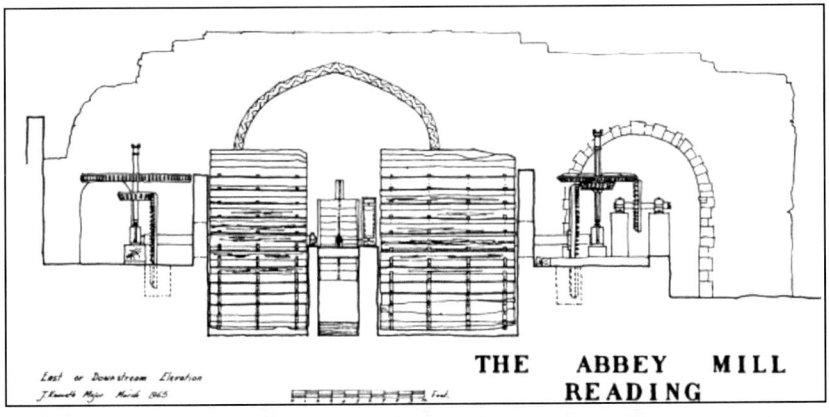

Roller mill workings [30]

Kenneth Major's drawing shows the two wheels. The one on the right, to the north, was dated 1934 and built by W Wilder & Sons Ltd, Crowmarsh, Oxon. This was the more recent of the wheels. The other was probably installed in 1860, as the design was of that period. Since its construction was identical it has to be assumed that the 1934 wheel was ordered to match the former and presumably replaced an earlier wheel. Both were 13ft 6ins in diameter. Whilst the northerly one was 10ft wide, the older, southerly wheel, was 7ft 6ins. The water was directed from the Holy Brook onto the wheels by means of two sluices or hatches operated from the floor above.

It is likely that the medieval wheels used the undershot method as the drop in the levels was insufficient to allow an overshot flow. The estimated drop of 5ft would suggest this.

Early 13th century undershot wheel. [31]

Left:

Aerial view of the building site around the remains of the Mill. This was the western wall. The eastern wall arches were destroyed before archaeological evaluation could be made.

The undershot mill wheels from the north east bank, just before demolition

The 1860s mill just before demolition in the 1960s

Mill photographs on this page [32]

PART 2. CHAPTER 6. ABBOTS WALK, THE INNER GATEWAY, THE ABBEY MILL

The Abbey Mill and the Holy Brook

The Holy Brook and the Abbey Mill.

Introduction to Part 3

So far we have looked at the area where the main ancient Abbey buildings once stood. We have seen that some still stand, albeit in ruins, and we have seen the buildings that now occupy the same land and have replaced them.

In the next section, Part 3, we shall continue past the Inner Gateway, along what is now the southern edge of the Forbury Gardens, as far as St Lawrence's church.

Despite the lack of any visible remains of the Abbey, we shall see that the basic ground plan of the area has changed very little. Although the buildings date back only to the 19th century, they often reveal a connection with their medieval antecedents.

PART 3   THE SOUTH SIDE OF THE FORBURY

CHAPTER 1 THE ASSIZE COURTS AND THE SHIRE HALL

The Assize Courts and the Central Police Station

The Assize Courts, Reading. 1864 [1]

In an earlier chapter we looked at the development of the justice system and the establishment of Reading Gaol. The Compter House, opposite the south east corner of St Lawrence's church, had served for many years as the home of the head constable and as the magistrates' court. However, with the growth in population and increased demands on the justice system during the 19th century, there was an urgent need to update its whole legal infrastructure.

In 1858 work was begun on the building of the new Police Station and Assize Courts next to the Abbey Inner Gateway.[2] Slade notes that *two archaeologically unfortunate episodes* occurred at this time. The first was in 1859 when Myres, the contractor building the new Courts, *excavated 30 cubic yards of stone* from the area. The other occurred in 1861 when *surplus soil from the Forbury, with whatever it contained, was used for filling the Portman Brook ditches*. In neither case was any attempt made to catalogue or even record the archaeology.

The architect appointed to design the Assize Courts was John Berry Clacy. He had been appointed Surveyor of Bridges for the eastern part of Berkshire. He failed to become Surveyor for Reading in 1851 but later became County Surveyor.

The fact that, as the architect and the County Surveyor, Clacy was given the contract to design the new Courts and Police Station, caused the local MP, John Walter to complain about the process, especially as the original estimate of £12,229 rose to £21,644 by the time of its completion. Clacy's justification was that several changes to his original plans had been demanded by the committee. These included not only *a long list of additional items* and an enlargement but most significantly that the building should be set back. This latter was to allow a better view of the refurbished Gateway, as the 1905 photograph shows.

1905, The Courts and the Inner Gateway [3]

The building was completed in 1861 along with the new Central Police Station to its rear. The end result was *the Baroque revival style building in channelled Bath stone ashlar* that today serves as the Crown Court.

The Police Station to the rear of the Assize Courts [4]

The Police Station, 1862 [5]

PART 3. CHAPTER 1. THE ASSIZE COURTS AND THE SHIRE HALL

The Shire Hall

2014 Berkshire County Council Shire Hall, now the Forbury Hotel

1902 Nos. 26 and 28, the Forbury, where the Shire Hall was to be built. Note the entrance to Suttons Seeds, with the royal coat of arms to the far right of the photo.[6]

Planned in the years just before the First World War, the design of the new Shire Hall for Berkshire County Council did not escape controversy. Half a century earlier the Courts had been placed in such a position as not to obscure the view of the Gateway along the Forbury and Abbots Walk. In 1908 Reading Corporation likewise refused Berkshire permission to erect a building that would have had a similar impact on sight lines.

The resultant plans, drawn up Warwick and Hall, allowed a good view towards the Abbey Ruins as one approached from the west and St Lawrence's. The commemorative plaque is still in place on the refurbished 'Forbury Hotel'.

Shire Hall [7]

Left: Plaque on the side of the building, which reads, *Berkshire County Council, 1911*

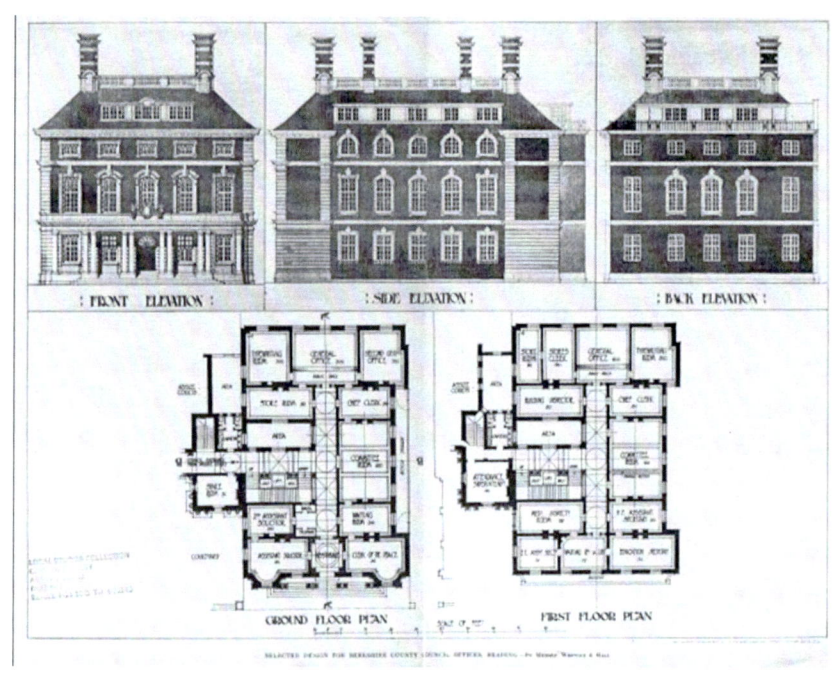

Shire Hall plans 1909 [8]

The Courts and Shire Hall at the start of the 21st century

View in 2012 showing the line of the building of the Shire Hall.

The Courts in 2014

PART 3 CHAPTER 2 BETWEEN SHIRE HALL AND ST LAWRENCE'S CHURCH

Historical background

The above modern aerial photograph shows the next area that we shall be looking at. This the section of the Abbey Quarter which has undergone most change between the 19th and 21st centuries.

The old Shire Hall (A) is on the right of the picture. To its west is the large open space surrounded, at the time of writing, by restaurants and office buildings.

The illustration on the next page shows the commonly accepted concept of how the land was used just before the dissolution of the monastery. It is considered that the area was part of the monastic gardens, possibly the Abbot's garden. This is likely, since it lies alongside the dwellings that most archaeologists consider to have been the Abbot's lodgings or palace. We should recall that the Abbey was a royal monastery where royalty and other nobles, with their courts, were entertained, and as such a formal garden would not have been out of place, even in a monastery.

In 1552, after the Dissolution of Reading Abbey in 1539, a survey of the property owners of Reading was made. The author of this survey was Roger Amyce.[1] It was conducted in the reign of Edward VI, but just one year before his death and the accession of Mary Tudor. One name, that of William Grey, (spelt Gray in some sources such as Dormer), stands out as a major landowner in the survey.

There is some uncertainly as to Grey's origins but we do know he was a colleague of Thomas Cromwell and Edward Seymour, the Duke of Somerset. We have already seen the role these two men played at the time of dissolution.

Grey married the widow of Robert Blagrave, one of Reading's leading families. A staunch protestant and Member of Parliament for Reading, Grey owned 197 out of 518 recorded houses, closes and tenements in Reading. He also owned land in Essex, Oxfordshire and elsewhere in the country. Grey died in 1551. The survey describes the lands that had been part of his estate. Most, if not all, of his Reading property passed to the Blagrave family after his death.

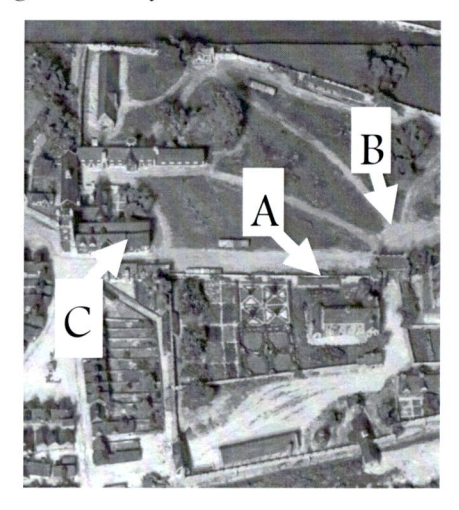

The plan to the right shows the Abbot's lodgings, A, and Inner Gateway, B, with the garden area reaching almost as far as the Compter Gate, C, alongside St Lawrence's church.
Copyright Reading Museum (Reading Borough Council). All rights reserved.

Amyce's Survey is a very detailed account of all the properties in Reading. Of particular interest to us is the section along the eastern edge of Market Place. Grey was in possession of virtually all these properties and their land. They stretched back towards the area we are examining at the moment and it appears likely that Grey's holdings reached into the 'garden space'. Whether this was the case or not, there is no doubt firstly that Grey owned a large proportion of the ancient Abbey's land and secondly that this was still not built over.

It is worth noting at this point something the maps and descriptions do not show, namely the contours of the area. To the north the land rises steeply from the Thames to the Forbury, including the land on which the Abbey stood. This latter is on quite a significantly higher level, rising, as it does, sharply from the Thames. The land then drops steeply back down to the Holy Brook and the Kennet, so much so that the garden would have been on a noticeable south facing slope, benefiting from the sun and with the Holy Brook providing water.

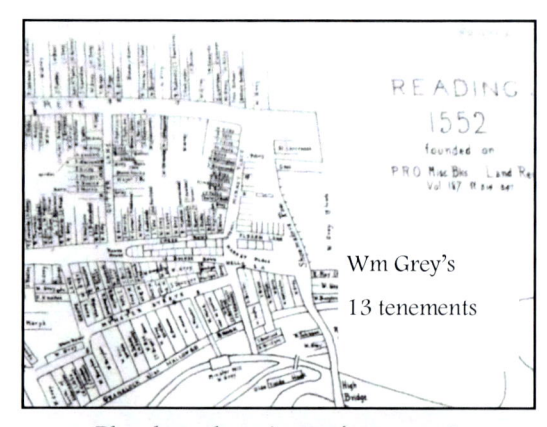

Plan based on Amyce's survey.[2]

PART 3. CHAPTER 2. BETWEEN SHIRE HALL AND ST LAWRENCE'S CHURCH

The next map (right) is Speed's, of 1610/11. Whereas other landmarks are lettered and named, the space to the west of the Gateway, and backing onto the Market Place buildings, is merely marked with a solitary tree. It lies in an enclosure above the more southerly of the two letters 'G' marking the sites of the stables.

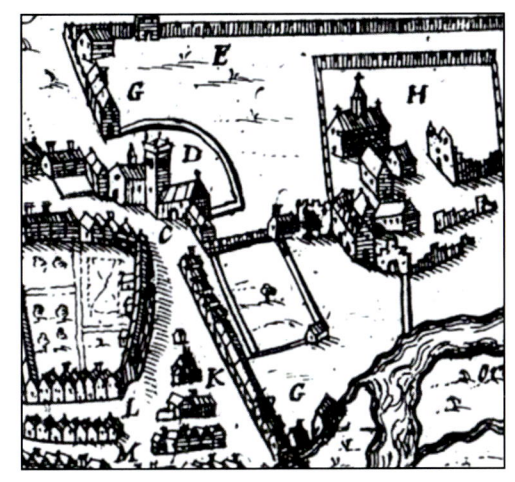

We have a detailed description of the Abbey area in the 1650 Survey at the end of the Civil War and which we looked at in an earlier chapter. The detail from the map of the Civil War defences (right) shows the Forbury Hill marked with four dots, the same stables as marked on Speed's map and the open space now marked with what look like several trees. In front of this is a semi-circular feature which is later referred to as 'the green'.

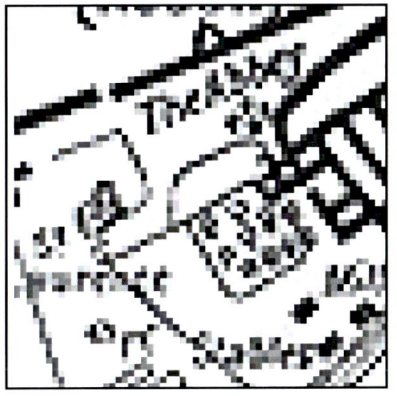

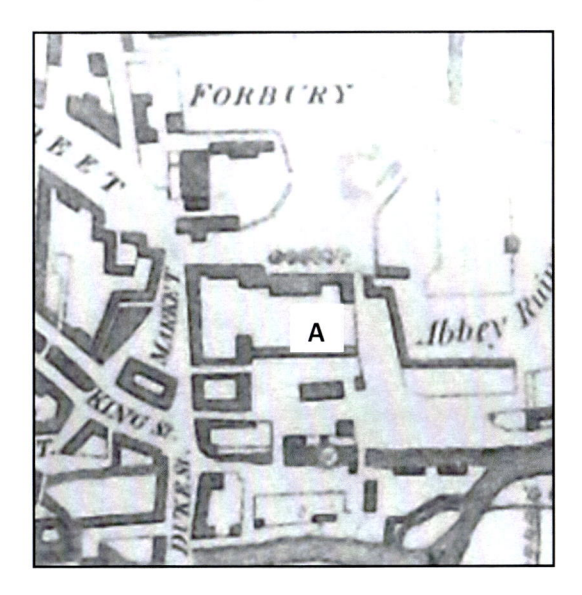

In 1798 John Man published this map, which shows the area surrounded with buildings, but the open space 'A' in the centre is still there. The semi-circular enclosure is not shown on Man's drawing, though there is a line of what appear to be trees which may indicate the boundary of the open space.

The Abbey Garden—the Open Space

The Two Gateways 1779. [3]

The above engraving, dated 1779, shows a wall leading to a large house, other buildings and so through to the Compter Gate alongside St Lawrence's church. The line of trees is present. If we match this 1779 drawing with Man's plan we can see that behind the wall there is the open space and the buildings appear to match the drawing.

The next illustration, dating from the first decade of the 19th century, shows the line of five trees, probably poplars, and what looks like a semi-circular patch in front of them.

These illustrations bring the maps to life, showing in one case the Forbury Hill, with St Lawrence's in the background and cattle in the foreground, and in the other, people, rich and poor, going about their daily business.

And so we can draw a fairly clear idea of what this southern edge of the Forbury looked like at the beginning of the 19th century.

However, as with much of Reading, this area was to undergo major changes over the next 200 years.

The 'green' from Forbury Hill. c 1800

PART 3. CHAPTER 2. BETWEEN SHIRE HALL AND ST LAWRENCE'S CHURCH

The plan shown on the right is an adaptation from Dr Hurry's work and refers to the Abbot's Garden of the 1650 Survey.[5]

Its nature as a garden area dating back to the founding of the monastery was therefore acknowledged after the Civil War.

Note the re-appearance of the semi-circular area later referred to as the 'green' which now also has the line of trees depicted in the late 18th century drawings.

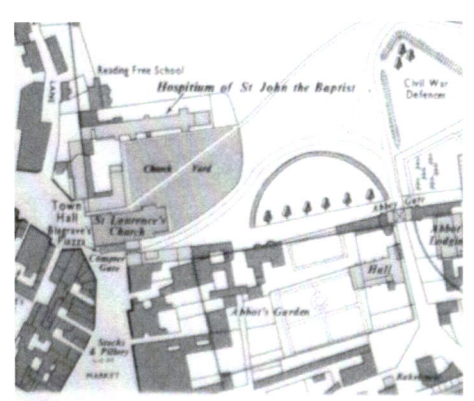

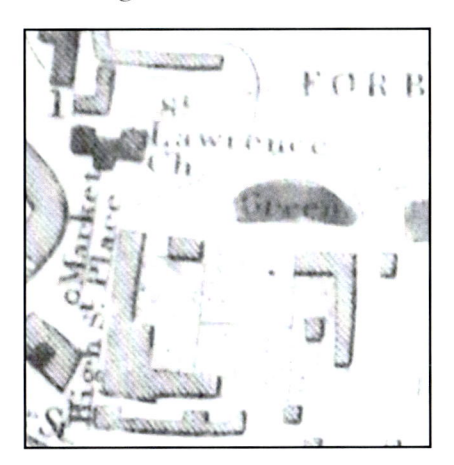

By 1840 the layout presents us with a now familiar scene. This extract from Snare's map of 1840 shows 'The Green' as a semi-circular space in front of carefully laid out gardens.

By looking at paintings, drawings and prints from the first half of the 19th century we can come to a clearer vision of what this looked like.

In a later chapter we shall be examining the Forbury, its development and changing uses over the centuries.

The drawing to the right is based upon Dr Hurry's plan. It is worth noting that this refers to the 1650 Parliamentary Survey and the 'Great Garden' mentioned in that Survey. In his original drawing Hurry has marked this as the *Royal Berkshire Seed Establishment*. The development of the 'seed establishment' helped create the Reading we know today. For it was the Sutton family, along with two other Quaker families, the Palmers and the Simonds, who were major players in converting Reading into today's industrial and commercial hub.

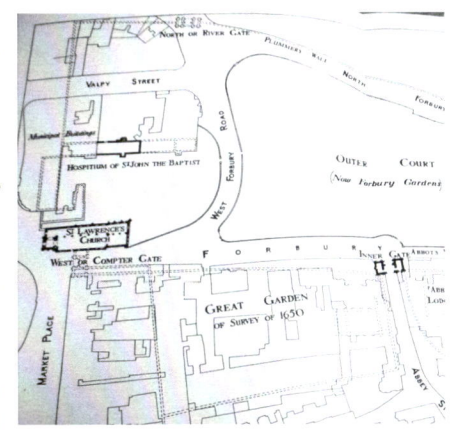

107

Sutton's Royal Seed Establishment

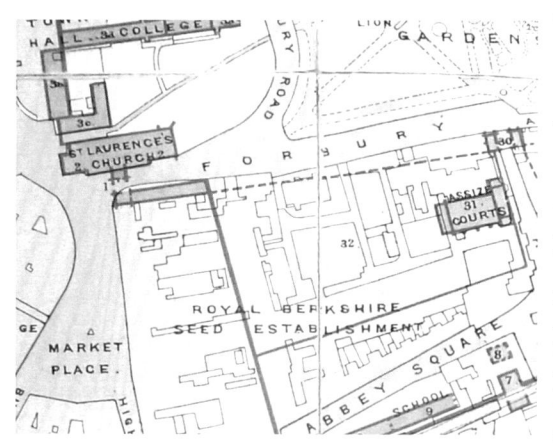

To the left is Hurry's original plan marking the *Royal Berkshire Seed Establishment*. Although at first the area between Suttons' Market Place headquarters and the Forbury Road entrance was open and used for seed beds, it soon became filled in with buildings related to seed and bulb production. To see how this happened it is necessary to look back at the growth of Suttons seeds.

John Sutton had begun his business in 1807 as a corn and seed merchant in King Street.[6] In 1832 he was joined by his sons, Martin Hope and Alfred. Martin Hope was a keen botanist and started to experiment with a trial seed ground. His success with his display of tulips led to the creation of a new business, a partnership between father and son, and they set up their business in Market Place. These are the dark buildings on the right of the photo. The frontage gave access to farmers as well as the general public on market days; to the rear were the trial grounds and seed beds. Suttons benefited from the arrival of the railway in 1840, enabling them to send their products all over the country quickly and reliably. The firm also took advantage of the new penny post to send free catalogues to potential customers, and used the postage system to deliver orders.

Sutton Seeds, Market Place, Reading

In 1858 Queen Victoria commanded that Suttons should supply the Royal household with seeds. The current Suttons website says that *the honour of the Royal Warrant has been bestowed on the firm ever since*. Consequently Suttons renamed their site and headquarters in Reading as *The Royal Seed Establishment*.

PART 3. CHAPTER 2. BETWEEN SHIRE HALL AND ST LAWRENCE'S CHURCH

From 1873, as the business expanded, the Market Place-Forbury site was developed. A new complex of offices and warehouses replaced the original Market Place-Forbury buildings and seed beds to the rear.

Apart from separate offices and store rooms for flower and vegetable seeds, bulbs, potatoes, grass and 'root seed', there were also recreations rooms for the employees, an exhibition area and a fire station with attached cottages for the firemen. There were stables and a house for the head groom and even a private post office to handle both internal mail and to organise despatch of orders. One source, Anderson, claims that in a single day it was recorded that as many as 15,000 items of correspondence, both letters and parcels, were handled by this post office.[6]

The result was that this area which, from the founding of the Abbey, had been a garden space, became built over and set the precedent for further 20th century development.

1920 Entrance to Suttons on the Forbury Road. Note the Shire Hall to its immediate left. Both above photographs are from postcards.

1902 photo showing the left gateway of the same entrance before the Shire Hall was built. [7]

The Prudential Building and Forbury Square

The 1960s saw major changes to the infrastructure of Reading, not least in its road system. Traffic congestion had become a significant problem. The planned new motorway, opening in the mid 60s, along with the introduction of new 'high-tech' industries, saw Reading become a transport and commuter hub. With improved rail services and the introduction of the '125' trains Reading's transport system required a total overhaul.

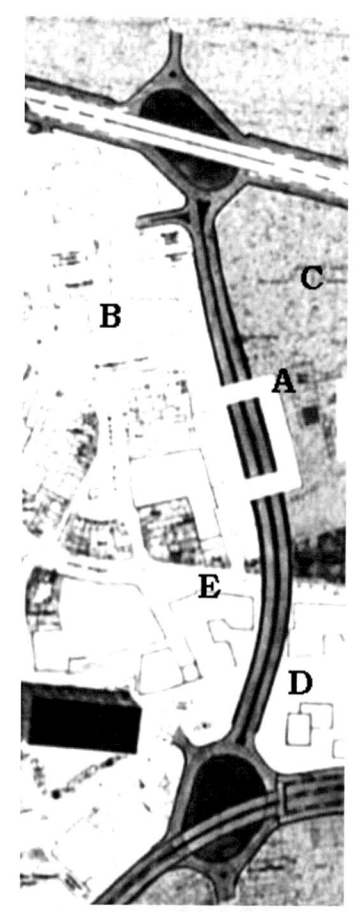

One solution was a proposed inner ring road, the 'Inner Distribution Road', (IDR). Much of this was completed and is in use today, in 2014. However the ring road was never completed. The 3rd stage, swinging northwards from the junction of Mill Lane and London Street, was planned as a flyover to cross the Kennet, and King's Road just to the east of Jackson's Corner. It would then pass under the new Prudential building, which had been designed with an arch to take a dual carriageway, and so through the western edge of the Forbury Gardens, joining a roundabout near the railway station. One plan was to put a section of the dual carriageway under a covered area linking the Forbury Gardens and St Lawrence's churchyard, possibly moving the Maiwand lion onto this section.

The photograph below shows the north of the Prudential building with its arch. The more southerly counterpart can be seen to the rear, through the arch. The project met with a great deal of public resistance. Moreover, under the

A. The Prudential Building
B. St. Lawrence's Church
C. The Forbury Gardens
D. The Kennet
E. King's Road [8]

The Prudential Building, 1986 [9]

PART 3. CHAPTER 2. BETWEEN SHIRE HALL AND ST LAWRENCE'S CHURCH

1974 local government reform, Berkshire County replaced the Borough as the highways planning authority. The County came to favour an alternative traffic solution, the so called 'Queen's Road scheme' which entailed the development of the Forbury Road, to the north of the Forbury Gardens.

Stage 3 of the IDR was abandoned and the Forbury 'saved'. Eventually in the 1980s the Prudential building was demolished and new plans were made for the area. However, in the process of constructing the Prudential, another important building was destroyed: number '22, the Forbury', also known as Pageant House. The abandonment of Stage 3 of the IDR, and the decision by the Prudential to move from its new building, resulted in yet more changes to this area. The photograph shows the open space that had started as the Abbey garden and which had undergone so many alterations.

The aerial photograph below shows the area in 2013, with the old Shire Hall (A), just appearing to the right and St Lawrence's church tower (B) on the far left.

c 1990 The 'Pru' demolished. Forbury Square being prepared for development [10]

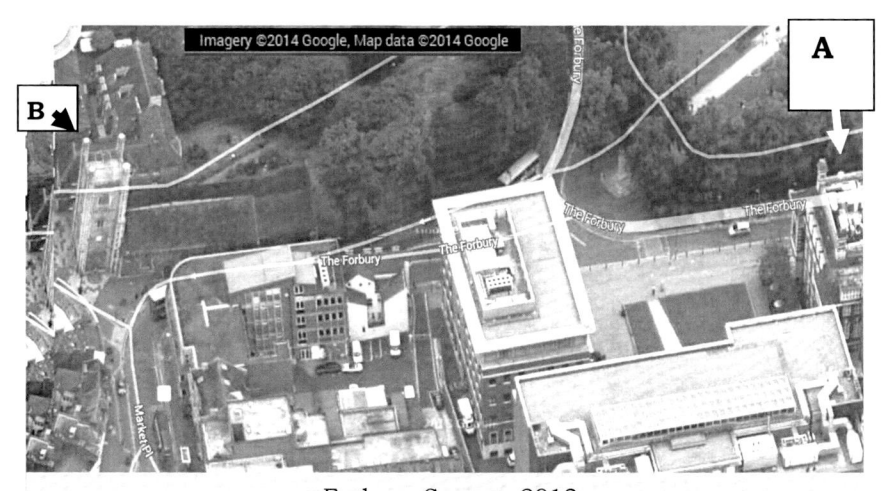

Forbury Square, 2013

Pageant House, No 22 The Forbury

Pageant House c.1900 [11]

Forbury Road c.1905 [12]

Pageant House in 1960 [13]

We have seen that this area saw many changes and several buildings were demolished, only to be replaced by others. One which merits particular mention, was Pageant House. This stood immediately to the west of Suttons grand entrance as can be seen in the photograph to the left. Above is a photo dating from around 1900 showing the frontage in some detail.

Remarkably, the building survived until the 1960s, when it was demolished to make way for the IDR scheme and the new Prudential building.

According to Lee in his book 'Reading As It Was', Pageant House, otherwise known as Forbury House, was built around 1760. If so, though much altered by the 19th century, it must be one of those in the 1820 illustration shown on the next page.

PART 3. CHAPTER 2. BETWEEN SHIRE HALL AND ST LAWRENCE'S CHURCH

The 'green' with ditch c.1820 [14]

One photograph, taken between 1900 and 1909, of the interior of Pageant House, shows a turn of the staircase with barley-sugar twist banisters. This style was originally of Spanish-Moorish origin and came to England from Portugal when Charles II married Catherine of Braganza.[15] On the wall, above the dado, are a picture and a large unframed chart or tapestry.

The transformation of this area from Abbot's garden and green space into a built-up conglomeration, which had begun in the middle of the 19th century, was completed by the middle of the 20th century.

We shall be looking at the 'Green' in front of Forbury Square in a later chapter. It is,

Pageant House staircase c.1935 [16]

however, worth mentioning that there is a strong case for thinking that, during Saxon and Viking times, this particular area of the Abbey Quarter was one of the first settlements of the future town of Reading. Yet very little archaeology was undertaken during these developments and building works; consequently much valuable information has probably been lost forever.

St Lawrence's Church and the Forbury Hill

PART 4   THE WESTERN EDGE OF THE ABBEY QUARTER

CHAPTER 1   ST LAWRENCE'S CHURCH AND THE COMPTER GATE

The Founding of St Lawrence's Church

In 1121 Reading Abbey was built at the eastern end of the triangle of raised land bordered by the River Thames to the north and the Kennet to the south. Over the last two centuries bones and artefacts dating back to Saxon times and earlier have been unearthed.[1] Kerry, writing towards the end of the 19th century, claims that the existence of Saxon burial remains indicates that a church must have been present somewhere nearby. He bases this on the argument that in the 8th century the Archbishops of York and Canterbury decreed that no church should be built without its burial ground and that no burial ground could be created beyond the precincts of a church. So when, in 1121, Henry I decided on this site for his new Abbey it is likely, he argues, that the old Saxon church was removed and St Lawrence's was built as its replacement. It may even be that the same patron saint's name was transferred to the new building, though it has been suggested that the original church was dedicated to St Matthew.[2]

This is speculation but based on some evidence. In 1966, when the present St James' church was being extended to the north, the architects reported: *We made one or two interesting discoveries… one of which was that the whole of the church area was built on a Saxon burial ground….*[3] This would place the original Saxon church somewhere in the area of St James' and the school, or just to its west in the Forbury Gardens. Further corroborative evidence for this theory is that the burial ground for the existing St Lawrence's remained, as contemporary Tudor documents indicate, just north of the nave of the ancient abbey church. Certainly it was only during the reign of Mary Tudor, in 1556, that the burial ground for St Lawrence's was moved to its existing site. One question, therefore, that remains is whether the 'St James' remains' were early Saxon or later burials.

Other sources claim that the original Saxon church was to the west of the 'triangle', possibly near to the Hospitium building on today's Valpy Street. It is possible that some of the existing fabric of the present church of St Lawrence can be traced to 1120, a year before the Abbey was founded, or even to a previous Saxon building.

Whatever its origins, much of what we see today of St Lawrence's is the result of development and changes culminating in the 16th century rebuilding. For instance, in 1196 Abbot Hugh II enlarged the church to double its original length and replaced the original tower. By extending the church eastwards he brought the whole building within the Abbey precincts. Two doors, one to the north, the other to the south, were also added. In addition the Abbot made an endowment to the church of the new Hospitium which he built at the same time. This consisted of an almshouse, just north of the church, with a refectory north of this leading to dormitories set at a 90 degree angle at its far end.

In 1458 the tower took on the form we see today, but with pinnacles at each corner. The number of bells was increased from three to five. In 1521 an arcade between the nave and the aisle was constructed by J. Cheney. This latter had been Wolsey's mason at Hampton Court. The font was added the next year. In 1611 Sir John Blagrave left a considerable sum of money, some of which was to be spent on constructing an arcade along the south exterior of the church. This was duly built around 1619 and the area later became known as Blagrave Piazza. Many later alterations were carried out in the 19th century.[4]

Before the Dissolution of the Abbey in 1539, the church itself was designed as a place of worship for the townspeople and for the large number of pilgrims who flocked to Reading. The Abbey church itself would be open for pilgrims coming to venerate the many relics, not least the hand of St James, held by the Abbey. Reading was no stranger to royalty. Many monarchs held court in Reading. Parliament also met here. On these occasions the Abbey church and its Chapter House, rather than St Lawrence's, would have become the focal point of royal and religious ceremony.[5]

The Compter Gate

Once built, the Abbey had four secured entrances to its precincts, in addition to the Inner Gateway. These led to the area referred to as the Forbury. The North Gateway stood approximately where the Rising Sun pub is today, at the junction of the Forbury and Forbury Road. The East Gateway was at Blake's bridge. The South Gateway, which also housed a porter's lodge, stood next to the stables where today the road called Abbey Square joins the King's Road. The most important entrance, however, was the West or Compter Gate. This was the main entrance to the Abbey. It too housed a porter's lodge but also contained a cellar, a hall, a buttery, three chambers and three garrets.

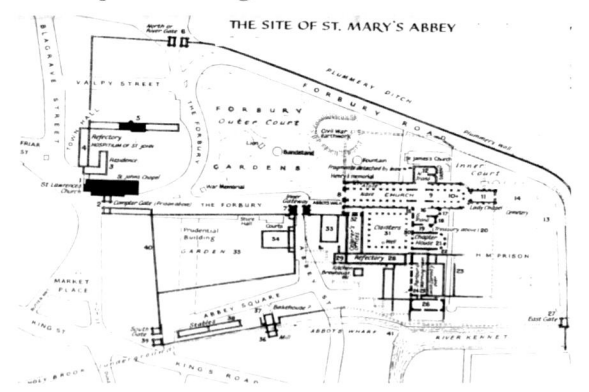

The Abbey in relationship to today's road layout, based on Hurry's map of 1909. The numbers refer to Hurry's plan.

PART 4. CHAPTER 1. ST LAWRENCE'S CHURCH AND THE COMPTER GATE

Left: The Inner Gateway c 1777 showing Abbots Walk leading to the Compter Gateway. Right: Detail from the same picture showing the Compter Gateway [6]

There was also a prison above the gateway. This latter is what gave the name to the gate, the word Compter being used in medieval times for a prison or lockup. Although there are numerous written records of the Compter Gateway there are remarkably few drawings. We saw above (p 40) how its use changed over the centuries. The picture on page 40 shows St Lawrence's around 1800, with the 'Hole', but the Gateway appears to have been removed by this date. The porch and whipping stocks had been removed by 1785.

The West End

These views are dated 1802 and 1820. The arcade, or Piazza, is to the right.[7] The Compter Gate has gone but the right hand drawing shows the gabled extension that had formed part of the gateway. In the left illustration notice also the flat roof frontage to the north aisle and how it is attached to the building to its left. This was the vicarage and the next building is the late 18th century Town Hall. Under the first set of windows of the vicarage there is an opening which was the entrance to a passageway under the vicarage, leading through to the churchyard at the rear. Today it is an open passage between Blandy and Blandy Solicitors' offices and the church.

Fox Talbot's early photograph of St Lawrence's confirms the details shown in the previous drawings. Notice however the fence in front of the west door. The north aisle still has a flat parapet, probably masking a pitched roof to its rear. The passageway under the vicarage leading to the churchyard is clearly visible. The state of the church in 1846 was such that major restoration was required. The architect chosen was Benjamin Ferrey.

Major alterations over the next 20 years were to bring radical changes, not only to the aspect of St Lawrence's but to the whole of the area, including the layout of the surrounding streets.

C 1846 St Lawrence's [8]

The following Board of Health map, held in Reading Library, shows the road layout and the relative positions of the main buildings in the 1850s.

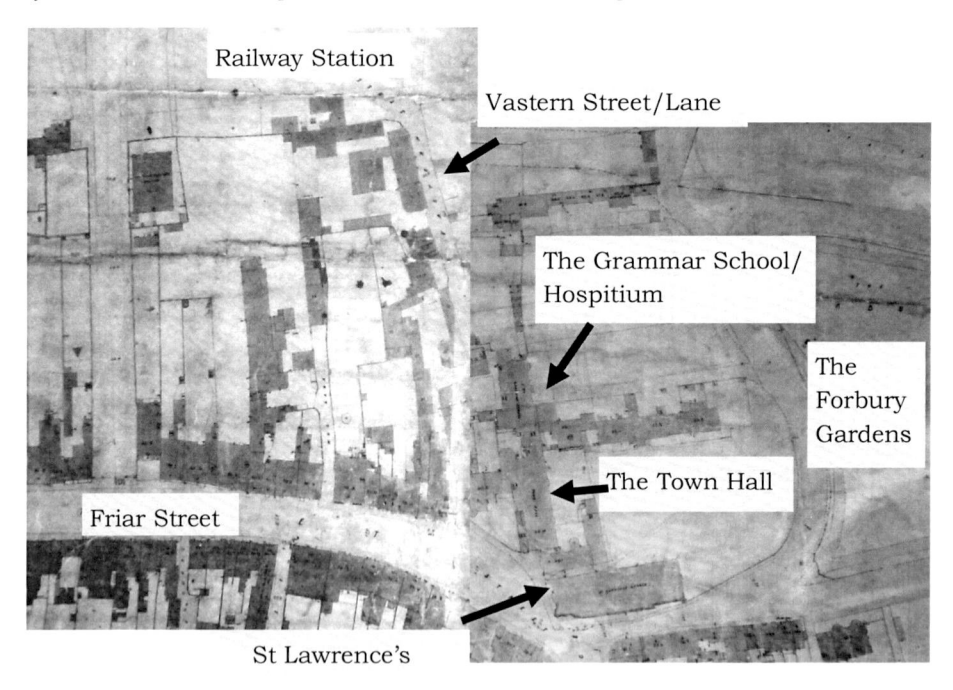

Board of Health 1853 survey

PART 4. CHAPTER 1. ST LAWRENCE'S CHURCH AND THE COMPTER GATE

The drinking fountain

In the hope of improving the facilities of the area, a public drinking fountain was installed in the Arcade in 1860. Also included were two water troughs for dogs. It was designed by Poulton and Woodman.[9] In 1867 a major restoration of the church was begun. Joseph Morris was the architect chosen and the work took two years. In fact Morris, who had been responsible for the two wing extensions at The Royal Berkshire Hospital in 1861, worked regularly over a period of several years on various projects at St Lawrence's including re-roofing in 1864.

In 1868 the Board of Health ordered the demolition of the Blagrave Piazza, which had been such a feature of the church for about 250 years. The area, it was claimed, was being used by vagrants and other socially undesirable elements of society. As we shall see shortly, the Corporation was also at this time planning major changes to the area, including new municipal buildings.[10]

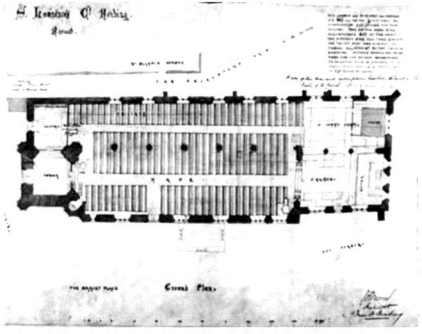

Work, mainly on the interior of the church, continued over the next few decades. The most significant projects included: 1886 – the organ chamber (Morris and Smallwood), 1886-90 - St John's chapel (SS Smallwood) and, in 1922 the Rood Screen, (Smallwood), completed by Smith and Son following Smallwood's death.

On the 10th February 1943 a lone German bomber dropped a stick of four bombs which fell in a line from Minster St to Friar Street, killing 41 people. Most of the casualties were in the 'People's Pantry' which was situated at the Friar St end of the Arcade. As the photograph shows Blandys' offices were totally destroyed and significant damage was done to St. Lawrence's. The church lost most of its stained glass and the west window was blown out. Following the blast the pinnacles were so unsafe that they had to be removed and were never reinstated.

Morris' ground plan, St Lawrence's,

One source says that the west window can now be seen in the churchyard behind the church.

However the 'Corpus of Romanesque Sculpture' website claims this is a *folly of brick and carved stones in the churchyard NE of church*. It further claims that: *In the centre, pieces of window tracery have been wrongly assembled* using *the carved stones from the Reading Abbey site*. [11]

Other bombs were dropped on Reading and Caversham in the course of the war but this incident appears to have been the only one resulting in fatalities.

The photograph, right, shows the church following restoration after the war. The pinnacles were not replaced. The work of restoration was given to FWB Ravenscroft, who was Diocesan Surveyor to the Archdeaconry of Berkshire. Ravenscroft came from a family of local architects and was, as Sidney Gold says, *an authority on local architecture and assisted John Piper and John Betjeman in their 'Murray's Berkshire Architectural Guide (1949)'*.

St Lawrence's 1950s. [12]

The photograph to the left is the structure variously described as the remains of the west window blown out by the bomb in February 1943 or as *wrongly assembled tracery*, either from the Abbey or from St Lawrence's.

PART 4. CHAPTER 1. ST LAWRENCE'S CHURCH AND THE COMPTER GATE

Another feature of this area is the statue of Queen Victoria. It was erected in 1887 to celebrate the 50th year of her reign. It was carved out of Carrara marble by George Simonds. Below is a photograph which was taken by HW Taunt shortly after the statue was placed in front of the Church and new Town Hall.

Simonds was also the sculptor of the Maiwand lion in the Forbury gardens.[13]

Inscription on the base of the statue of Queen Victoria

The Three Faces of No 1 Friar St

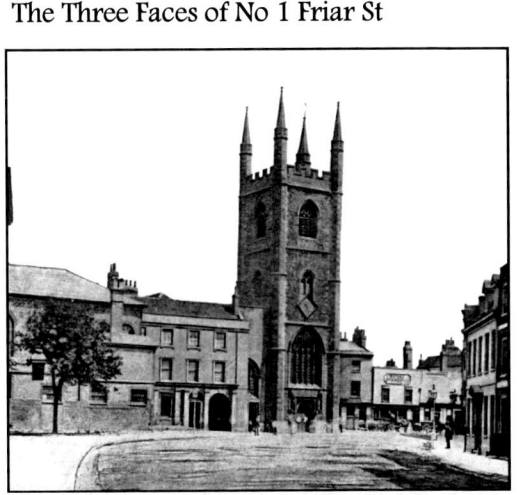

St Lawrence's, the Vicarage and the Old Town Hall, c.1870 [14]

The buildings to the left of the church occupy the space which approximates to the 'Residence' of the Hospitium. The space to the immediate left became the vicarage of St Lawrence's.

However the vicarage later moved alongside the grammar school dormitory, just to its east. With the rebuilding of the Municipal Buildings the famous firm of solicitors, Blandy and Blandy, commissioned new offices more in keeping with Waterhouse's new Town Hall. They were designed in the late Victorian 'Queen Anne Revival' style and the architect was William Frederick Albury and can be seen in the 1885 photograph over-page.

We have seen, however, that in February 1943 an air-raid destroyed Blandys' offices. Their post-war replacement contrasted with the style of the earlier building and with the gothic elements of the church to the south and the neo-gothic of Waterhouse's town hall to the north.

The New Town Hall and St Lawrence's, c.1885 [15]

Blandy and Blandy, solicitors c.1979 [16]

The East End

These two pictures (A and B) are catalogued by Reading Library as dating from c1800 and c1820. However they demonstrate the difficulty in relying on sketches. They show significant differences to the east end of the church. At first sight it would appear that the more southerly gable has been extended between the two dates. The number of windows has increased from two to seven and the gable is much broader. However in pictures dated around the 1860s the gable is again narrower in appearance and the number of the windows openings changes. This may be a problem of the artists' ability to handle perspective but this would not explain all the discrepancies.

PIC A c.1800 [17]

PIC B c.1820 [18]

PART 4. CHAPTER 1. ST LAWRENCE'S CHURCH AND THE COMPTER GATE

A hundred and thirty five years separate pictures C and D. Apart from the loss of the pinnacles on top of the tower, just visible in picture D, the east end of the church has changed very little.

PIC C 1860 [19]

PIC D 1995 [20]

CHAPTER 2

THE HOSPITIUM AND THE MUNICIPAL BUILDINGS

The Hospitium of St John

Hospitium—Dormitories

Hospitium— Refectory

Hospitium—Residence house

St Lawrence's church

Copyright Reading Museum
(Reading Borough Council).
All rights reserved.

The Abbey's charter demanded that the *alms of the monastery* should be *bestowed on the poor and strangers*. Irrespective of the status and wealth of the travellers, the Abbey had a duty to provide for the physical as well as the spiritual needs of those who came to Reading. These included the ever-growing number of pilgrims.

The first Hospitium most probably occupied the area immediately north of the church, approximately where Blandys' solicitors stands as of 2014.

By the time Hugh II became Abbot, in the 1180s, the number of visitors had grown to such an extent that this small house could no longer cope. Consequently between 1189 and 1193 the new Hospitium of St John was built. At the same time the church of St Lawrence was also annexed by the Abbey as part of the Hospitium. This was with the agreement of Hubert Walter, Bishop of the Diocese of Salisbury, in whose jurisdiction the church lay. The new agreement provided for the upkeep of 13 poor men and 13 poor women from the revenues of St Lawrence's. In addition 13 men were to be sustained from the daily distribution of the Abbey's alms. Pilgrims and other travellers were to be maintained from the profits of the mill at Leominster, one of the Abbey's properties.[1]

PART 4. CHAPTER 2. THE HOSPITIUM AND THE MUNICIPAL BUILDINGS

THE PARTS OF THE HOSPITIUM

1. The Residence, or Almshouse

The Almshouse housed the 26 poor men and women mentioned above. It lay just to the north of the church and was connected to it by a private entrance, possibly a wooden cloister, leading into the chapel of St. John in the north chancel. The poor women were known from the start as 'sorores' (sisters). They were the wives of men who had held some office in the town who, in their widowhood, had fallen on hard times.

They took religious vows, including that of celibacy. They had a prioress who therefore acted as their superior. In short they became a small religious community of what today we would call 'nuns'. Their needs were supplied by the Abbey and we have records showing, for instance, that one sister received a daily allowance of one loaf and two quarts of ale. On feast days the Abbey distributed an extra allowance of 1d or a dish of meat from the Abbey.

It would appear that the term 'fratres', or brothers, for the men came later. Nevertheless similar rules were applied. Both the men and the women shared in the Abbey's duty to care for visitors and pilgrims. As such they were not only the beneficiaries of alms but helped in looking after those who came to stay in the Hospitium.

Comparisons of population and wealth are always thwart with difficulties. However it is worth making an estimate of how much the Abbey was spending on the care of the needy of the town. Thirty six poor people in their old age and infirmity, being looked after by the Abbey, most probably represented between 0.5% to 1% of the population. The care was generous and unstinting. If we take even the lower figure that would be the equivalent of about 900 people in Reading today. Impossible though it is to make direct comparisons, the most conservative estimate must be that in today's terms the care was costing the Abbey around £8 million per annum.[2]

2. The Refectory

This was a substantial structure lying north of the church and was about 40 metres long and between 6 and 9 metres wide. It stood approximately where Waterhouse's Town Hall stands today, (cf p 122). The exact nature of the original structure is uncertain. The photograph on the next page shows a hall with a wooden roof and a row of stone pillars down the middle. As we shall see there is a suggestion there was such a feature in the Reading Hospitium refectory. However this may have been added at a later date or it may be even have been a feature of the building erected in the second half of the 15th century. The importance of the refectory lies in the obligation the monastery had, as we saw above, to provide at least two days food and lodging to visitors, be they pilgrims or other travellers. It was therefore an integral part of the monastic establishment.

The town benefitted in no small part as a result of the Abbey's own increasing prosperity. The monastery gave work to the local inhabitants and, as Reading grew as a place of pilgrimage, the Refectory was a focal point in the town.

3 The Dormitory

Running at right angles to the east, from the northerly end of the Refectory, was the Dormitory. It was over 65 metres long. This is where the only remaining section of the Hospitium can be found today, although, as we shall see, very little of the original building is extant. The first building dated back to the work of Abbot Hugh II between 1189 to 1193.

The two photographs below, taken from the south in St Lawrence's churchyard, span a period of just over one hundred years. The differences are clear to be seen, even in this timeframe. This building is all that remains, in any form, of the original Hospitium. In the period from around 1200 to 1438 the dormitory would have housed pilgrims and visitors to the town.

However in 1438 it would appear that a new Hospitium was built to replace, in part or in whole, that founded in 1193. St Lawrence's church also benefited from alterations as at the same time its tower was reconstructed and the nave altered.

c.1880 [3]

c.2013

PART 4. CHAPTER 2. THE HOSPITIUM AND THE MUNICIPAL BUILDINGS

The First Reforms

The Abbey's relationship with St Lawrence's church and Hospitium was also changing. It would appear that by the time Edward IV came to Reading in 1480 the Hospitium was no longer functioning as previously. On account of the plague the King and Parliament had moved from London to Reading in 1466, 1467 and 1468. The records show that several members of the House of Commons had died as a result of the plague. The twenty-six 'fratres' and 'sorores' were no longer being sustained by the Abbey and it was claimed that the Abbot was appropriating money, that should have been used as alms to the poor and needy, for other unspecified purposes. The Abbot promised the burgesses of the town that the money hitherto used for the Hospitium would be spent on creating and maintaining a new Free Grammar school. This did not happen and, following representations by the burgesses, Henry VII ordered that the matter should be attended to. By 1485 Abbot Thorne I had converted the Refectory and Almshouse into a Grammar school with an endowment of £10pa, in addition to some private endowments. It was recorded that *William Dene, a rich man and servant of the Abbey of Reading, gave 200 marks in money towards the advancement of this school.*[4] In 1486 it received the name *Royal Grammar School of Henry VII*.

However the story is not as straightforward as appears at first sight. Naxton, in his history of Reading School, points out that there is evidence of a pre-existing school. In the Abbey's *Close Rolls* (meaning confidential), of 1242-1247, we read that *rex rogat rectorem scolarum Rading quod Radulfium ... una cum filio Willelmi.. admittat nutriendos et instruendos.* (The King asks the rector of the scholars of Reading to admit Rudolf and William and that they should be provided for and educated). This leaves the question open as to whether there was a fee-paying school in Reading before the establishment of the Free School by Henry VII. Whether the dispute was more a matter of providing a free school to replace an existing school or merely providing a school of any description, is open to investigation and further research.[5]

The Dormitory continued to be used to house visitors, especially poorer travellers, until the Dissolution in 1539.

The Hospitium 1539—1786

With the Dissolution of the Friary the burgesses hoped to move from the Yield or Guild Hall near the Kennet and to adapt part of the old Friary into suitable premises for its meeting rooms. We have seen how Greyfriars was converted into a 'hospital' or workhouse for the poor, eventually becoming a town 'Bridewell'. However the members of the Corporation never really settled into Greyfriars as it proved less suitable than they had at first imagined.

By 1578 the Corporation had moved into the Hospitium Refectory. There is some controversy as to whether it was at this point that an upper floor was created by inserting a new level, or whether the hall was merely partitioned off. According to Hurry the burgesses occupied a new upper level of the Great Hall, having put in a floor to create a two storey building. In this scenario the school continued to occupy the ground floor. Hurry claims that a row of pillars stretched down the centre of its 120ft length (36m), supporting a series of pointed arches. There is some dispute also as to the use of the Dormitory and Refectory. A minority of sources say that the school was also housed in the former and only moved back to the old Refectory when, in 1625, King Charles I moved to Reading on account of the plague in London. At this point the old Dormitory area was converted into stables. According to Slade, the Court of the Exchequer occupied the Town Hall and the Court of Augmentation moved into the School House. This was for a matter of just a few weeks. Whatever the exact location of the school, the old Refectory building of the Hospitium was the meeting place for the Corporation for the next two hundred years.

We have seen how the Parliamentary government commissioned a detailed survey of the King's property in 1650. Unfortunately this did not include the old Hospitium area as this was now deemed to be the property of the Corporation of Reading and not of the King. It would appear that the Dormitory was still used as stables. The School House (Refectory) had been converted into an arsenal during the Civil War but had reverted to its original use during the Commonwealth.

By 1785 the town was seeking to improve its appearance. The Reading Paving Act of the same year was supported by public subscription. The list included members of the mayor's family and the Catholic owner of the 'Reading Mercury' newspaper, Mrs Anna Maria Smart. The Corporation now turned its attention to their meeting room. Daphne Phillips claims that the structure was so unstable that a row of pillars had been installed to support the overhead arches. It is not clear if this is the same row of arches alluded to by Hurry.

Whatever the case it became clear that large gatherings in such a confined space were increasingly impracticable: so much so that a meeting to choose Parliamentary candidates had to be moved to the Forbury as the Hall was no longer large enough to accommodate the crowd. An alderman of the town, Charles Poulton, designed a new Town Hall which comprised a large assembly room with an adjoining council chamber. This was built on the same site as the Refectory of the old Hospitium, alongside St Lawrence's vicarage, as the illustrations A and B show.

PART 4. CHAPTER 2. THE HOSPITIUM AND THE MUNICIPAL BUILDINGS

A. 1802 Poulton's Town Hall to the far left. [6]

B. Poulton's Town Hall c 1865 [7]

The assembly room was lavishly decorated in the prevailing late 18th style and the Meeting Chamber hung with portraits of some of Reading's famous sons such as Archbishop Laud and John Kendrick. The opening was marked in August 1786 with a grand ball and a performance of works by Handel and Haydn.

These two illustrations show Poulton's grand hall as it was nearly a century later. Picture A shows the main chamber just before the changes brought about by Waterhouse, which we shall see shortly. Picture B is from the 'London Illustrated News', dated 1865. The 'Father Willis" organ, installed in 1864, is visible in both pictures.

A. c1875 The Town Hall chamber [8]

B. Reading Industrial Exhibition 1865 [9]

Reading Grammar School

The building of the new Town Hall created a problem for the Grammar School. In 1781 Richard Valpy had taken over as headmaster. This same year, as we have just seen, the Corporation determined on rebuilding the Town Hall. By 1786 the work was complete but no provision had been made to rehouse the school. Whilst the plans were being drawn up Valpy had offered to pay for the improvements to the school room. In 1672 a new floor,

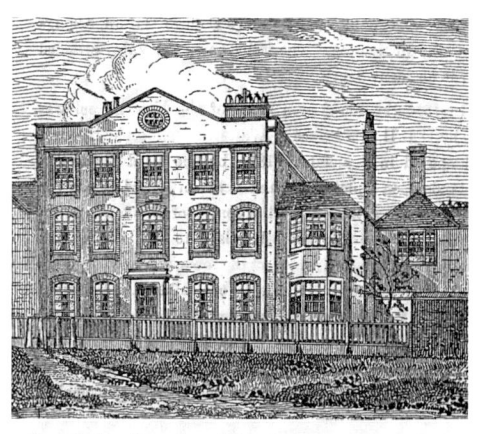

C. Valpy's school house. [10]

installed for the Corporation, had reduced the headroom in the lower school room to just 8ft. Poulton's design of the new Town Hall mean that the lower schoolroom was deprived of much of its light. Valpy now asked that the Corporation should provide alternative accommodation to replace the loss of the old Refectory building.

PART 4. CHAPTER 2. THE HOSPITIUM AND THE MUNICIPAL BUILDINGS

When this was refused Valpy came to the decision that the school would have to move.

He therefore went ahead and built a new schoolhouse, picture C on the opposite page, at his own expense.

A. Valpy's school buildings in 1820 [11]

B. Reading School Havell 1816 [12]

This was a substantial extension to the house that a previous Headmaster, Haviland John Hiley, had built in 1731 for 20 boarders.

Valpy's new school house, shown on page 130 (C), can be seen in its overall context in pictures A and B on this page. The Senior Assistant Master's House can be seen to its immediate left in picture A.

The ancient Hospitium dormitory, to the far left in picture B, provided extra accommodation for the boarders. Note its distinguishing turret behind the wall which is obscured slightly by the tree in the foreground.

Victorian developments

Changes to this part of Reading during the 19th century were greater than in any other period until the second half of the 20th century. As the focus of the town moved towards the new railway station the whole road structure was altered. The municipal buildings, St Lawrence's churchyard and the Hospitium all became separated from the rest of the Forbury by a new road system. This corresponded with the rapid growth of the existing population and the arrival of newcomers into the town. It was during this period, as the British Empire expanded, that Reading became famous as a world manufacturing centre. Suttons, Huntley and Palmers and Simonds became household names, not just in Britain but throughout the world. In the age of an unprecedented building boom Reading was renowned as a centre of brick making.

We have seen the changes to the main buildings in this specific area towards the end of the 18th century with completion of the new town hall and the expansion of Reading School. But one of the first hints of the unprecedented changes to come is in a letter written in 1837 by the Catholic priest of the town, the Reverend Mr Francis Bowland. The Catholic 'Chapel of the Resurrection' had been built in 1811 by a French émigré priest, the Reverend Mr Francis Longuet. We do not know its exact location; all we do know is that it was on Vastern Street, or Vastern Lane as it was sometimes called. Tradition suggests that it was where the Rising Sun pub stands today, but it may have been elsewhere, possibly near the junction of today's Valpy St. and Blagrave St.[13] We know that it consisted of a two storey house, with an attached chapel. However in early 1837 the Reverend Bowland wrote to his Bishop in London expressing concern that the new railway company was threatening to acquire the land on which the house and church stood. Within the Catholic community this led to a frenzy of activity and planning which finally resulted in the laying of the foundation stone of St James' church, at the eastern end of The Forbury, in December of the same year.

Whether the priest acted rather hastily or whether the chapel was in real danger we shall probably never know. What is certain is that within three years the railway had arrived and the whole north side of the Forbury had been altered. The water meadows had been replaced with shunting yards and two stations had been built.[14] By 1850 the Great Western and South Eastern railway stations were fully operational. In 1853 a road was built from just south and east of St Lawrence's churchyard, alongside the edge of the Forbury. Although this had the beneficial result that no traffic could cross the Forbury, it also ensured that the Forbury became cut off from the area occupied by the school and St Lawrence's churchyard. We shall be looking at this in greater detail in a later chapter.

PART 4. CHAPTER 2. THE HOSPITIUM AND THE MUNICIPAL BUILDINGS

We saw earlier that in 1853 The Board of Health drew up a detailed map of Reading. If we look closely it is possible to make out the outline of the proposed road between what we now call the Forbury Gardens and the section to its west. Colonel Blagrave, who owned all this land, had given permission for the road to be built to prevent carts and other traffic using the Forbury as a short cut to the north, especially to the new railway yards along the northern part of the Forbury.

The next two pictures of the railway show just how significant the changes wrought by its arrival were on the town.

1853 Board of Health Survey

1850 South Eastern Station [15]

View north of the Forbury, approximately from where St. James' church stands. This shows the South Eastern railway station. In the distance to the left is the Great Western Station. To the right is the original terminus of the South Eastern Railway at Forbury Road, with a train at the platform.

1842 Great Western Station [16]

This artist's impression shows Station Road as a raised causeway, with the "down" station and goods shed to the left, and the "up" goods shed, refreshment room and station to the right. The engine shed is between and behind the two stations.

133

If the arrival of the railway was a major contributory factor to the development of the Forbury area, other changes were due to complications resulting from the historic nature of land tenure following the Dissolution of the Abbey.

We have seen that in 1539 the ancient Abbey lands had reverted to the Crown. We also saw how the Blagrave family acquired the crown leasehold of the western part of the Forbury. This created a complicated property and land ownership system and one that caused legal disputes throughout the period following the Dissolution of the Abbey. Two examples spanning over 50 years serve to illustrate the problem. The first was during the Headship at Reading Grammar School of John Spicer between 1750 and 1771. He attempted to prevent the public from accessing the area where the boys were accustomed to play cricket. The townspeople organised a cricket match on the same ground to make the point that this was not the school's private property. The Corporation supported the townsfolk and Spicer conceded. A second incident occurred in 1813. Valpy claimed that the rent he paid to Blagrave gave him priority, if not sole rights, of usage of the land around the school. The corporation replied that *the inhabitants of this borough have an established right to walk, exercise and divert themselves in and upon the Forbury and every part of it at their free will and pleasure.* Valpy abandoned his claims after a series of fights between his pupils and the town's youths.[17]

If skirmishes between town and school were infrequent and fairly quickly resolved, a far greater threat to the existing land tenure was built into the legal agreement that Valpy signed with the Blagrave family and Reading Corporation. When Valpy bought the land for his new schoolhouse it was on a 'lease for life' basis. This meant that with the death of the leaseholder the freehold owner could reclaim the land. Thus it was possible for an individual or group to own the building but only on leased land. There were several 'lives' on the school lease but in September 1866 the last of these, John Jackson Blandy, died. In the same year the School Commissioners also reported on the dreadful state of the school. It had only three boys; the accommodation, offices and classrooms were all condemned. Consequently the lessors and the Corporation refused to renew the lease. In addition to this the Corporation, in 1860, had bought the western part of the Forbury from Colonel Blagrave for £6010. In this manner the buildings and land around the old town hall and school buildings were opened up for development. With the resignation of Robert Appleton, the Headmaster, the school closed in 1862 and the buildings were vacated.[18]

Having set the scene for events in the late 19th century we shall look next at how the area, which had been dominated by St Lawrence's' church, the Hospitium and its outbuildings for over 750 years, was to change so radically and assume the face of Reading we know today.

PART 4. CHAPTER 2.   THE HOSPITIUM AND THE MUNICIPAL BUILDINGS

The Municipal Buildings 1870—1939

By the second half of the 19th century the Corporation was looking at ways to improve the Municipal Buildings. In 1864 W H Woodman had put in the fine plasterwork ceiling which is in today's Victoria Hall. This is possibly after an original design by Charles Poulton. In 1871 we come across the earliest drawings for the new Town Hall by Alfred Waterhouse. This was erected between 1874 and 1876. Waterhouse skilfully incorporated Poulton's assembly rooms, notably the Victoria Hall, into his design.

As early as 1877 it was decided to extend Waterhouse's 'small town hall'. The architect Thomas Lainson, along with his son, also Thomas, was engaged to design the extension. Lainson's additions include the Large Town Hall, with a balcony for the Father Willis organ, and the rooms which housed the newly formed 'Reading Schools of Science and Art', which eventually had their own entrance in Valpy Street. These buildings were opened in 1882. In 1897 the complex was completed by the addition of the School of Art which, according to 'The Builder', in March 1900, is listed as *Art Gallery and Other Additions to Public Buildings*. This was designed by William Howell of the architect firm Cooper and Howell. The sculptor of the external terracotta friezes was William Charles May. These friezes represent *Ancient Britain, Roman Life, Literature and Science*. The panel of Henry I founding the Abbey was by Charles Pinker. The complex was officially opened by the Prince of Wales in 1898.

Waterhouse's Small Town Hall c1877 [19]

Left: Municipal Buildings 1887.

Right: Drawings for Lainson's Extension c.1880. [20]

It was during these years that Vastern Street (Lane) was replaced by Blagrave Street and Valpy Street.[21] The new Municipal Buildings replaced what was left of Reading School. This moved to its new site in 1871 on land bought from the Redlands Estate and in a building designed by Alfred Waterhouse.

The Cradle of Learning

Since the reign of Henry VII and the founding of the Grammar School, this part of Reading had been associated with education. With the removal of the Grammar School in 1871 to Erleigh Road, a new chapter in the history of culture and learning in Reading was about to begin.

This emerged from a government scheme to establish *schools of science and art*, throughout the country. Centred on the newly founded South Kensington Museum (1857), following the success of the Great Exhibition (1851), and under the aegis of the Department of Science and Art, lecturers were sent out to towns and cities around the country, using whatever accommodation was available. In Reading classes were held in West Street, and in Valpy's old Grammar School building.

1897 School of Art Valpy St entrance [22]

The scheme was part of the philanthropic educational movement but also fitted well into the spirit of 'self improvement' which was a feature of the Victorian era. With regards to the former, in the early 1870s, Hubert Sutton, of the Sutton seed family, seeing the need for a permanent centre, bought St Lawrence's vicarage and rented it to the College, at a nominal rate, to be used for Reading School of Science and Art.

By 1878 the old school dormitory, in what was left of the Hospitium, was in danger of being pulled down. The proponents of this plan noted that little of the original Hospitium was extant, the old Tudor windows had been removed and it had been *cruelly disfigured in many ways*. However the mayor, Arthur Hill, bought the building and presented it to the town. It was used for a variety of purposes by the Corporation, including that of Junior Library. This was considered a temporary measure as it was clear the structure of the building required major restoration.

PART 4. CHAPTER 2. THE HOSPITIUM AND THE MUNICIPAL BUILDINGS

In 1891 it was proposed that *the old Hospitium could be restored in such a manner as to preserve many of its original features.* One suggestion was that it could be converted to house the Duke of Wellington's Silchester Collection, which had been deposited with Reading Museum. Reading's architect, Slingsby Stallwood, was honorary curator of the collection. Although this suggestion was not realised, the building was renovated and adapted to house the newly founded School of Science and Art. Stallwood was the architect.[23]

At the same time the University Extension College movement was gathering momentum. During the 1880s Oxford University, especially Christ Church College, was sending lecturers to non-university towns. The success of the Kensington experiment, mentioned above, had shown that the people of Reading were more than receptive to the idea. As there was an almost ready-made grouping in the School of Science and Art it was a small step to establish an official Extension College in September 1892.

1904 The plate by the door reads: "University College, Reading." There is ivy growing on the multi-angular stair turret, and the end wall of the Town Hall is to the right. [24]

In 1898 the Prince of Wales officially opened the complex of buildings. In 1902 it was granted University College status.

The first Principal was Halford Mackinder, a Reader in Geography at Oxford. He found that he had an able secretary in Francis Wright, who had been administering the School of Science and Art. Mackinder then made an appointment which was to have long term benefits. William Childs, arguably more than any other individual, championed the cause of creating Reading University. In 1903 he succeeded Mackinder as Principal.

1890 St Lawrence's vicarage is the last house on the right. [25]

Ordnance Survey 1879

The County Court offices

Original site of the School of Art in Valpy's old Grammar School, 1870-1880

The vicarage

School of Science & College Head-quarters

St Lawrence's Church

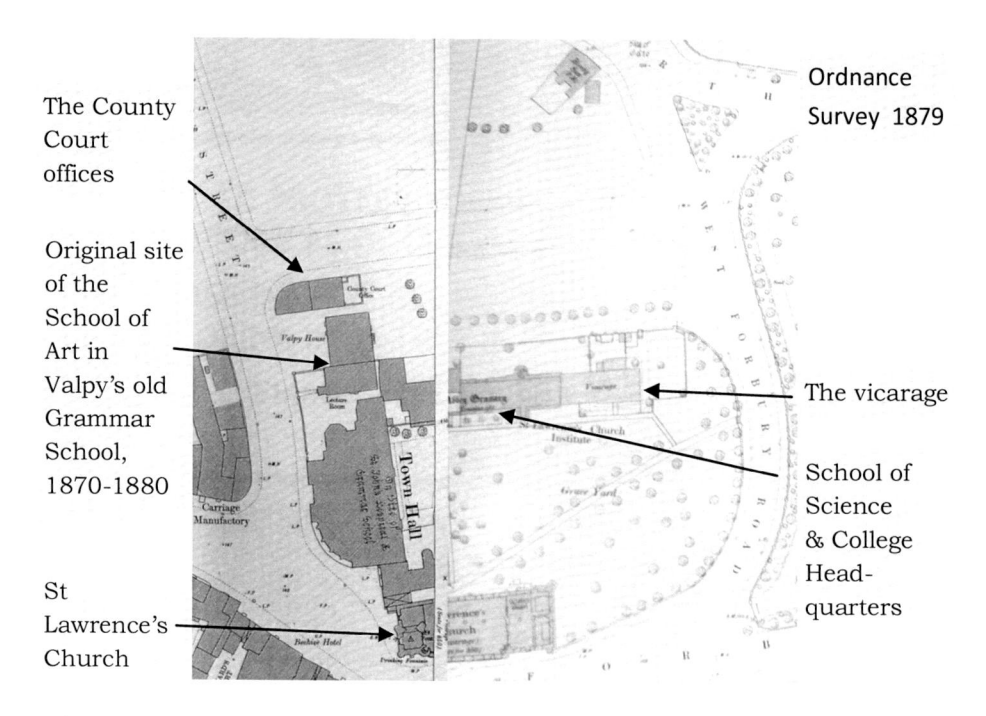

In his account of the early days of his career in Reading Childs noted that on his arrival in Reading in 1893 the *College was housed in three buildings: the School of Art, awkwardly detached and indistinguishable from the municipal offices, the School of Science, where were also the College headquarters; and the vicarage now linked up with the School of Science, and adapted to profane uses with devastating ingenuity.* By this he meant that the old vicarage was used first as a library then as the senior common room.[26]

In 1903 Childs was appointed as Principal of the College following Mackinder's resignation in 1902. As there was no room to expand, the College moved to the London Road site in 1906. Twenty years later it received the Royal Charter and became Reading University.

The vacated site gave Reading Corporation the opportunity to consider extending its offices into the area formerly occupied by the College.

Once again plans were proposed that would have entailed the demolition of what remained of the Hospitium. However pressure from many sides resulted in a rethink. In 1908 the Corporation accepted a design by the noted architect Slingsby Stallwood which incorporated what was left of the ancient Hospitium building into the extended Civic Offices. With the establishment of a Museum and Library alongside the Municipal Buildings, it could be justly claimed that this part of Reading, which had for over 400 years been a centre for education, continued to be the cultural heart of the town.

PART 4. CHAPTER 2. THE HOSPITIUM AND THE MUNICIPAL BUILDINGS

In fact we should recall that the Abbey had been one of the great repositories of learning, with a magnificent and comprehensive library. It had been consulted by scholars throughout the middle ages and even by Henry VIII himself. These new buildings devoted to learning and culture ensured that a thousand year old tradition now reached into the 20th century, if not beyond.

The British Dairy Institute

The photograph to the right, looking east along Valpy St, shows the College buildings. The furthest of these was to become the British Dairy Institute. Originally designed by Stallwood, the building was modified by William Ravescroft in 1898.

College buildings c.1900 [27]

The photograph below shows the same building taken from the north western corner of The Forbury, with Valpy St just visible to the right. The words 'British Dairy Institute' are on the side of the first large turret. The Institute had moved to Reading from Aylesbury in 1894, occupying the new wing of the College on the corner of Valpy St in 1896.

c.1900 British Dairy Institute [28]

Drawing of the Dairy Institute, c 1898, to the left and the old Vicarage to the right. The gateway to St Lawrence's churchyard is just left of centre.

Alongside is an illustration from the 'Berkshire Chronicle' of 1898 showing the Dairy Institute from the west. An article was written to mark the official opening of the Institute by the Prince of Wales. It is also interesting in that it gives a very detailed description of the interior and workings of the building.[29]

We read that *the New Buildings, which are on the east of and attached to the old vicarage buildings, fill up the whole area that was once the Vicarage gardens.*

The article describes how the building has a 10ft wide corridor from which the *various rooms new and old are reached.* On the ground floor there is a Hall, 45 by 35ft, and 19ft high. We then read about the various laboratories and a detailed description of the work carried out in each part of the building.

In 1896 the Royal Agricultural Society selected Reading as an examination centre for the National Diploma in Dairying. In 1912 the Institute moved to a new location on Redlands Road. The Board of Agriculture recognised the importance of the Institute by creating the Research Institute in Dairying and the combined departments of Agriculture and Horticulture became a Faculty of the University College. In the meantime the Institute acquired several farms in the area.

Today Reading University enjoys a world-wide reputation in all areas of agriculture.[30]

PART 4. CHAPTER 2. THE HOSPITIUM AND THE MUNICIPAL BUILDINGS

Reading Police Station and Magistrates' Court

Vacated by the 'Institute', the building was converted into the town police station and magistrates' court. The photograph below was taken in 1979. In 1981 the building was demolished.

Police Station and Magistrates' Court, c.1979 [31]

St Lawrence's churchyard and entrance
from the Forbury c.1820 [32]

The illustration above demonstrates how much the area had changed over the hundred years between 1820 and 1920. Although the church and the churchyard remained, new buildings now reached across into the churchyard and new roads had been constructed separating St Lawrence's from the Forbury.

In the next part we shall see how and why the Forbury itself changed over the same period and became the Gardens that we know today.

PART 5 THE FORBURY GARDENS
CHAPTER 1 THE WAR YEARS 1793–1815

The Forbury and the Military

We have already seen how, by the late 18th century, the Forbury and the lands around the Abbey ruins had passed into the hands of the Blagrave and Vansittart families. We also saw how eventually these latter passed to the Wheble family and how, subsequently, the whole area, except for the prison, became the property of the Corporation of Reading.

We shall now turn to the land we now know as the Forbury Gardens and how it came to pass that it became such an important green space in the heart of Reading.

Before the outbreak of the French wars one of the main uses of the Forbury was as an assembly place for displays and pageants and there had been several attempts to improve its facilities. In 1755 Richard Simeon paid *5 guineas towards the expense of repairing the road through the Forbury and beautifying the other part thereof.* In 1766 Francis Annesley paid *10 guineas for the improvements ... in the Forbury.* Annesley was noted for his desire to better the Forbury, specifically the Hill, and had been involved in raising money for this purpose.

Possibly one of the most magnificent celebrations occurred in 1789. There was news that George III had recovered from his 'illness'. The festivities began with a banquet for 283 people in the newly built Town Hall. When the mayor announced the toast of 'God Save the King' a 21 gun salute was sounded from the Forbury. Records state that the cannon had been *placed on the hill in the Forbury.* The account further relates that the *whole company, preceded by the band of music, went in procession to the Forbury, where a display of fireworks was exhibited.* [1]

With the outbreak of war against the French, in 1793, the Forbury became a focal point of military activity. The Berkshire Militia, part of the national militia, was based mainly on 'Bulmershe Heath'. However Reading had its own militia with its training and parade ground in the Forbury. The Captain was the Mayor of Reading, Martin Annesley, and their full title was the 'Reading Volunteers'. The militiamen were paid out of government funds, though they had to provide their own uniforms. Lack of military engagement with the enemy did not prevent the Volunteers displaying their enthusiastic support for the war. In 1794 Martin Annesley gave a banquet in the Town Hall for 300 people

PART 5. CHAPTER 1. THE WAR YEARS 1793–1815

including the officers i*n their full uniforms.* They only saw service once. Bizarrely that was in Reading itself and did not involve any enemy French troops. Irish dragoons were based near Reading. It was reported in 1795 that a group of Irish soldiers kicked away the scaffolding supports whilst some labourers were working on a building. This led to a fracas, ending up with a near pitched battle between the Irish soldiers and townspeople in the Forbury. The Volunteers were called in to re-establish order.

By 1798 the threat of invasion appeared imminent and an unpaid voluntary force was created, with a branch in Reading. This was called the 'Loyal Reading Volunteers', often referred to as an 'Armed Association', no doubt to distinguish it from Captain Annesley's 'Reading Volunteers'. They comprised around 150 men drawn *from among the principal inhabitants (of Reading) who were no longer averse from taking the ranks.* There are several records of their parades, usually starting in the Market Place and ending up in the Forbury where they entertained the crowds with manoeuvres and band music. Their uniforms were blue with scarlet facings and they wore either caps or helmets depending on the occasion.

An even greater cause for celebration came in October 1797 when Admiral Duncan famously won a major victory against France and its allies by defeating the Dutch navy at the battle of Camperdown.[2] It was reported that the Volunteers *were drawn up in the Forbury whence they marched to the Town Hall and fired three excellent volleys.*[3]

By 1798 the Armed Association could boast over 200 members drawn chiefly from *the most respectable tradesmen and housekeepers of this borough.* In the autumn of the same year there was a combined *colourful spectacle* involving both the Reading groups, as well as the Woodley Cavalry and the 15th Light Dragoons. This was staged to celebrate Nelson's successful campaign in the Mediterranean.

In the early years of the 19th century the Forbury continued to be the setting for military parades. Sometimes it was one or other of the groups mentioned, sometimes a combined operation. On one occasion, in 1804, the Oxford Loyal Volunteers met with the Reading Volunteers in the Forbury. However by 1806 the Armed Association had been disbanded. As the threat of invasion lessened the enthusiasm of the volunteer groups appears to have waned. In 1809 the Woodley Cavalry, the Royal Berkshire Regiment and the Reading Volunteers did take part in a joint grand parade in the Forbury to celebrate the King's birthday. It was reported that the Forbury was *gaily decked with trophies of naval victory, won by our gallant townsmen.* This is interesting on two accounts. We know that Reading was famous for its sail-cloth industry but we also learn that Reading men were in the Navy. Secondly, it was the last time such joint exercises took place. Later in 1809 there was a mutiny among the local militia in the

Forbury itself when some of the men who had not been paid their 'marching guinea' refused to obey orders. As a result the Reading Volunteers were disbanded.

Nevertheless in October of the same year more celebrations were held in the Forbury to mark the 50th anniversary of King George's reign. This was a splendid occasion, with tables in the Forbury for the townspeople to eat a *fine fat ox*, with beer and bread being provided.[4] Although there were celebrations in 1813 to mark Napoleon's defeat at Leipzig, the military element all but disappeared. The focus moved to other reasons for celebration in the Forbury. Fireworks became increasingly popular and are mentioned in several reports. In 1814, to mark the peace with France at the Treaty of Paris, the Forbury was once again the centre of festivities but this time the main attractions were the *rural and ludicrous sports* of donkey races, jumping and running in the sack, smoking matches, dancing and of course fireworks.

The move away from military spectacle was possibly linked with the way the military was viewed by some of the inhabitants of Reading and the surrounding countryside. The 'mutiny' may have been about 'pay' but it could also have been connected with the use of the military towards the suppression of riots and demonstrations for higher agricultural wages and for lower food prices. We shall return to this point shortly. In the meantime we should note that the importance of the Forbury as a focal point for demonstrating loyalty to the crown, and as a rallying point in support of the war, cannot be overestimated. These were uncertain times, politically. The 'republican' and 'democratic' ideals of the French Revolution were spreading throughout England as well. There was no guarantee of 'loyalty' from either civilians nor the military themselves. But note the names given to these militia and the stress on loyalty. Note also that there was virtually no chance that any of these 'volunteers' would ever meet an enemy Frenchman in anger, yet there were frequent military parades, displays and manoeuvres.

We should remember that in Reading at the time there were over 300 French priests, exiles from revolutionary France. These men were no friends of the Revolution. We know from the detailed letters of one of these priests, François Longuet, that he felt very much at home in Reading and that he had been made very welcome by the townspeople. He was also a close personal friend of several Protestant clergymen. We have several examples of gratitude and loyalty to the Crown by these French priests.[5] It should be noted that they were under the direct protection of the Prince of Wales, so any attack on them was tantamount to an act of treason against the monarchy itself. This demonstrates both the importance which the Crown and Government put on retaining the good-will of these exiles, and also the extent to which the exiles themselves identified with the British principles of 'Liberty', as opposed to those expounded across the

PART 5. CHAPTER 1. THE WAR YEARS 1793–1815

channel. Two examples serve to illustrate this point, both written by French refugees in Reading.

The first is in a letter by François Longuet. A few years before his death in 1817 he wrote the following to a Protestant clergyman and friend in Wallingford: *I hope my Dear Doctor, you will take all this as coming from a Catholic Man, who is sincerely convinced of the truth of his religion and bears no malice nor antipathy to those who differ from him; only I wish I could save all men and above all your nation whom I love more and more from day to day, for she is the only one, who protects oppressed justice; our King* [6] *at last is forced to come and take exile among you, you have the most right to our gratitude; as to me I look upon you as one good friend and I am sincerely grateful to you, and to your Nation; I would very willingly sacrifice everything to save an English person of any description; I feel a great satisfaction when I can oblige any English person, I daily pray for the prosperity of the good and generous England; may She and her children be blessed to the end of the world.*

A few years earlier another French priest, a Reverend Mr Leguay, wrote several pieces of poetry, one of which he entitled 'A Letter to the English Nation and especially to the Inhabitants of Reading'. In this he praises the virtues of the English crown and thanks the people of England, and particularly the people of Reading, for offering him and other exiles, including the King of France, a place of refuge and safety.[7]

If these Frenchmen presented no threat to the loyalty of the people with whom they mingled, there were also many 'enemy' prisoners of war held in and around Reading. These came from all over Europe. It is most probable that some of these supported the republican and democratic ideals of the Revolution. Among them were the Danish captives. A memorial to one of these can be found on the south wall of St Mary's, the Minster church.

A notable prisoner was Admiral Villeneuve, commander of the French fleet at Trafalgar. He was held at Bishop's Waltham in Hampshire with his retinue of around 200 men. Villeneuve also stayed at Sonning and it appears he attended at least one ball in Reading. He was allowed to attend Nelson's funeral. The Admiral was released on parole the next year, 1806. He died in mysterious circumstances on his return to France and was found with several stab wounds to his chest. A verdict of suicide was passed although there has always been the suspicion that Napoleon ordered his murder.

So we return to the question about the purpose of the militia, how it was employed and how it was viewed by at least some of the inhabitants of Reading and the surrounding area.

There can be no doubt about its first role for training military personnel, some of whom may have intended to join the regular army. However there was a very real fear of invasion and the militia was needed as an internal security force in case the French crossed the Channel. Had this happened, the enemy French troops, and their allies, would have been met with a well trained, well armed and disciplined force, both infantry and cavalry, throughout the nation. This strategy was initiated in 1793, when the British Government came to the conclusion that the regular army would not be able to counter an invasion. In 1794 Parliament passed an Act which allowed the Lords Lieutenant of each county to raise volunteer forces. Infantry volunteers came from unskilled ranks whilst Yeomanry recruits were drawn from farmers and tradesmen. Their officers came from the gentlemen of the county.

The Berkshire Yeomanry first appeared in Abingdon, and it is interesting that even at this early stage it was recognised as fulfilling a twofold role. Certainly it had to be ready to answer the call by the Crown in the eventuality of invasion. However it had a second and more immediate purpose. It was also at the service of the Lord Lieutenant or Sheriff to supress riots *within five miles of Abingdon*. As for Reading we have seen how and when the two volunteer groups were formed. It was only in 1798, with the immanent threat of invasion, that the second cavalry group was formed in Berkshire. This was the Woodley Cavalry commanded by Henry Addington, later to become Lord Sidmouth and Prime Minister.

The Yeomanry was never called into active service against the French and their allies. In fact their only action was to suppress the agricultural riots and disturbances referred to above. The first of these was at Thatcham in 1800, when over 300 people were dispersed by the appearance of the Cavalry. When looking at the pomp and splendour of the parades in the Forbury we should recall that the military manoeuvres, though no doubt a source of pride, reassurance and even entertainment for many, were also a way of demonstrating power and control and acted as a warning to those with subversive intent, social or political.

Memorial on the wall of St Mary's Minster church to a Danish prisoner of war

CHAPTER 2 THE FORBURY 1815 TO 1840

The Lay-out of the Forbury

The year 1840 marked as sudden a break in the social, economic and commercial life of Reading as had the Dissolution of the Abbey, three hundred years beforehand, or the founding of the Abbey four hundred years before that. This was due to the arrival of the railway. At a stroke, old commercial enterprises were devastated, the Kennet and Avon Canal lost most of its business, coaching companies had to readjust to accommodate the impact of the new railway and one of Reading's commercial mainstays, the cheese-fair, all but collapsed overnight. But other opportunities presented themselves. New commercial activities grew up around the railway itself. Entrepreneurs, such as the Sutton family, used the railways to expand their businesses and transport their goods reliably and quickly. The town's population was given another boost to its numbers and the foundations were laid for Reading to become a world trading centre for beer, biscuits, bricks and seeds.

So 1840 is a good date to make a break in the story of the Forbury and of the Abbey Quarter. We have seen how the Forbury had been used by the military during the war years of the late 18th and early 19th centuries. But the Forbury, even during this period, continued with its more traditional role as a place of commerce and entertainment. It was also an open space, with free public access, where problems of 'anti-social behaviour' were frequently reported.

The increasing activity also undoubtedly had an effect on the appearance of the Forbury. It is clear that there was a distinction in the minds of the people at the time as to the uses of different parts of the Forbury. The far eastern section was now the prison. Just south and to the west of this there were the ruins. Here there were several houses and by 1812 the National School buildings had been erected. The river bank of the Kennet, as it was joined by the Holy Brook and flowed past the south wall of the prison, was an area for relaxation. Moving further westwards, between the modern site of St James' church and the Hill, was a open space bordered by the Plummery wall to the north. To the south there was another wall around the Gateway school with what appears, from contemporary prints, to be a garden with tall trees. Next came the Hill, which was to be the centre of much debate. To the west of this lay the open space in front of the Gateway and the houses on its southern edge, leading to St Lawrence's. This southern section was separated from the great open space by a semi-circular ditch and fence. To its north we find the part of the Forbury where the fairs and military parades took place. Further west again lay the churchyard of St Lawrence and, by 1800, the newly constructed buildings of Dr. Valpy's Grammar School.

READING'S ABBEY QUARTER

The Open Space

One of the most important uses of the Forbury was as a location for Reading's annual Fairs. We have seen how these had been established over the previous centuries. There were four seasonal fairs: February- cattle and horses, May- cattle and horses, July-cattle (The only one not held in the Forbury—see p 164), September (Michaelmas) - cattle, horses, hops, the hiring of servants and, most important of all, cheese. This was of such significance that the Michaelmas Fair was often referred to as the Cheese Fair.

This event featured entertainment and games. In addition there were stalls in Market Place and New Forest ponies for sale. To get a flavour of what these fairs must have been like we need only look at the report, given above (p.144) for the festivities laid on in 1813 to celebrate Napoleon's defeat at Leipzig.

The open space to the east of the Hospitium buildings was also the home of Reading Cricket Club and the boys of the Grammar School used it as a playground and to play cricket. We have already seen the 1791 drawing, A, above, when examining the Abbey Gateway but it is worth looking at it from a different point of view.

A. The Forbury as seen through the Abbey Gateway, 1791 [1]

There are two paths leading across to the Hill, just out of sight to our right. These paths still have echoes in today's Forbury and are clearly visible on the 1840 map, D. It should be noted that in drawing C the level of the gateway through to the churchyard appears to be the same as that of the Forbury itself. There are no steps up to the churchyard as exist today. Photograph B shows today's path from the churchyard gateway to the northern edge of the Hill. This follows almost exactly the same path as shown in the 1820 illustration and map C.

B. The Forbury today

PART 5. CHAPTER 2. THE FORBURY 1815–1840

C. The Forbury in 1820 [2]

It is worth commenting on the state of the ground. In the earlier illustration, A, the furthest path is in reasonable condition. By 1820, illustration C, it looks churned up and muddy. It also appears that other pathways have been formed and that they are much wider, indicating increased usage with wider vehicles. Concern over the state of the Forbury was to be an issue over the next few decades.

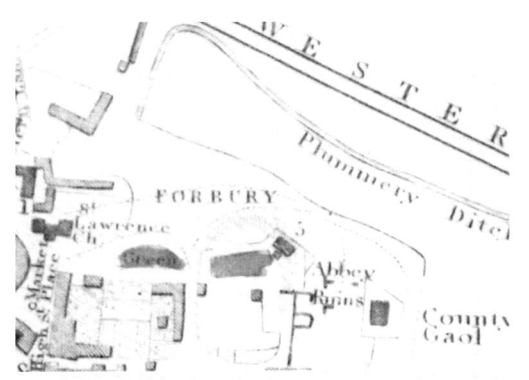

D. 1840 John Snare's map not only includes the new railway but marks the semi-circle as the 'Green'. The footpath is also shown.

There was growing awareness of the state of the paths, roads and public places. This had manifested itself in the first Paving Act.[3] This was not an issue that passed without comment at the time. John Man, school teacher and leading light of the town, wrote a spoof article, published in 1824, in the 'Reading Mercury'. Man had been a keen supporter of the Paving Act and subsequent attempts to clean up the town. This piece shows him in a very different light and we can well understand why one of his ex-pupils admired him so much as a teacher. The following is an extract from a much longer article purporting to be by-laws for those using the new paved areas.

Ladies bonnets are not to project more than seven inches from the head two inches of trimming allowed. Leghorns or Cobbetts in their natural state, to be cut by inspectors.

Hoops found trundling on the pavement in dirty weather, to be seized and forfeited; half to the inspector. If the weather be dry, the drivers to be seized and the hoops re-turned. Little boys making bear-traps to be well splashed for the first offence, second offence, transportation to the Forbury. No unqualified person to use a pea-shooter in the streets, under a penalty of five pounds, besides forfeiture of the engine and ammunition.[4]

On the left of picture C, page 149, the ditch which formed the boundary to the 'semi-circle' or 'green' can be clearly seen; as can the footpath leading from St Lawrence's referred to above. The Forbury, it should be recalled, extended much further to the west than today, including as it did the area north of the Hospitium buildings.

The Hill[5]

There had already been several attempts to make the Forbury and its Hill *a commodious and pleasant resort for the inhabitants* of Reading.

In 1790, prisoners from the County Gaol now situated at the eastern end of the Forbury, had erected railings around the Hill. But by 1813 it would appear that these had all but vanished and the Hill was in a poor state. The social unrest that we noted earlier was not eased by the hard winter of 1816-1817. The consequent increase in unemployment did afford the opportunity to use labour to try to shore up the hill by building a retaining wall around its base.

The Forbury Hill [6]

It is now that we encounter a Mr Joshua Vines. He held the tenancy for the Hill and he was passionate in his concern for its preservation. He blamed the *mischievous pranks of idle boys* for its deteriorating state and paid for remedial work out of his own pocket. In 1830 he campaigned for financial help to erect some iron railings to prevent cattle and the 'mischievous' children from causing more damage. In 1833 he planted two oak saplings to help stabilise the soil. He was, however, criticised for preventing the children from enjoying the *soft verdant sward with which the hill is so richly clothed.* Furthermore his oak trees were not considered to be in keeping with the existing *venerable elms.*[7] However the elms were themselves in a dangerous state and in 1836 a large branch fell, nearly causing serious injury to a gentleman and some children. The branch did damage the iron railings which Mr Vines again replaced at his

PART 5. CHAPTER 2. THE FORBURY 1815–1840

own expense. The Hill was considered a great vantage point from which to view the rustic picturesque landscape across the Thames and the village of Caversham with its rolling hills and majestic skyline beyond; truly a highlight of the Forbury Promenade.

1850 The Railway Yards [8]

All this was to change in the late 1830s with the arrival of the railway. There were mixed opinions as to its benefits. Many regretted the loss of the view but some suggested that the sight of the railway and its stations, shunting yards and workshops, might themselves become *a very fashionable promenade.*

The Green

The final section of the western part of the Forbury is the Green; the semi-circular area which reached from the western edge of the Inner Gateway almost to the wall surrounding St Lawrence's churchyard. We have already seen how this was portrayed over the centuries. Its origins are open to debate. Darter considered that it dated only as far back as the 17th century Civil War. Kerry suggests that it was in fact the remains of the 9th century Danish fortification, which itself was on the site of a Saxon settlement. He argues that it was once a circular fortified encampment, strategically placed on the highest point of the area lying between the Kennet/Holy Brook rivers to the south and east and the Thames to the north.[9]

What we see in 18th and 19th century illustrations are the remnants of its surrounding ditch. If Kerry is correct then the original circular defensive ditch was most probably filled in during the construction of the Abbey buildings, especially the Inner Gateway and the large house to its west, so leaving just the most northerly segment, which remained visible until the middle of the 19th century. We have also seen (p103-113) that the land lying within this proposed circle had most probably been a garden attached to the monastery and that after the Dissolution it retained this horticultural characteristic until the development of Sutton's seed establishment, again in the middle of the 19th century.

Some More Events in the Western Forbury 1800-1840

The military displays and fairs were not the only events that took place in and around the Open Space, the Hill and the Green.

There was an on-going disagreement between the leaseholders and owners of the land on one hand and the townspeople on the other. We have already seen how the Corporation jealously guarded its rights vis-à-vis the claims of such as Blagrave and Valpy. In October 1809, on the occasion of the celebration of the 50th anniversary of George III's accession, a meeting was held on the Hill, independent of the Mayor and Corporation to *assert and maintain inviolate the Right of the People to assemble and express their own sentiments in their own style, on all public occasions.* The controversy over rights of access and use continued until the Corporation bought and took control of the whole area in the second half of the 19th century. For instance the Corporation, as late as 1852, had to check the advance of the railway onto the open area which included the *public promenade* by the old wall; that is the Plummery wall.

From 1798 the Corporation ruled that *wild beasts and shows of other description were to be confined to the Forbury.* Prior to this, fairs, entertainments, stalls and animals had occupied the town's streets, especially those in and around Market Place. We should note that the Corporation's ruling was consistent with its drive to gentrify the town, part of this campaign being the implementation of the Paving Act and the building of the new Town Hall.

The exhibition of exotic animals became a favourite and essential part of Forbury festivities. One such event took place in 1814. Gillman and Atkin's Grand Menagerie was one of many to follow. This event featured a Camera Obscura, possibly similar to the one pictured here as demonstrated on Plymouth Hoe in 1827. By means of the lenses in the top part, panoramic images in colour were

PART 5. CHAPTER 2. THE FORBURY 1815–1840

projected onto a white surface, probably a sheet, in the darkened room, or 'camera obscura', below.[10]

In order to obtain as panoramic a view as possible it was necessary to place the cabin at a high vantage point. It is worth noting that the Green was chosen for this, partly because the surrounding ditch prevented cattle and other animals from intruding on the show. More importantly it was, as mentioned, a strategically high point in the Forbury, commanding views over the Thames Valley and across to Caversham.

In 1816, following Napoleon's final defeat at Waterloo in 1815, a temporary building was erected in the Forbury to mark the end of the war. The main attraction was the *military carriage with all its curious apparatus in which Bonaparte made his campaign in Russia and in which he escaped at Waterloo.*

Two years later the continuing confrontation over usage rights flared up again, and once more it was the contentious Dr Valpy, Headmaster of the Grammar School, who was involved. He objected to an auctioneer selling horses on the part of the Forbury that Valpy considered his territory. Although the auctioneer retreated, Valpy met a more determined adversary in a Mr Winkworth, an *intrepid asserter of the rights and privileges of the borough,* who drove his horse and cart outside the Head's study several times to emphasise his rights. He was not challenged by Mr Valpy.

An inexplicable celestial object appeared over the Hill during the Michalemas Fair of 1820. *It appeared first as a pointed star, rather larger than a crown piece and continued so for one and a half hours, seeming stationary over Forbury Hill.*

One of the Forbury's recurring favourites was Wombells' menagerie and its associated brass band. After Mr Wombell's death, his widow carried on the tradition well in to the 1850s and it was always keenly anticipated by the townsfolk.

Another remarkable event was the balloon flight by Charles Green. He is credited with having made more than 500 flights over a period of 30 years or so after his first flight in 1821. A volunteer from the town went with him on this flight. He was Henry Simonds of the banking and brewery family. The balloon travelled 50 miles or so north east and landed at South Mimms. Balloon flights became a perennial feature of the Fairs. Gingell of Vauxhall Gardens also came to Reading and offered flights in 1831.

On other occasions there were animated waxworks with the *application of mechanism to wax figures.* Even preaching figured as entertainment as in 1829 when *the Dissenters of all denominations turned out their pastors.* It would seem that each 'learned gentleman' was allocated space or 'a station' around the

Forbury from which to proclaim their message to what were referred to as *numerous auditories.*[11]

If these gentleman were no doubt proclaiming high morals, the fairs and gatherings also attracted the less socially conscientious among Reading's population. Crime was controlled by the local magistrates. In 1821 an officer from Bow Street came to the May Fair. Some twenty seven years earlier a young officer in the 15th Light Dragoons helped control the crowds. His name was Samuel Taylor Coleridge. By the end of our period, in 1841, Reading had a local police force which kept an eye on proceedings. Clearly there was a need. It was noted that a *swell mob* had arrived. In the same year John Murray in 'Blackwood's Magazine' wrote,

Who would suppose, for example, that those young men at the corner, dressed in the height of the Cockney fashion, bedizened with mosaic jewellery, and puffing their cigars, are members of the swell mob – thieves, in short, and pickpockets? They are exchanging cards: truly so they are; but, if you observe, the cards are pawn-brokers' duplicates of the plunder of the preceding day – yet you say it is impossible: they are young, of genteel address, and look like gentlemen; how is it you can detect their dishonest calling? At this moment a policeman is turning the corner – mark with what instinct of self-preservation the crumpled duplicates are crammed into their respective pockets ...

Pickpockets and confidence tricksters were undoubtedly a problem. In 1830 one poor innocent from the countryside, on associating with a prostitute or *nymph of the pave*, found she had stolen the £65 he had taken from selling his wares at market. This was a considerable sum if one considers that £50 was considered a good year's wage.

Horse thieves were another danger. Today we may be reminded not to leave valuables in our cars, whereas in 1814 the advice was not to leave valuable horses unattended in neighbouring meadows, as thieves gathered several days before and after fairs. The advice: *Safer to leave them in a reputable livery stable.*

If crime was a problem, albeit generally of a petty nature, the punishments were extremely severe. We have seen that the regime of the Forbury Prison and House of Correction was not a gentle one. In 1830 four pickpockets were sentenced to a month on the treadmill. Several months hard labour were likewise not an unusual punishment for theft.

Darter recalls how one man, starving and destitute, stole a loaf of bread. He was found guilty and the magistrate ordered that he should be tied to the back of a

PART 5. CHAPTER 2. THE FORBURY 1815–1840

cart and whipped from his place of incarceration at Greyfriars to his house. He died of his wounds.[12]

We saw that the arrival of the railway, in 1840, radically altered the character of the town. It also changed the numbers and types of people coming to Reading. The Great Western station opened in March 1840. The September Fair of that year attracted coachloads of visitors travelling from London and eventually extra trains were laid on to cope with the throng. We shall be examining the long-term effects of the coming of the railway in the next section. However it should noted that it was the Forbury Fairs which continued to attract the greatest number of visitors to the new Reading.

The coming of the railway was just too late for the Coronation of Queen Victoria on the 28th June, 1838. The Forbury once again was the focal point of the town's celebrations:

From dawn to a very late hour ... in the afternoon rural amusements were resumed in the Forbury and much diversion by the dipping in flour, wheeling, blindfolding, climbing for mutton, pig chasing etc etc' In the evening on the Green one of the most brilliant illuminations perhaps ever exhibited out of the metropolis ... upwards of 8000 lamps were employed. The fad of sending up lighted balloons was as popular in the 1840 as today. The newspaper reported that *fire-balloons, might be dispensed with. Last evening, a large balloon of this description passed over the town, and being caught by the draught at St. Lawrence's tower, entered the belfry-window, and passing through the opposite window, blazed up, threatening the fabric... it however subsided without damage.*

The day ended with fireworks on the Hill.[13]

Although not strictly in the part of the Forbury we are looking at here, one other event took place which was to have long term significance for the area. In May 1839 Reading Horticultural Society held its annual show in the Ruins.[14] These shows had previously been held in the Town Hall. The extra space and *the beautiful view* offered by the location guaranteed the success of the event. Reports indicate that the Society tidied the area and provided its own marquee.

To a great extent this heralded in a new stage in the use of the Forbury and one that has left its mark on the Reading we know today.

CHAPTER 3 THE CREATION OF THE FORBURY GARDENS 1840 –1860

Not only was there a rapid growth in an appreciation of the Forbury as a place for public recreation but other factors changed the townspeople's attitude to the area. The first of these was the arrival of the railway. The second was a change in the nature of the land ownership of this part of Reading. We have seen that following the Dissolution of the Abbey the land had been divided up and ownership, often through long-term leases, became complex, frequently leading to disputes over rights of usage.

The Coming of the Railway

We have also seen that the impact of the arrival of the railway was such that the economic focus of the town altered radically. An area which had been of little financial significance became the trade hub of the town. During the middle ages, and even before, the Thames had been the focal point for trade, both downriver to London and upriver to Oxford. Although this had continued to some degree, the main routes, both for trade and personal travel, had moved to the east-west links from London to Newbury and so onto Bath, especially from the start of the 18th century. Queen Anne had made Bath both famous and fashionable. In her search to ease the painful consequences of her debilitating arthritis, in the form of gout, the Queen made frequent visits to that city. Although Anne herself wanted nothing more than peace and quiet the result was that Bath became a fashionable resort, a status it retained throughout the 18th century and beyond. The Bath Road, linking London to Bath, became one of the major routes in the country.

Reading was well placed to benefit from this increased traffic. Along with the general growth in trade and prosperity over these years, the whole infrastructure necessary to maintain such an arterial trade route developed in Reading as elsewhere along the road. Farriers, wheelwrights, victuallers and livery stables were but a few of the trades that thrived. Inns and hostelries prospered the length of the road. In Reading many old and long-established inns grew and

The King's Arms, Castle Street today.

PART 5. CHAPTER 3. THE CREATION OF THE FORBURY GARDENS 1840 –1860

flourished whilst many new ones were founded. In the centre of the town the George and the Ship are two surviving examples.

The King's Arms, at the far western end of Reading, was one of the most renowned and exclusive of these inns. It was requisitioned by the government during the French Wars at the end of the 18th century to house over 300 émigré French priests who had fled France under the threat of death. We are fortunate in having contemporary etchings of the Kings Arms, possibly made by these refugees. Today a fine cedar of Lebanon stands in the grounds. In all probability this was planted as a sapling by the refugees as a token of gratitude to the King and people of Reading for their help during their time of persecution and exile.[1]

The King's Arms c.1800.[2]

Roads were not the sole means of transport along the east-west axis. The Kennet, which flowed alongside the Abbey before reaching the Thames, likewise offered scope for improved transport and communication. In 1715 The Kennet Navigation Act sought to develop this facility; in 1718 John Hore of Newbury was appointed as the engineer. His plans were to shorten the distance of the Kennet between the two towns, and so reduce travelling time, by straightening out the meanders. This would cut the distance by about 11 ½ miles to around 18 ½ miles. The townspeople of Reading vigorously and even violently opposed the scheme as they feared it would damage their position as the centre of trade for the whole surrounding area. During the work of canalising the Kennet in the 1720s a mob of about three hundred, led by the Mayor, Robert Blake, owner of the wharf by Blake's Bridge, attacked and destroyed some of the workings.

It took some time for the citizens and traders of Reading to realise that, far from being detrimental to trade, the canal could bring prosperity. By the 1740s attitudes had changed and Reading became an important junction in both river and road transport between London, to its east, and Oxford and Bath to its north and west. Following the survey by the engineer John Rennie, the Canal's route west of Newbury took a more southerly direction. It was completed in 1810. By 1815, London and the great port of Bristol were finally connected, as planned by the Kennet and Avon Canal Act of 1794,

Opening this trade link with Bristol gave Reading an even greater role in the transport infrastructure of the Industrial Revolution throughout the south of England.

Significant though these 18th and early 19th century improvements were, transportation of goods by water and road was subject to the vagaries of the weather. The river link between Reading and London was particularly prone to drought and frost. The hard winter of 1813-14 saw the town suffering considerably from lack of coal and other essentials. Those employed in the transport industry were reduced to penury. Times of drought likewise saw disruption in traffic between the capital and Reading. The freezing conditions of the winter of 1813-14 were followed by a long period without rain, causing several weeks of further delays. At such times goods from the West Country frequently had to be unloaded at Reading's wharves and transferred to wagons for onward transport by roads which, it has to be said, were themselves often unsuitable for any traffic, let alone heavy goods.

The prospect of a faster, cheaper and more reliable transport system proved an attractive alternative. Not all favoured the railway however. Its opponents included those whose interests lay in the existing system: barge operatives, road hauliers with their related industries and landowners who felt their estates would suffer as a result of railways being driven through them.

Opinion in the town as to the benefits of the railway was divided, as reflected in the columns of the local press. The 'Reading Mercury', a liberal-leaning paper, whose proprietors, the Smart/Cowslade family, had supported the campaign behind the Great Reform Bill of 1832 and Catholic Emancipation (1829), was in favour of the railway whilst its rival the 'Berkshire Chronicle', a Conservative paper founded in 1825, without opposing it, took a more critical stance.[3] In 1835 the Parliamentary Act allowing the construction of the railway was passed and building began almost immediately. In March 1840 the Great Western reached Reading.

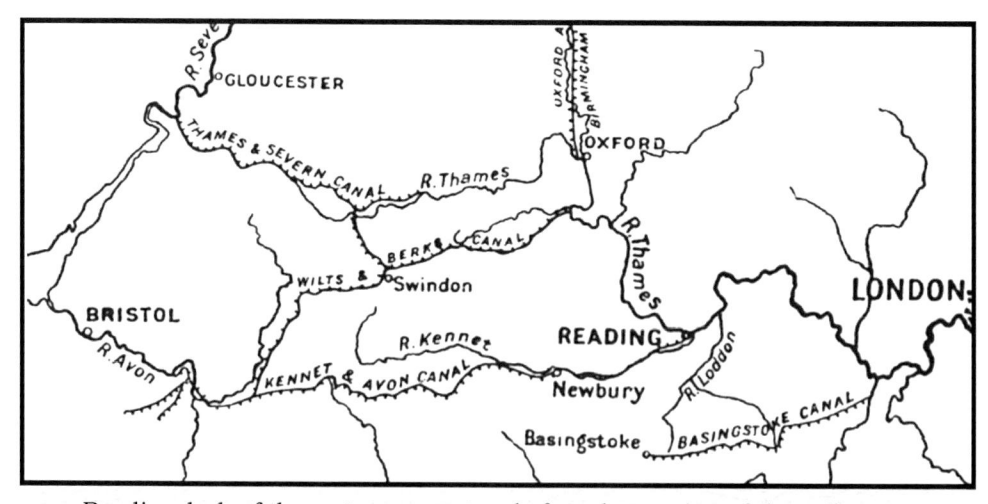

Reading: hub of the waterway system before the coming of the railways.

PART 5. CHAPTER 3. THE CREATION OF THE FORBURY GARDENS 1840 –1860

Picture A is of Reading's Great Western Railway Stations in 1842. This artist's impression shows Station Road as a raised causeway, with the "down" station and goods shed to the left, and the "up" goods shed, refreshment room and station to the right. The engine shed is between and behind the two stations. St. Peter's Church, Caversham, appears among the trees in the background.

A. The GWR Stations, 1842 [4]

There was a great deal of excitement surrounding the arrival of the railway. The opening took place on the 30th March, 1840. The 'Reading Mercury' reported large crowds lined up along the platforms, in the Forbury and, for those lucky enough, from the vantage point of the Hill. The occasion was marred by the death of one of the workmen, Henry West, only a few days beforehand following a freak whirlwind which blew him off the roof on which he was working. A memorial to him was erected in St Lawrence's churchyard.[5]

View B, of both the Great Western and South Eastern Railways at Reading, was drawn from a more easterly perspective, possibly from the Hill. In the distance, to the left, the "down" and "up" stations of the Great Western are visible. The "up" station has an overall roof. Also shown is the wooden viaduct over Vastern Lane, labelled 'Road' in the catalogue, with a train on it. Two railway signals are visible. To the right is the terminus of the South Eastern Railway with a train at the platform. The Forbury Road is in front of the station.

B. Reading Stations c1850 [6]

The next view, C, is yet further to the east. It shows a landscape which is still rural, with the River Kennet in the foreground. In the distance are St James' church, the towers of St Lawrence's and St Mary's and the spire of St Giles' church.

C. The junction of the Rivers Thames and Kennet c1840 [7]

The Eastern Forbury – The Pleasure Gardens 1854 –1860

We saw earlier how the Wheble family acquired that section of the Abbey Ruins and the Forbury which had belonged to Lord Bexley (p63). We also saw how, in 1843, James Joseph Wheble had sold a section of this land and how Abbots Walk was built there. The area containing St James' church and other buildings was handed over to the Catholic authorities but Wheble still owned the eastern section of the Forbury, including the Hill.

The Hill was causing problems in several ways. First of all its stability became a matter of concern. In 1845 the railings had to be removed to allow more soil to be pitched into *the hollow* so that more trees could be planted. Evidently the railings were replaced but it was claimed *the practice of using them to beat carpets should be prevented as it shakes the foundation which supports it* (the Hill). In fact following heavy rain the earth on the north side of the Hill forced out the retaining brick wall around its base, making it unsafe either to walk on the Hill or along the promenade at its foot.

There was also a question as to who was responsible for maintaining the seats. In July 1854 the tenant who ran a beer stall on the Hill had broken up the benches, ordering anyone not buying his beer or cigars to leave the area. The Corporation recognised that it was private land but also invoked the ancient rights of free access to the site. The townspeople took this a stage further when a crowd of around seven to eight hundred people *refreshed with supplies of beer*, presumably not from the tenant's establishment, smashed up the beer stall, removed his notice and in so doing also destroyed the gas light which adorned the Hill.

James Joseph Wheble was keen to rid himself of this troublesome business, and no doubt of his even more troublesome tenant. Wheble preferred to sell the land to the Corporation rather than to a private developer. Although this would only cover the eastern section of the Forbury, including the Hill, there was a feeling of optimism that the area could be converted into a retreat and promenade *judiciously restricted to the well-behaved classes*.

Consequently Wheble sold the land to the Corporation for £1200. He himself contributed £400 whilst the residents of Abbots Walk also gave £400, with the Corporation finding the balance. By November 1854 the Hill and 'other land and hereditaments' had become the property of the Town. Wheble received a civic vote of thanks for his public spirited actions.[8] It is worth noting that if Wheble had instead chosen to sell his land to a private individual, at a much higher price, it is highly unlikely that Reading would have the gardens we know today.

The town lost no time in planning this *feature of attraction to the town*. In 1855 the Board of Health asked for plans, with a limit of £1000, to be spent on the

PART 5. CHAPTER 3. THE CREATION OF THE FORBURY GARDENS 1840 –1860

improvements. By September work had started. A boundary wall was begun, to enclose the area from the north. The wall was to be built of brick with iron railings between its pillars. A fountain was to be placed in the centre of the area, the slopes of the Hill were to be planted with evergreens and a summer house constructed in the north east corner. In October the decision was taken that the new gardens should be given a *botanical character*. By the January of 1856 a building belonging to the South Eastern railway, which had been built encroaching on the Forbury land, was removed. On the 23rd March, Easter Sunday, the gardens were officially opened and despite the time of year, the lack of plants, and a rather drab appearance, several hundred people attended this important event in the town's history.

Work continued apace and by July the fountain had been installed. The gardens became a regular venue for the Royal Berkshire Band, who at first performed on the Hill. They soon discovered that it was better to play on the flat grass area so that by August it was reported that on *Tuesday evening last upwards of 3,600 people entered the grounds*.

The area became known as the Pleasure Gardens, under the direction of a head keeper, Mr Davis. Sutton Seeds, as we have seen, had their nurseries across from the Forbury. These in many ways became an extension of, and added to, the 'botanical' nature of the gardens as they were already open to the public to enter freely. In the autumn of 1856 Suttons were given charge of supervising the planting of numerous shrubs and deciduous trees in the Pleasure Gardens.

Illustration A, dated at around 1860, shows just how densely planted the Hill and adjacent area were. The gateway which had previously led to the buildings to the east of the Abbey Gateway, was retained as an entrance to the Pleasure Gardens. It is visible on the far left of the illustration.

A. The Pleasure Gardens c 1860 [9]

The original wall was replaced by a new wall with iron railings. It stretched from the Abbey Gateway to the Forbury Road just west of the Hill.

The Corporation now owned the Ruins and the eastern section of the Forbury but there was no connecting route between the two. The Board of Health, which was charged with the responsibility of administering these areas, had appointed Mr Davis, the Head Gardener, in charge of both sites. In 1858, following discussions with James Joseph Wheble, along with Fr. Ringrose, the Catholic priest in charge of St James', the Corporation could announce that *arrangements have been made by the trustees of the Roman Catholic chapel to give up to the board sufficient ground for the purpose of effecting a connection between the Forbury Gardens and the Abbey ruins.*

The wall and railings

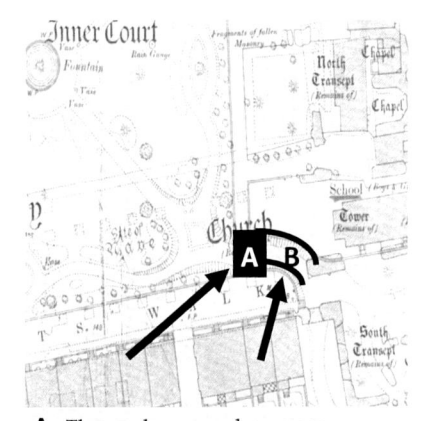

A The underground passage

B The parcel of land given by the Catholic Church and Wheble to the Corporation.

Extract from the 1879 Survey

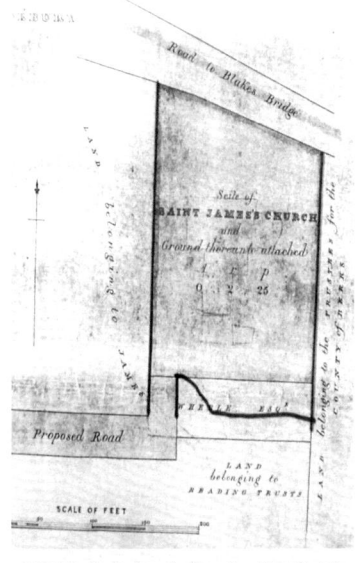

1858 Original deed of gift [10]

This consisted of a short tunnel from the south eastern corner of the Gardens, leading to the arch between the south aisle and the old cloisters of the ruined abbey. Whilst digging out the subterranean passageway, underneath the existing pathway, some stones and flint from the Abbey were uncovered and these were

PART 5. CHAPTER 3. THE CREATION OF THE FORBURY GARDENS 1840 –1860

used in constructing the archway of the underground passage.

It should be recalled that at this time Britain was at war. The three years of the Crimean War ended in 1856. In June 1857 the Sebastopol gun was presented to the Corporation. It is of more than passing interest, and rather poignant, to note that a member of the Wheble family, the Reverend John Wheble, brother of the same James Joseph who had sold the Hill to the Corporation on such favourable terms, had died whilst serving as a Catholic chaplain in the Crimea. He became a victim of dysentery whilst serving at Sebastopol and died aged 29 en route to hospital at Balaklava on the 3rd of November 1854.[12]

B. The Hill and **Russian gun** c 1865 [11]

On Sundays the gardens were closed between 10am and 1pm to allow the garden attendants to go to church. Not all the visitors to the Pleasure Gardens were as law abiding as their founding fathers had hoped. Entrance was certainly not restricted to the *well-behaved classes* and it became necessary for assistants to Mr Davis to be appointed. Flowers and plants were being dug up and removed, in some cases almost as soon as they had been planted. The old problem of *mischievous children* also had to be addressed. By 1860 Mr Davis was sworn in as a special constable to give him extra powers to help in these endeavours. The Russian gun also attracted the attention of other miscreants. Twice in the same year that it had been placed on the Hill it was fired during the night, breaking windows in the houses along Abbots Walk. The gun was *muzzled and capped,* though somehow the next year, in March 1858, its oak carriage was blown up. It was decided to leave it on the Hill and in 1859 the cannon was mounted on a stone plinth and surrounded with iron railings as can be seen in illustration B, above.

This was not the only annoyance that the residents of Abbots Walk had to suffer. They made numerous complaints about the noise and dirt resulting from the proximity of the railway. The early morning routine of steaming up, and the noise of the shunting and work yards were a continual cause of complaint. Little was achieved as the railway management merely replied that this was the cost that Reading had to pay for having such a successful railway coming through the town.

The Western Forbury 1840 –1860

If there was an improvement in the facilities, upkeep and management of the eastern part of the Forbury, the opposite was true for the western section. The whole area was still in the ownership of Colonel Blagrave. The arrival of the railway resulted in increased traffic over the Forbury, cutting deep ruts into the ground and causing almost impassable muddy areas in wet weather. This was not helped when the Mayor of Reading, in 1841, ordered that at the St. James' Fair *all cattle shall be exposed for sale in the Forbury and nowhere else*. Previously, although much of the Fair had been on the western section of the Forbury, cattle could be shown and sold on the streets of the town, especially Friar Street and West Street. Moving cattle onto the Forbury naturally caused much more damage to the ground.

In 1848 The Public Health Act created local Boards of Health with powers to purchase land. Reading's Board of Health was to have significant long lasting impact on the face of the town and specifically on the Forbury area. We have frequently referred to the Board of Health Survey of 1853. With regards to the Forbury, the newly created Board of Health was concerned about the detrimental effect the Railway was having on the area. It was reported that *the disgraceful state of the Forbury caused by vehicles being driven across it to and from the railway station* required urgent attention.

On page 133 we looked at the Board of Health Survey map of 1853 which shows the line of the new road which was intended to reduce the problem. However, at the next Michaelmas Fair of 1854 a local newspaper reported, *there are heaps of oyster shells, manure and other refuse from the late fair, which, being exposed to the heat of the sun, emit an effluvia annoying to persons either passing to the Reigate Railway Station or to the Forbury Hill*. In 1855 it was reported that the path between Market Place and the Abbey Gateway was deep in mud.

The situation was worsened by continuing arguments over the rights of the landowner, Colonel Blagrave, and his various tenants. For example, Blagrave had protested at the mayor's decree of 1841 regarding the decision about moving the cattle onto his land for St James' Fair. The Corporation referred him back to the Elizabethan Charter which gave the town overall rights over the Forbury. The Board of Health suggested that *the wisest course for the board* (was to) *effect a purchase under the Land Clauses Consolidation Act*. In short they would buy the western section of the Forbury from Blagrave. In March 1860 negotiations were completed. The Corporation became the owners of the western section of the Forbury together with the western part of the Inner Gateway.

PART 5. CHAPTER 3. THE CREATION OF THE FORBURY GARDENS 1840 –1860

The Abbey Ruins South of the Chapter House

One section of the old Abbey was still in private hands. This was the area between the Kennet and the Chapter House which had belonged to Richard Buncombe as shown on the map on page 64. There was the perennial concern about the need to keep *the mischievous and badly-disposed in order or to check their practices.* The problem appears to have been particularly acute in this area. Not only did the Corporation wish to keep better order in the town but it now aimed at acquiring what was left of the ancient Abbey lands still in private hands. In 1859 the sale was agreed at a price of £700. Not only did this cover the remaining part of the Abbey Ruins but it also included the north bank of the Kennet as far as Blake's Bridge.

Raising the money was, as ever, complicated by the wish to use a mix of public subscription and private donations. A Grand Summer Fair, held in July 1859 with music and fireworks, was poorly supported and raised only £21. However by the end of the year an appeal by the Board of Health to *gentlemen residing in the neighbourhood of the town,* raised £500. When the Buncombe estate offered to include the cottages along Abbey Walk, the outstanding balance was forthcoming. One of these cottages was designated for the use of the Head Gardener.

In late 1859 work began on the area. A terraced walk along the north bank of the Kennet, reaching from Abbey Street to Blake's Bridge, was created and planted with horse chestnut trees. This was to become Chestnut Walk. By May 1860 the levelling and turfing of the area was completed, allowing Reading Horticultural Society to hold a Grand Floral Exhibition in the new area. *A tent of immense size... 90 feet by 120* was erected occupying the whole of the central space.[13] The show was repeated with even greater success over the next two years.

By the late 1850s it was clear that the Corporation and people of Reading viewed the Forbury and Abbey Ruins as a place for public relaxation and entertainment. Different parts fulfilled various requirements but the scene was set for the area to become the green space we know today.

The next chapter will look at how the Forbury took on its final shape, along with many of its well-loved landmarks.

CHAPTER 4 THE CREATION OF THE FORBURY GARDENS 1860-1919

The Two Forburys

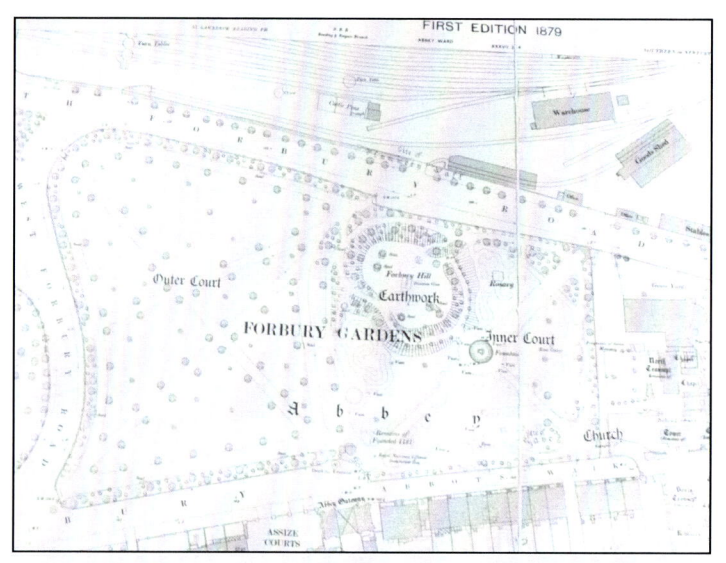

Plan of the Forbury Gardens, Ordnance Survey 1879

There were some negative aspects to these developments. Professor Slade comments on the fact that no proper archaeological surveys were made during this time. The Corporation was intent on ameliorating the amenities of the area, partly to justify the time and money they had spent on its acquisition and restoration. A contemporary architect and antiquarian, J C Buckler, who had undertaken an earlier survey of the ruins, commented that the treatment by the Corporation had *proved destructive in the extreme,* with ancient walls removed or pierced to make way for footpaths, open spaces and flower beds. He concluded that *it would be hard to find another instance of such callous barbarity as the present age has witnessed here.* However the great majority of public opinion supported the Corporation and the Board of Health. [1]

One fact that cannot be disputed is that, just over 300 years after the Dissolution of the Monastery and the division of its property, the greater part of the area, except that occupied by the prison and Abbots Walk, was once more under a single ownership and, most important of all, was in hands of, a public body: Reading Corporation. The Corporation lost no time in getting to work on the new combined Forbury. The distinction between the two parts, the Pleasure

PART 5. CHAPTER 4. THE CREATION OF THE FORBURY GARDENS 1860 –1919

Gardens and the western area, was maintained; indeed the separating wall was retained. Improvements were immediately made to the western area. A pit was dug and the gravel extracted used to level the area and form a uniform layer for a parade ground surrounded by grass and gravelled walks.

On the 16th of August 1861 the Mayor, his mace bearers and other dignitaries officiated at the official opening. The Mayor also accepted a drinking fountain which William Palmer had specially commissioned for the Gardens, and which stood at the main entrance opposite the Inner Gateway. This was described as *of exceeding chaste and beautiful design*. It is just visible, to the left of the gas lamp, in the above photograph dated by Reading Library as between 1890 and 1900 .

The drinking fountain c1890 [2]

The early 1860s saw more improvements such as the installation of three lights and the conversion of the pond, immediately to the east of the Hill, into a rose garden or 'rosary' as it is marked on the 1879 OS map. This replaced the pond which, unlike the water in the fountain basin, had become a *mass of dried weeds and rushes*. More seats were added, iron gates erected to keep animals out and a green house installed.

The Hill became the venue for regular performances by various bands. The Rifle Corps was prominent among these. Initially there were complaints that it was too loud and in 1862 the weather became so bad that the band moved to the more sheltered position of the Abbey Ruins. However it was soon discovered that the acoustics of the Ruins were not as good as in the Pleasure Gardens, so the band retuned to the Hill. In June 1863 a platform was built on the Hill for the band, along with a flagpole which was felt to be a fitting complement to the Sebastopol gun.

We saw that the cannon had been fired on several occasions by miscreants, but in March 1863 it was fired to celebrate the visit of the Prince of Wales, following his tour of the town. Since it had been capped in 1853 it must be assumed that it was made usable again. A commemorative oak tree was planted on the Hill and, in the spirit of earlier fairs, rustic sports were staged including *bobbing for oranges, diving for eels, climbing the greasy pole etc etc*. An ox was roasted for general consumption. Unfortunately this was spoilt by a group of 'roughs' who forced their way into the Forbury and dragged away the roast. This did not appear to deter the great majority who went on to enjoy a firework display from the Hill and the release of a 'fire balloon'. The whole of the town, including the Forbury and the Gateway, was lit with an *extensive illumination of small oil lamps*. In the same year, 1863, the western part of the Forbury acquired a new parade ground with trees planted around it.

We have seen that vandalism appears to have been a major problem in the town. Once again it caused upset when over twenty of the trees were damaged. The guilty party was caught on this occasion, fined and sentenced to 21 days hard labour.

If deliberate vandalism was a problem, so was the design of the area. There was no fencing around the western section except for some boundary chains. These were constantly damaged by children swinging on them. Moreover, animals being driven to the cattle sheds to be transported by rail would frequently wander into the western section of the Forbury, causing damage.

There was a proposal to erect gymnastic equipment in the gardens, but it was not followed through. In 1866 the Victorian passion for physical exercise culminated in a plan to build a gymnasium. But once again nothing was achieved. The problem was that the Corporation knew that the space needed to be improved to bring it in line with the Pleasure Gardens. This, however, conflicted with its traditional use as an open area for parades, free public games and the like. It was even suggested that a new market could be placed on the site.

The purchase of Kings Meadow in 1869 changed the whole dynamic of the debate and at a stroke solved the problem. Kings Meadow consisted of an area of around 12 acres which was bought from John Knollys. The map on page 12 shows it as King's Mead. It had originally been called 'Abbot's Mead' before the Dissolution. Yet another section of the ancient Abbey was now in the possession of the town and it was designated for the activities previously held in the western Forbury.

There was some danger to the Forbury when a suggestion was made to sell the western section to pay for the acquisition of Kings Meadow. This was not taken up. Instead the Corporation followed advice that *the time has arrived for enclosing ...* (the western portion) *of the Forbury*. Although this had the result of combining the two parts, to some extent, the western section was to be known as the Outer Forbury. The wall separating it from the Pleasure Gardens was removed and it was replaced with a temporary fence. Partly to save money, but also to distinguish it from the botanical part of the Forbury, it was decided to cover the Outer Forbury with turf but that it should not be *laid out for flower beds*. It was clearly designated for gentle recreation. Circuses, for example, were forbidden. Along its western border the chains, which had achieved little and been the cause of much trouble, were replaced with a wall.

PART 5. CHAPTER 4. THE CREATION OF THE FORBURY GARDENS 1860 –1919

The year 1870 saw a significant change in the management of the whole Forbury garden area. Mr Davis, the Head Gardener, left. He had overseen the development of the gardens and, as much as any individual, created the Forbury as we known it today. Instead of employing their own gardener and caretaker, the Corporation contracted the work out to a Mr George Phippen, who owned the Victoria Nurseries along the Oxford Road and a florist shop in Broad Street. Phippen, and his wife, were given the contract to supply and maintain the horticultural aspect of the gardens. It was agreed that the Outer Forbury should be put in good order by the Corporation, before the contract began, and that the Phippens would not be allowed to sell their produce in the Forbury. This arrangement continued until George Phippen died suddenly in 1893, after which his wife more than ably continued the business until her death in 1922.

At the same time the Corporation also employed a keeper who was responsible for maintaining order throughout the Forbury and Ruins. Repeated instances of vandalism and theft continued to be a problem; so much so that additional special constables had to be appointed. The strength of the fear of the 'rough' element in society can be judged by the reasons given for maintaining a ban on nursemaids and children using the Outer Forbury. In 1876 it was cited that the grounds were being turned into a *rough and common playground*. In 1885 the ban on allowing people to walk on the grass was upheld and as late as 1904 the Corporation forbade the playing of games in the Forbury, the Abbey Ruins and Chestnut Walk.

The two photographs, A and B, are by Taunt. A is from the west and B from the east. They show the two portions of the combined Forbury. The fence and shrubs between the two sections were removed in 1873. They give us an excellent and unique view of the Forbury soon after the creation of the outer Forbury. Note the decorated west wall and entrance in A.

A. c.1870–71 [3]

The lower photograph, B, shows the eastern Pleasure Gardens. The keeper's thatched shelter is in the centre of the picture. There are iron railings between the two sections of the gardens. Also visible are the wall and railings separating the Gardens from Abbots Walk.

B c.1875 [4]

We saw above (p72ff) that St James' school was built in 1872. As the school does not appear on this photograph it must have been taken before this date.

In 1871 the Corporation undertook the repair of *the walls of the Abbey Ruins with cement so as to render the same secure.* Contemporary comment called this a defacement of the old walls and proposed that *the new plastering be hid with a sprinkling of mould.* This suggestion was not carried out but it is interesting that the Corporation faced the same challenges regarding the preservation of the Ruins as today. We can also observe that some of the problems we encounter today may have their roots in the solutions proposed and implemented 150 years ago.

The Maiwand Lion

On the 27th July 1880 the British army, along with Indian troops from the Bombay Army, suffered a terrible defeat west of Kandahar in Southern Afghanistan. Brigadier General Burrows commanded the field brigade and Brigadier General Nuttall, the cavalry. The two and a half thousand British and Indian troops faced an overwhelming force of twelve thousand regular Afghan troops and experienced tribesmen, who were also well armed with more modern and heavier Armstrong guns than those supplied to the British troops.

The Maiwand Lion 1887 [5]

The British infantry who formed the bulk of the force were from the 66th Foot, renamed the Royal Berkshire Regiment in 1882.

Of the combined British-Indian army, 969 were killed. Reports of the actual number of men lost do vary but it is likely that the 66th lost 286 dead and 32 wounded; over 60% of their number. The battle was commemorated by Kipling in his poem 'That Day'. William McGonagall also wrote about Maiwand in his poem 'The Last Berkshire Eleven: The Heroes of Maiwand'. The title is taken from the report that eleven men of the 66th were honoured by their opponents, after the battle, for protecting their colours so valiantly. It is said that Arthur Conan Doyle based the character of Dr Watson, in his Sherlock Holmes stories, on Surgeon Major Alexander F. Preston who was wounded at Maiwand.

PART 5. CHAPTER 4. THE CREATION OF THE FORBURY GARDENS 1860 –1919

The Forbury is the site of the Maiwand Lion. It was designed by George Simonds, who made the suggestion that the Memorial should take the form of an angry lion. He undertook detailed anatomical studies of lions at London Zoo before embarking on the project. He then made twelve models from which he selected two to be converted into a full size sculpture. One of these was then cut into nine pieces for final enlargement and casting in iron. Young's of Pimlico were the ironmasters. The inscription along the base of the Lion records both the sculptor's and the ironmaster's names. There is no truth in the rumour, which persists to this day, that Simonds committed suicide on completing the sculpture because it was anatomically incorrect. Simonds was a renowned sculptor with other works in Reading, see p121. He even has the distinction of having one of his pieces, 'The Falconer', displayed in Central Park, New York. He went on to become chairman of Simonds Brewing Company in 1910 and died in 1929.

Private Nightingale in 1930 with his Afghan medals

The lion is reputed to be the largest free standing statue of a lion in the world. The head alone weighs 5 tons; its total weight exceeds 16 tons. The pieces were transported separately and brought to Reading to be reassembled and placed on the specially prepared plinth. This consisted of four brick pillars, one for each paw, surrounded by a terracotta pedestal. The cost of the Lion was £900 but subscriptions exceeded this amount, raising £1088-12-3d, which allowed for a memorial window to be commissioned and placed in St Mary's Minster. The unveiling of the Lion took place in December 1886, with the Mayor officiating at a full civic ceremony. The picture of the Memorial on the previous page is dated c.1887 in the Reading Library catalogue. By 1910 the terracotta facings of the plinth had deteriorated to such an extent that they had to be replaced. The original plinth was enclosed in a Portland stone structure, with the names of those commemorated transcribed onto bronze tablets and fixed to the new plinth.

The Lion on its new plinth, 1912 [6]

The Bandstand

The Bandstand, 1904 [7]

Military tattoos, parades with bands, musicians accompanying the many types of festivities, had become an integral feature of the Forbury and the Abbey Ruins. Whilst the parades had taken place on the eastern section it had become increasingly common for the bands to play from the Hill. They also played in the Ruins and on the grass in front of the Hill. The musicians themselves, on most occasions, appear to have expressed a preference for the Hill but at other times found this inconvenient. It seems that the acoustics of the Ruins were not good and we saw that on one occasion, when this area was used, the band moved back to the Hill. Despite the popularity of bands, however, there was no agreed permanent place from which to perform. Indeed in 1880 the Corporation forbade the use of the Hill to bands on account of the damage that *children and others* were causing to the gardens. Yet a proposal to erect a permanent bandstand, described as an *ornamental orchestra,* was not followed up. By 1884 this injunction against performing on the Hill had been overturned and the bands retuned to the site.

In 1895 a public subscription was launched to provide a *handsome iron structure.* The target was £350 but this was not reached so a wooden bandstand with a red tiled roof, designed by George Webb, was erected in its stead and officially opened by the mayor on August 26th 1896. By 1909 the wooden floor had become unsafe and the Corporation replaced it with another, made of concrete and asphalt, in 1910.

PART 5. CHAPTER 4. THE CREATION OF THE FORBURY GARDENS 1860 –1919

Memorials to Henry 1

The Forbury Cross

Dr Jamieson Hurry, a medical man, adopted Reading as his home town and became one of its greatest and most popular historians. In 1900 he published his book 'Reading Abbey' which is still one of the most readable and authoritative sources for anyone interested in the history of the town. True, there are opinions that today have to be questioned in the light of more recent research, but the town owes him a great debt of gratitude for his pioneering work in making both the man in the street and the 'authorities' aware of their responsibilities towards the architectural heritage of Reading.

Henry I memorial cross 1910 [8]

One of his lasting memorials is the 20 foot cross in the Forbury which Hurry donated to the town. It was officially unveiled on the 18th June 1909 and was placed near the area of the west end of the destroyed nave of the Abbey church. (cf p 36). It was designed by William Ravenscroft and carved by Maile and Sons of London from grey Cornish granite [9]

The Chapter House Commemorative Tablets

It should be noted that the cross was never intended to mark the burial place of Henry I to whom it is dedicated. Hurry was well aware of the fact that Henry I had been buried *in front of the high altar*. In fact, two years later, in 1911, Hurry made another gift to the Borough to mark the coronation of George V. This consisted of two large square tablets made of Forest of Dean stone. They commemorate the first and last Abbots of the Abbey and were placed on the east wall of the Chapter House, near the site of Henry I's original

Memorial tablet to Henry 1 [10]

Summer is icumen in tablet. 1920 [11]

tomb which, we have seen, most probably lies under St James' school.

These tablets were joined in 1913 by another matching tablet, also donated by Hurry. This was placed on the north wall of the Chapter House and inscribed with the words of the 13th century song *Summer is icumen in.* Reputedly written in Reading, this musical 'round' is the oldest known example of six part polyphony and even possibly the oldest known piece of independent melodic counterpoint.

The Victoria Gate

In June 1897 the nation celebrated the Diamond Jubilee of the accession to the throne of Queen Victoria. At the south west corner of the Forbury a pair of iron gates was installed to commemorate the event. The left gate as one enters reads 'Victoria Gate 1897' and the right gate 'Forbury Gardens'. Both gates have the crest of Reading Town with the five maidens' heads. The surrounding Latin motto reads 'S COMMUNITATIS RADINGIE'. The 's' stands for Sigillum which translates as 'seal'. So the phrase means *The seal of the Community of Reading.*

PART 6   PLANS AND DEVELOPMENTS 1919 – 2000

CHAPTER 1 PLANS AND DEVELOPMENTS 1919 –1939

The War Memorial

The War Memorial in the 1930s [1]

After the Great War there were plans for a memorial to be placed near the Victoria Gate. A design and a plaster model were made for a stone plinth surmounted by a bronze statue of Victory. However only about £1000 of the £8000 was raised and in 1922 the plans were shelved.

In 1931 Councillor Sainsbury revived the campaign and eventually a new monument was designed by Leslie Gunston, sculpted by John Harvard Thomas and constructed by the long- established Reading firm of Collier and Catley.

Unveiling ceremony July 1932 [2]

On the 27 July 1932, the anniversary of the Battle of Maiwand, the 'Reading and Berkshire War Memorial' was unveiled by the Lord Lieutenant of the County, Mr. J. H. Benyon,

Proposals for Developing the Forbury

Shortly after the war, in 1922, Mrs Phippen, the Forbury gardener, died. Her two daughters, who had acted as her assistants, were replaced with Mr Loader who by 1923 had brought the grounds back to *a much brighter and orderly appearance.* He looked after the Gardens until his retirement in 1938.

This not only brought to an end a period of continuity from the founding of the Gardens, but ushered in a new era of development and proposals for development. These included supplying electricity to the bandstand in 1927 and tar-paving the paths around the Gardens. The popularity of the Gardens for band performances continued. The Gardens were also used for other events. Political meetings were not allowed but Reading authorities offered alternative sites such as Hills Meadow for such gatherings. Religious groups were permitted to use the grounds. In 1930 the Reading branch of the League of Nations set up a loudspeaker system to broadcast the speeches of Stanley Baldwin and Lloyd George. When in 1935 the Salvation Army held a rally in the Forbury, a loudspeaker van was provided for General Evangeline Booth. The main use of the gardens, however, was as a place of relaxation and casual visiting by the public. In 1918 this had been extended by relaxing the rules forbidding the use of prams. *Perambulators drawn or propelled by hand and used solely for the conveyance of children* were now permitted in the Forbury Pleasure Ground.

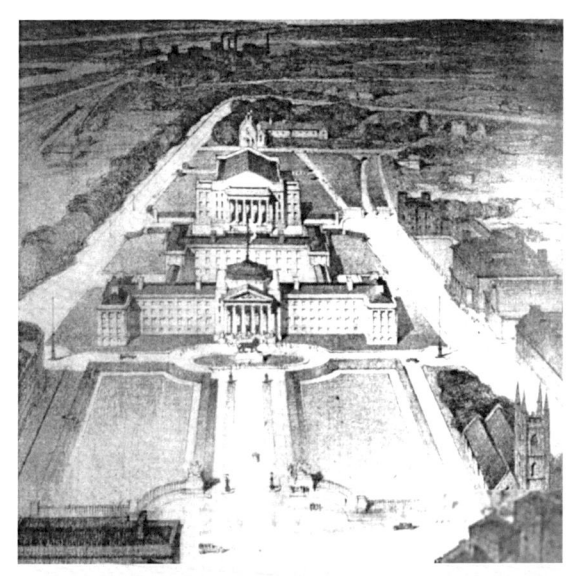

Plans for the Forbury 1928 [3]

With regard to the ancient buildings of the Ruins an important event was the recognition in 1915 that these were to be given Ancient Monument status. HM Office of Works stated that Reading Abbey had *been included in certain lists of monuments which the Ancient Monuments Boards of England, Scotland and Wales considered to be of national importance.*[4]

Any such monument now fell within the jurisdiction of the Commissioners of Works, who were entitled to receive notice from the owner of *any proposals to demolish or remove in whole or in part structurally alter or make additions to the monument.*

PART 6. CHAPTER 1. PLANS AND DEVELOPMENTS 1919 – 1939

The importance of this may be judged when we see that as early as 1927 the town planners had their eyes on the Forbury for a new town hall and municipal building complex.

The illustration, opposite, of the proposal shows St Lawrence's Church in the bottom right hand corner. The churchyard has all but vanished and the Maiwand Lion has been brought forward. The new municipal buildings occupy the whole area of the western section of the Forbury, in line with the Inner Gateway, and the Ruins are in the distance. The Hill, it seems, would have been removed. Although nothing further was reported about this plan it appears to have formed the basis of a much more serious project in 1935, some eight years later.

There was almost universal agreement that the existing Municipal Offices were no longer suitable. Suggestions for a new site included Hills Meadow and London Road. But the favoured location of the Council was the Forbury. The new plan would have involved about one tenth of the Gardens and the idea was supported by the 'Reading Mercury', and some sections of the public. However a vocal and increasing number of people opposed the plan. Debate and discussion rumbled on until 1937 when the Council rejected the scheme by 32 votes to 12.

The Abbey Wall

One plan that did proceed involved the area around the remnants of the south side of the ancient Refectory wall. This had become known as the Abbey Wall. Reading Borough owned the eastern corner, shown in the modern photograph on the next page. The remainder to the west was in the hands of Berkshire County Council, except for the very last cottage in the row. The land north of the wall was part of the properties along Abbot's Walk.

The Abbey Wall cottages c 1925. [5]

Cottages had been built along the wall but these were in a poor state of repair. By 1926 Berkshire had plans to replace these with a row of police houses. Although Berkshire Archaeological Society considered that the cottages had contributed to the fact that the wall had not been knocked down, they were subsequently demolished. After negotiations between the two planning authorities, it was agreed, in 1931, that Berkshire would not build beyond an agreed line so as not to obscure the view of the wall, on condition that Reading would acknowledge ownership of, and responsibility for, its maintenance. We shall see more of this in Chapter 3.

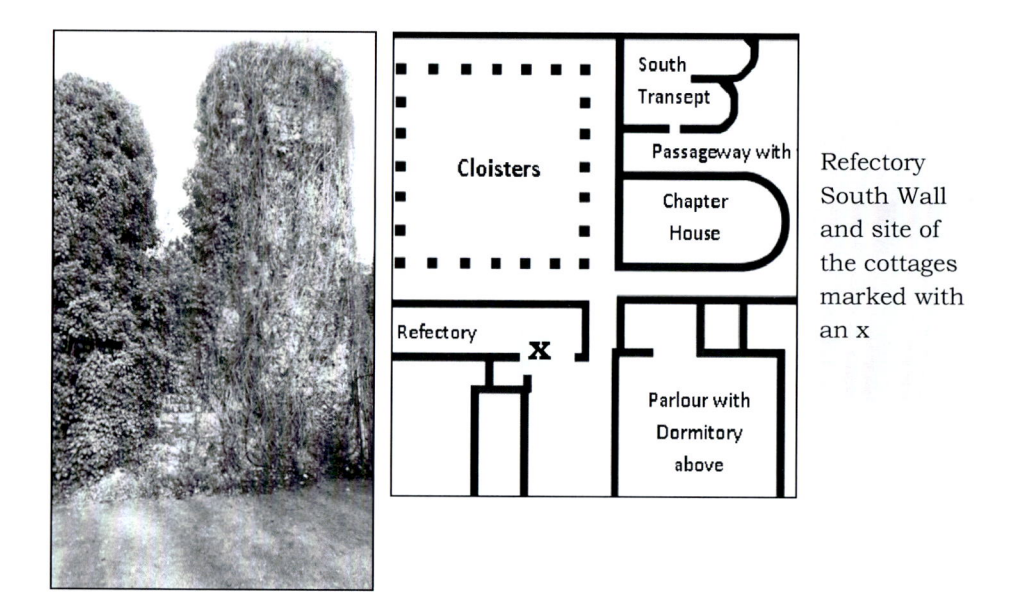

Refectory South Wall and site of the cottages marked with an x

The Cloisters were the heart of the monastery. They led to the Church, the Chapter House, the Refectory and the Monks' private quarters.

CHAPTER 2   THE WAR YEARS   1939–1945

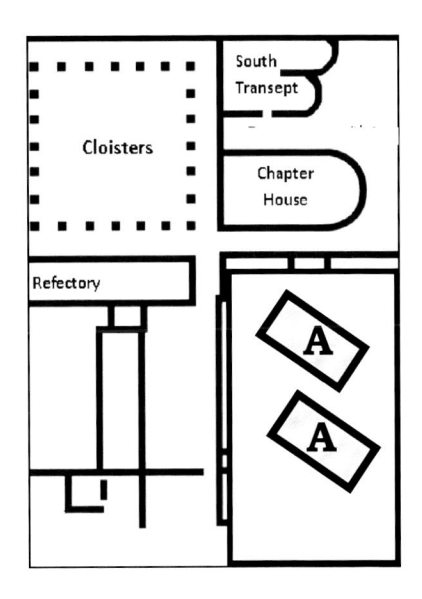

Entrance to one of the air raid shelters. Wessex archaeology

With the onset of war in 1939, plans were made to build air raid shelters and trenches for children in the area of the ruins. Slade writes that this would have compromised any future archaeological surveys and that the plans were never realised. However excavations by Wessex Archaeology have uncovered air raid shelters in the dormitory part of the Ruins, both marked with A on the plan. Moreover members of today's St James' parish who attended the school recall their air raid drills and being taken to these underground shelters.

Another building in the area, the Inner Gateway, became part of the Borough's ARP (Air Raid Precautions) organisation. During the Second World War, the ARP was responsible for the issuing of gas masks, pre-fabricated air-raid shelters such as Anderson and Morrison shelters, the upkeep of local public shelters, and the maintenance of the blackout. The ARP also helped rescue people after air raids. Some women became ARP Ambulance Attendants, whose job was to help administer first aid to casualties, search for survivors, and, in many grim instances, help recover bodies, sometimes those of their own colleagues.[1]

Apart from the tragic bombing of February 1943 the area suffered little damage during the war.

CHAPTER 3   PLANS AND DEVELOPMENTS 1945—2014

The Abbey Wall Area

The post war period ushered in a period of further development. The town's infrastructure evolved alongside the growth of new industries and commerce. We have seen (page 110ff) how Stage 3 of the planned IDR was abandoned, thanks largely to the intervention of Berkshire County Council (BCC). But the town's growth put further strains both on its outdated administrative buildings and on its transport infrastructure. Although the planned IDR route was rejected, its replacement, the Queen's Road solution, was to cause further problems. Neither scheme incorporated a fully circular route around Reading; hence bottlenecks were created. With regards to the administration of local government, both the 19th century municipal buildings of Reading Town and the County's Shire Hall, along the Forbury, were totally inadequate.

Berkshire appeared to have saved the Forbury from development with its rejection of Stage 3 of the IDR. However it had itself, in the 1960s, been responsible for an even greater threat to the integrity of the Ruins, specifically in the area stretching from Abbot's Walk, through the Cloisters and down to the Abbey Wharf. BCC had become owners of much of this property. The County planned to site its new purpose-built Shire Hall, a ten storey building, in this area. This time a combination of public objections and Reading Council's opposition persuaded the County to abandon the scheme. Instead it was replaced with the plan to build a new Shire Hall at Shinfield. One consequence of this was the archaeological excavation which was carried out between 1964 and 1967 in the area of the Mill, the Cloisters and south of the Refectory.[1]

Nevertheless the County still owned much of the property from Abbots Walk to the King's Road. It allowed two archaeological excavations during the 1970s, by Reading Museum, in the Cloister and Refectory areas. In 1980 the County announced the decision to sell its Abbey land for office development. BCC was required by law to sell this for the best possible price. It entered into negotiations with MEPC (Metropolitan Estates & Property Corporation) who planned a large scale office development over the area.

Reading Council and Reading Civic Society, with much public support, opposed the scheme. The Borough lodged a formal objection with the Secretary of State for the Environment, but the minister would not intervene. However the situation altered when changes in planning legislation made the Borough the planning authority for the area. By 1983, following extensive negotiations, Reading came to an agreement with MEPC concerning the nature of the development. The Council negotiated changes to the design of the planned buildings, which were now felt to be more in keeping with the area. MEPC also

PART 6. CHAPTER 3. **PLANS AND DEVELOPMENTS 1945 –2000**

made a significant contribution to the costs of an archaeological survey of the site, the finds being passed to Reading Museum for professional conservation.

One problem concerned the remnants of the Abbey Wall. In 1986 MEPC, having gained permission, demolished part of its western end to help clear land for the main building works. This section was not in fact part of the ancient abbey but had been added in the 19th century. Reading Council, however, was not consulted and a subsequent agreement was reached between the two parties that Reading would be kept informed about any future developments.

The Forbury Road

Forbury Rd under construction. 1989 [2]

1844 view of the same stretch as shown in the 1989 photo.

We saw above how Stage 3 of the IDR plan was shelved and replaced with the Queen's Road solution. This eventually took shape in the 1980s. By 1989 work was under way to convert the Forbury Road, north and east of the Forbury and the Prison, into a dual carriageway. One consequence was the final removal of any traces of the Plummery Wall. However, in acknowledgment of its existence, a new wall was built along one section of the dual carriageway. This replaced the one listed by the British Listed Buildings record of 1978 as a *mid 19th century wall on site of and probably incorporating the mediaeval Plummery wall. Dwarf wall of mixed flint and random rubble and brick with low mid 19th century railings.*

The Abbey Mill

We have seen (page 89ff) that the Abbey Mill, otherwise known as Soundy's Mill had all but been demolished in the 1960s. The dispute between the County and the Borough over ownership and maintenance continued until 1984 when negotiations were opened once more between the two authorities.

In 1988 it was agreed that the freehold of the Mill and the responsibility for maintaining the Arch and the banks of the Holy Brook would pass to the Borough. The County made a one-off grant payment of £1500 towards the restoration costs.

In 2009 a new building was completed alongside the mill. Designed by Sheppard Robson architects, it is known as the Blade and is 86 metres high.

The Abbey Stables and Reading Library

In monastic times the Abbey stables were situated near the southern gateway. These would have served as livery stables for well-to-do visitors to the monastery. Unlike the Compter entrance, this Gateway and the stables led directly to the Abbot's quarters. The stables lay alongside the Holy Brook to the west of the Abbey Mill. The land rose sharply upwards towards the Abbot's garden and the Inner Gateway. Just how much of an incline this was can be judged today when climbing from the level of the Holy Brook to the Forbury Gardens. This would have been a warm south-facing slope offering a refreshing end to the discomforts of medieval road travel. Ostlers, employed by the Abbey, occupied the adjacent buildings and were at hand to care for the travellers' horses and no doubt their baggage. Following the Dissolution of the Abbey the stables remained in use, as demonstrated by their appearance on Speed's map of 1611 (page 8) and the Civil War map of the 1640s (page 9).

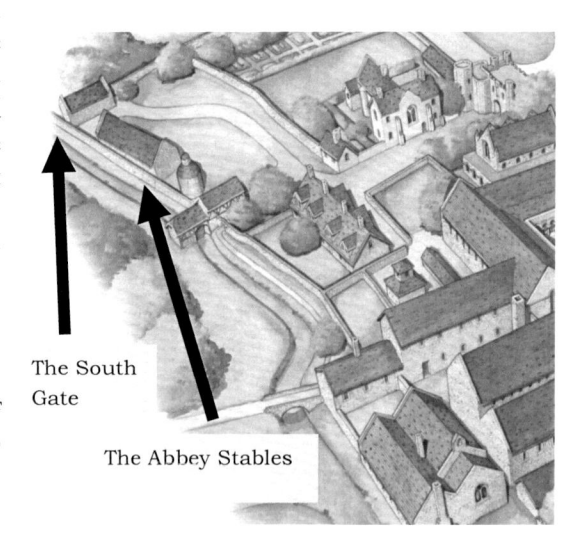

The South Gate

The Abbey Stables

PART 6. CHAPTER 3. **PLANS AND DEVELOPMENTS 1945 –2000**

A. Abbey Square, South side.1983

B. 1983 King's Road [4]

However by the 20th century the appearance of Abbey Square and King's Road had changed significantly. Photograph A shows the rear of the building, in photograph B, which faced onto King's Road at the corner leading to Abbey Square. This is where the Central Library was built in the 1980s.

The 1971–1973 Excavation of Reading Abbey [5]

Under the direction of Dr Slade a detailed investigation of a small area of the ancient Abbey was excavated. This covered the section of the apse which lay within the prison grounds.

This thorough investigation of the area uncovered a variety of tiles and footings. It also confirmed the existence of Saxon influence in the area, dating back to the 5th and 6th centuries. The report runs to 79 pages.

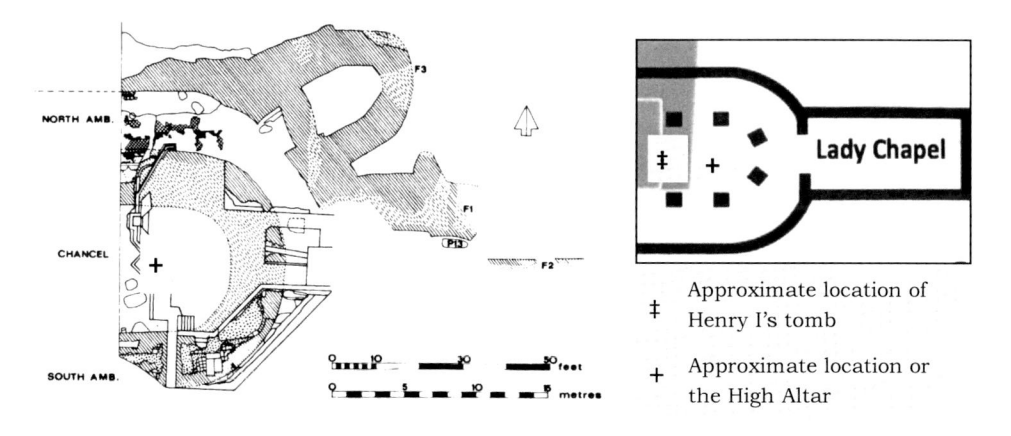

‡ Approximate location of Henry I's tomb

+ Approximate location or the High Altar

The drawing to the left is taken from the official report of the 1971-1973 excavations showing their extent with the approximate location of the High Altar added. The diagram (right), from a section of the plan used throughout this book, shows the area of the Abbey Chancel that the excavations covered.

Reading Central Library 1985 – 1914

This set of pictures shows the changes that took place during the building of the Library and some of the archaeology that was uncovered.

The first photograph, dated 1979,[6] shows The Holy Brook, looking down-stream from where the Central Library was later built. The backs of the buildings in King's Road are to the right, and there is a building over the stream which hides the arches of the Abbey Mill.

The next photograph,[7] taken during the excavations in 1983, shows the partially excavated foundations of the stables, before the new Central Library was built on the site. The view is to the east, with the Holy Brook behind and below the wall to the right. The line, A-B, which has been superimposed on the photograph, denotes a cross section on a plan for the archaeological survey.

The third photograph,[8] also dated 1983, shows the excavations of the foundations of the stables. The view is to the south. The Holy Brook is hidden behind the wall.

PART 6. CHAPTER 3. **PLANS AND DEVELOPMENTS 1945 –2000**

This fourth photograph,[9] taken in 1984, shows the Library under construction as seen from the roof of the Prudential Assurance building. The piling has been carried out, but the Holy Brook has not yet been covered over.

Below is a photograph of the purpose-built Reading Central Library, formerly Berkshire and Reading Central Library. It was opened on December 4th 1985 by HRH the Duke of Gloucester, and replaced the Berkshire Central Library which had been situated since 1885 in the Municipal Buildings in Blagrave Street.

The Holy Brook runs under the building. The bridge to the bottom left of the photograph is where the stream briefly makes a reappearance before going underground beneath the Library to emerge on the far side.

At this point I should note that without the Library's records, and most of all the kind help the staff of Reading Library, this work would not have been possible.

And so a photograph of Reading Library is a fitting note on which to end this survey of Reading's Abbey Quarter.

POSTSCRIPT

In May 2014 it was announced that a memorial to Trooper Potts, who won the VC during the First World War, would be placed alongside the Forbury Gardens on its southern edge opposite the Crown Court and the old Shire Hall.

The artist Tom Murphy at work on the maquette

Trooper Potts, VC

Frederick William Owen Potts was born and raised in Edgehill Street in the Katesgrove area of Reading. He trained as an engineer, at University College, Reading and before the war worked for the Pulsometer Engineering Company Ltd, now SPP Pumps Ltd based in Theale. He joined the Berkshire Yeomanry in 1907.[1]

His unit was sent to Gallipoli in April 1915 via Egypt, landing at Suvla Bay, Gallipoli Peninsula, on 18 August. On the 21st August, facing heavy opposition, the regiment retreated; 154 of the 323 soldiers from the regiment who advanced did not return. Trooper Fred Potts and Trooper Arthur Andrews, both from Reading, were wounded in the attack. As Fred crawled back to the British lines he came across the severely wounded Arthur, who was unable to move. After some time Fred found a shovel and strapped Arthur to it and, over a 48 hour period, he managed to get both Arthur and himself back to safety. He was awarded the Victoria Cross, the first Victoria Cross awarded to a man from the Yeomanry in the war. He was hailed in the press as *The Hero with the Shovel*. He was 23 at the time.[2]

After the war Fred became a master tailor and Master of the Aldermaston Masonic Lodge. He died on 2 November 1943 at the age of 50. His ashes are interred at Reading Crematorium. Trooper Potts is Reading's only VC holder.

The man he rescued, Arthur Andrews, was born in 1891 in Reading. He was apprenticed to a local bicycle maker on leaving school. After the war he worked for Great Western railways as an instrument maker in their telecommunications & Signalling Works. He died in 1980, aged 89.

POSTSCRIPT

At the time of writing the 'Trooper Potts VC Memorial Trust' is working to unveil, on 4 October 2015, a memorial to both men, and the men of the Berkshire Yeomanry. The memorial will consist of a life size sculpture in bronze, by Liverpool artist Tom Murphy, depicting the rescue of Trooper Andrews by Trooper Potts. It will be set on a plinth of Portland Stone measuring 7ft high by 10ft long and 3ft 6ins wide. There will also be a Roll of Honour in bronze, set on a separate plinth of Portland Stone, listing the names of the 409 men of the Berkshire Yeomanry who lost their lives in service of their country in the wars of the 20th Century.[3]

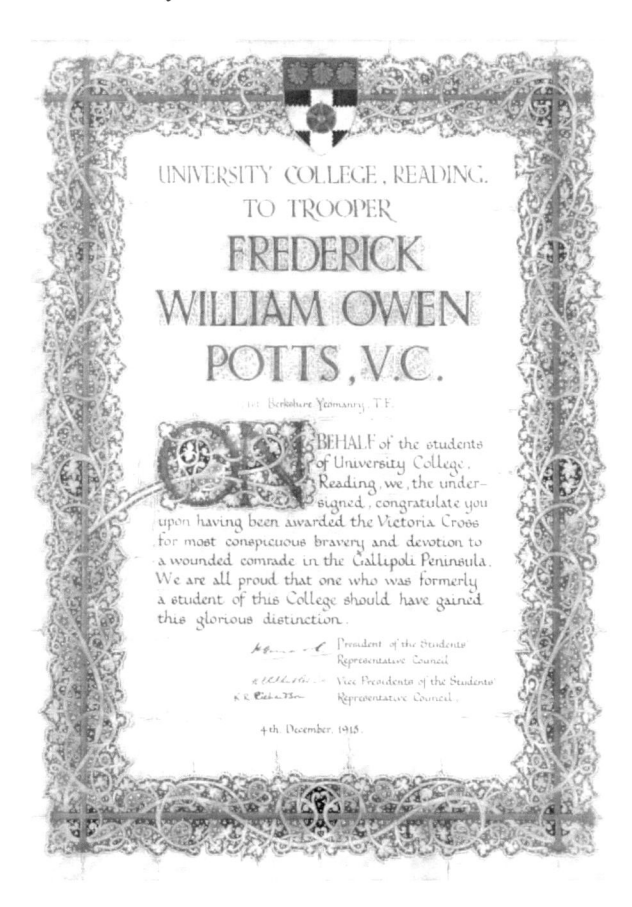

Illuminated scroll presented to Trooper Potts VC by the Students' Council of University College, Reading, in December 1915.

CONCLUSION

During the research for this work it was announced that the Prison was to close, so ending an 800 year feature of town life. However as some landmarks change, or are lost, new ones, as we have seen in the case of Trooper Potts, appear.

The Abbey Quarter is a time capsule. Within its precincts there lies a thousand year old story of the town of Reading and its people. Its buildings and open spaces tell a tale of good times and bad times, of hope and despair, of war and peace. Sections of the Abbey were left in ruins, almost forgotten, whilst other parts became the hub of town life. The buildings have changed and will continue to change but the echoes of past days may still be heard for those who listen; the spirits of times past are still to be seen for those who look.

The probable site of the earliest burgh of Reading is within what we now call the Abbey Quarter. Although most of the original buildings have long since vanished, we should recall that, with the arrival of the Cluniac monks and the building of their Abbey, this was the birthplace of modern Reading.

Today the town is left with only a few scattered memories of its past. The town, and maybe one day 'city', will no doubt remain, even grow and prosper. Yet those icons of our history, the stones and buildings of our past, are the cement which binds our todays with our yesterdays: a bond which unites all the generations and all the people who have lived in our town.

Even as new and exciting features are added there is the constant danger of losing the most ancient of those stones and buildings: the last remnants of the Abbey. Should this happen the very soul of Reading's heritage would be lost.

Reading's Abbey Quarter: the Ancient and the Modern [1]

Heraclitus: πάντα ρεῖ καὶ οὐδὲν μένει

APPENDICES

APPENDIX A Reading Abbey's Wealth at the Time of its Dissolution, 1539.

Source: Hurry p87ff from the *Ministers Accounts 30-31 Henry VIII No 85*.
The completeness and accuracy of these figures has been disputed. Nevertheless they do show that Reading was amongst the most prestigious and wealthiest religious establishment in the country at the time of the Dissolution.

Annual income:

St Peters' Westminster	£3,977
Glastonbury	£3,508
St Albans'	£2,510
St John's of Jerusalem	£2,385
St Edmundsbury	£2,336
Reading	£2,116

APPENDIX B Inscriptions on St. James' Font, The Reading Abbey Stone.

The great Abbey of Reading was commenced ad 1121 and the conventual Church was finished ad 1125 and consecrated by St. Thomas of Canterbury ad 1164. The foundation stone of St James's Church was laid Dec 14th 1837 and Divine Service was first performed therein on the Feast of the B V ad Nives Aug 5th 1840.

This interesting though mutilated specimen of ancient sculpture, once a capital, was discovered Jan 24th 1835 most curiously concealed within the site of the Abbey Church and from surpassing elaborate decorations it then received the denomination of the READING ABBEY STONE. It is now humbly restored to the service of the one true God in the converted form of a baptismal font.

APPENDIX C The Discovery of the Reading Abbey Stone by James Wheble

Extracts from Wheble's letter to the 'Reading Mercury' 1835 and quoted in the 'British Archaelogical Journal' of April 1881 in Albury's paper about Reading Abbey.

The excavators having, in the progress of their labours, passed across the North aisle of the Choir end of the Church… came upon the perfect base of one of the great pillars. … On penetrating downwards through this coat of grouting, about three inches thick, it

appeared that there were two other coats, of a nearly similar cement, before the natural soil was reached… The attention of the persons in charge of the excavation, was … aroused, on seeing what first appeared to merely a flag stone… That it was within the Choir, and only few feet from the Nave, seems easy of proof.

To what use, then, was it originally intended to be applied ? Was it adapted to support in part a sarcophagus, or rather a slab, on which reposed some recumbent figure ? Could it have been the basement for a Holy Rood or Cross? or for a font? or a paschal candle? or a chaunter's desk? … Why was it deposited, enveloped in all its cerements, in such curious concealment?

A footnote states that

The moulding at the square central bottom part seems to preclude the idea of a capital to a clustered column.

Since the inscription on the brasses states that the Stone was 'once a capital' it would seem that Wheble had, by 1840, for some reason changed his opinion as to its use.

APPENDIX D   Roger Amyce.

Roger Amyce's ancestry is uncertain. His father may have been John Amyce or Amyas, a yeoman of the crown under Henry VII and a serjeant-at-arms (sic) from about 1520 until 1526 or later. The first mention of Amyce is in February 1537 when he obtained a lease of the manor of Kingsbury in Somerset.

Amyce is included in a list, possibly dated 1538, of those who had access to Thomas Cromwell at any time or by appointment, described as among *the gentlemen most meet to be daily waiters upon my said lord.*

Amyce was appointed general receiver for the former estates of the abbeys of Glastonbury and Reading. This exempted him from serving in the French campaign of 1544 and accounts for the fact that he was returned as Reading's member of Parliament in 1545 along with Thomas Vachell.

APPENDICES

APPENDIX E   Record of Marriages and Burials at Reading Abbey

The following were married at Reading Abbey:

- Prince Lionel of Antwerp, Duke of Clarence, son of King Edward III, m. 9th September 1342 to Elizabeth, daughter and heiress of William De Burgh, Earl of Ulster.
- Prince John of Gaunt, Earl of Richmond, later Duke of Lancaster and King of Castile and Leon, son of King Edward III, m. 13th May 1359 to Blanche, daughter and heiress of Henry, Duke of Lancaster. The ensuing celebrations lasted for fourteen days.
- Princess Margaret, daughter of King Edward III, m. 19th May 1359 to John Hastings, Earl of Pembroke.
- Princess Philippa, daughter of Prince Lionel of Antwerp, Duke of Clarence and Earl of Ulster, m. February 1359 to Edmund Mortimer, Earl of March.
- King Edward IV, m. 1st May 1464 in secret at Grafton Regis, Northants, to Elizabeth Woodville, widow of John Grey, Baron Grey of Groby and daughter of Richard Woodville, Earl Rivers. The marriage was publicly announced to the world at Reading Abbey on 29th September 1464.

The following were buried at Reading Abbey:

- King Henry I of England, 1068-1135, (bowels, brains, heart, eyes & tongue at Rouen). He was buried in front of the High Altar.
- Queens Matilda and Adeliza, wives of Henry I, were supposedly buried here. However the former is also thought to have been buried in Westminster Abbey and the latter at Afflighem in Flanders.
- Empress Maud of the Holy Roman Empire, Countess of Anjou and claimant to the throne of England, daughter of King Henry I. Probably only part of her was buried at Reading. Her major burial was originally in Bec Abbey and her remains later removed to Rouen Cathedral. Camden recorded her Latin epitaph as *Great at her Birth, Greater than any Man, but Greatest at her Death; Here lies a wife & parent, the daughter of Henry.*
- Prince William, Count of Poitiers, d.1156, aged two, eldest son of King Henry II. He was buried in front of the High Altar, at the feet of King Henry I.
- Princess Constance of York, c1374-1416, wife of Thomas Le Despencer, Earl of Gloucester & daughter of Prince Edmund Langley, Duke of York. She was buried in front of the High Altar.

- Prince John of Cornwall, 1232-1233, son of Prince Richard, Earl of Cornwall and Holy Roman Emperor.
- Princess Isabella of Cornwall, 1233-1234, daughter of Prince Richard, Earl of Cornwall and Holy Roman Emperor.
- Reginald, Earl of Cornwall, 1100-1175 illegitimate son of King Henry I by Sybil Corbet.
- Anne, Countess of Warwick, 1443 –1449, daughter of Henry Beauchamp, Earl of Warwick, who lived at both Warwick & Caversham Castles. Anne died aged six at the Palace of Ewelme, Oxfordshire, where she was in the care of her step great-grandmother, Alice De La Pole, Duchess of Suffolk. The location of Caversham Castle has not been established.

Sarcophagi and skeletons discovered in the Abbey grounds.

1786 Leaden coffin with almost perfect skeleton and leather fragments.

1815 Stone sarcophagus unearthed in the nave of the church.

1841 Stone coffin in the inner court of the prison grounds whilst excavating mould to adapt the surface for gardening purposes.

1841 Whilst levelling ground around St James' a stone coffin was unearthed similar to one discovered in the prison grounds.

1867 John Mellor found in the Forbury, at a 'depth of seven feet' a leaden coffin, pieces of tile, human bones and a skeleton but no further record of his activities survives. See Reading Mercury 7th September 1867.

1873 Digging at gaol uncovered skeletons and Purbeck marble.

1927 Near the Hospitium several skeletons discovered and reburied in St. Lawrence's churchyard.

1960s Human remains uncovered to the north of St James' Church whilst the North Aisle was being built, The contractors reported this as a Saxon burial ground, (see page 115).

Many other unrecorded fragments of human remains have been discovered in the area.

SOURCES AND FURTHER READING

Many of the sources are referred to in detail in the notes and may not appear here.

Barres-Baker, M.C.   *The Siege of Reading April 1643.*   2004

Battle of Maiwand   http://www.britishbattles.com/second-afghan-war/maiwand.htm

Berkshire Archaeological Journal; (BAJ). See notes for detailed entries.

Childs, W.M.   *Making a University.*   1933

Coates, A.   *English Medieval Books.*   1999.

Darter, W.   *Reminiscences of Reading by an Octogenarian.*   1888.

Englefield, Sir Henry.   *Reading Abbey.* Archaeologia Vol VI 1779

Ford, B. et al.   *Under the Oracle.*   2013

Gold, S.   *A Biographical Dictionary of Architects at Reading.*   1999.

Gordon Spriggs, F.   *History of Greyfriars Church, Reading.*   2013

Guilding, J. (ed).   *Diary of the Corporation of Reading 1431 - 1654* in 4 volumes

Hurry, J.   *Reading Abbey.* 1901

Hurry, J.   *Rise and Fall of Reading Abbey.* 1906.

Kemp, B. et al.   *Guide to Reading Abbey.* 1988.

Kerry, C.   *A History of the Municipal Church of St. Lawrence, Reading.* 1883.

Lee, R.J.   *Reading As It Was.* 1973.

Maiwand Lion Restoration: Rupert Harris. http://www.rupertharris.com

Mullaney, J and Mullaney, L.   *Reformation, Revolution and Rebirth.* 2012

Newcombe, D.G.   *Henry VIII and the English Reformation.* 1995

Parliamentary Survey, 1650.

Philips, D.   *The Story of Reading.* 1980.

Preston, A.   *Demolition of the Reading Abbey.* 1935.

Sharp, M.   *The History of Ufton Court.* 1892.

Slade, C.   *Excavation of Reading Abbey 1971-73*, BAJ.

Slade, C.   *The Town of Reading and its Abbey.* 2001

Southerton, P.   *Reading Gaol by Reading Town.* 1993.

Tomkins, C.   *Eight Views of Reading Abbey.* 1805

Verey, A. et al.   *Berkshire Yeomanry.* 1994.

Victoria County History; A History of the County of Berkshire: Volume 2 (1907), pp. 62-73

Wheble, J.   *The Reading Abbey Stone.* BAJ 1880-81, 87–90.

Wykes, A.   *Reading: A biography.* 1970.

READING'S ABBEY QUARTER

NOTES

These are numbered per chapter. Illustrations in Reading Library have a seven digit number. This is the Library's 'horizon number'. It is unique to each illustration and the reader may use this to refer to the picture on the Library's website. The initials 'RL' (Reading Library) prefix this number in the following notes.

PART 1 AN HISTORIC OVERVIEW   Pages 1-19

Part 1 Chapter 1.   The Abbey Quarter under the Tudors. Pages 1-8

1   The spelling of this church has varied over the centuries. For consistency I have used a 'w' rather than 'u' through the book but there are strong arguments for the use of both.

2   'Fidei Defensor', Defender of the Faith. This title was granted to several monarchs by the Papacy. It was conferred on Henry in 1521 as recognition of his book, *Assertio Septem Sacramentorum* (*Defence of the Seven Sacraments*), which opposed Luther and defended the doctrines of the Seven Sacraments, the sacramental nature of marriage and the supremacy pf the Pope.

3   *Letters relating to the suppression of the monasteries,* Camden Society, p 226. The Commission had visited Reading a year earlier in 1538, resulting in the suppression of the Franciscan Friary of Greyfriars.

4   As a mitred Abbot and member of the House of Lords, the Abbot of Reading should have been tried by his peers in Parliament.

5   For a more complete listing and sources see *Reading Abbey,* Hurry chapter 1X and X. See also *The Demolition of Reading Abbey,* by A. Preston and *The Berkshire Archaeological Journal Vol 39 No. 2 1935.* See also Appendix A for the relative wealth of Reading Abbey compared with other religious houses.

6   The first recorded use of the title 'Mayor' dates to Henry VII's Charter of 1487. This Guild Charter refers to the *Majori et Burgensibus Radingiae.* However the Mayor was still chosen by the Abbot.

7   Patent Rolls 2, Edward VI, Part V.

8   Charter granted by Elizabeth I to the town of Reading, 23rd September, 1560. RL Call no R/EB

9   Dictionary of National Biography, 1885-1900, Volume 53: Speed, John.

Part 1 Chapter 2. The Abbey Quarter in the 17th and 18th Centuries . Pages 9-20

1   Brod, M. *The Case of Reading.* 2006.

2   Lord Clarendon *History of Rebellion and the Civil Wars in England* vol. vi p125

3   For a detailed examination of the Great Ditch see page 29ff.

4   Englefield, H. *Observations on Reading Abbey* in Archaeologia, 6, pages 61-66. 1782

5   RL 1205198

6   RL 1167190

7   RL 1167191

8   RL 1168349

NOTES

9   RL 1168344

10 RL 1167209

11 RL 1168352

12 cf p 6

13 The Earley Charity is one of the largest local grant-making charities in central southern England. It was founded in 1990 by the merger of two historic local charities: the Englefield Charity and the Earley Poor's Land Charity. Its website notes that it may have been founded as early 1711. Cf www.earleycharity.org.uk

14 An estimate for the site of the High Altar can only be approximate. The location of Henry I's tomb depends on the position of the High Altar and is based on the following sources: Gervase of Canterbury (1141-1210) *Opera Historica vol I, in ipsa Ecclesia ante altare sepultum est* (He is buried in front of the High Altar in that Church), also quoted by the Monk of Malmesbury in *De Gestis Regum Anglorum vol 11*. See Apendix E for a list of those known to have been married and buried in the Abbey.

15 Slade C. *The Town of Reading and its Abbey*. Op. cit. p 51.

16 ibid. p 48. This sketch plan is used throughout the book to help the reader locate the approximate positions of the various parts of the Abbey being discussed. It is based upon the diagram on the inside back cover in Reading Museum's booklet *Reading Abbey*. However, as we shall see later, the exact relationship between St James' Church and the line of the northern wall of the Abbey's north transept is not certain.

PART 2   FROM ABBEY RUINS TO TODAY'S BUILDINGS   Pages 21-97

Part 2 Chapter 1   The Monks' Private Buildings   Pages 21-26

1   RL 1162571
2   RL 1167206

3   BAJ vol 64 *Paving Tiles of Reading Abbey* Cf Slade; *A Guide to Reading Abbey* by Kemp, Slade. Fasham, and Stewart, 1991; *Excavations at Reading Abbey*, 1985-6, BAJ 73, 1986-90; Friends of Reading Abbey (FORA) website: http://readingabbey.org.uk/fora/lesabbey/interpretationdetail.htm

4   Parliament convened at Reading in 1265. Hurry states that the authority for this is the *Annales de Dunstaplia* (Rolls series) p255 but it is not mentioned in Parry's *Parliaments and Councils of England*. Hurry, *Reading Abbey*, p35. It met in 1440-41 and again in 1452, though the session was adjourned owing to an outbreak of the plague in Reading. In 1453 Parliament met in the Refectory and again in 1544. The source for this is Stubbs' *Constitutional History*. On Michaelmas Day, 1464, Edward IV announced his previously secret marriage to Elizabeth Woodville to a Council of the Peers of the Realm at the Abbey. Cf. Hurry ibid p40-41.

5   RL 1167133

READING'S ABBEY QUARTER

6   RL . 1167896

7   See page 177 and for a detailed analysis see the FORA website, see note 3 above.

Part 2 Chapter 2   The Abbey Church Pages 27–41

1   Englefield, H. *Observations on Reading Abbey*. Archaeologia 6

2   Coates, C. *History and Antiquities of Reading*. 1802

3   Berkshire Chronicle 19 Feb 1831

4   Wessex Archaeology. See data posted on their website in 2008. This includes a map of the finds in the Forbury area

5   Slade C. *Historic Towns : Reading* : Volume 1, *Maps and plans of towns and cities in the British Isles, with historical commentaries, from earliest times to circa 1800* ; 1969. General editor M. D. Lobel.

6   Redan; a type of angled fortification with an open back, shaped like a 'V' to allow a wide angle of fire and to protect walls alongside from close attack.

7   In a late 12th century Psalter from the Abbey, *Psalterium cum glossa; Cantica reliqua, cum glossa Benedicite, Te Deum etc* t here is a note added, presumably after 1314, in a fly leaf. It reads *Capella beate Marie Radingie cepit edificari per reverendum patrem nicholaum abbatuem xiii Kal Mai anno domini M.CCC^{mo}XIIII°.* (A chapel of the Blessed Mary was begun to be built by Abbot Nicholas on the 13th day of the Kalends of May – i.e 19th April – in the year of the lord 1314).

8   For a detailed account of early prisons see Southerton *Reading Gaol by Reading Town*, chapter 2.

9   Reading Mercury 1786.

10   Guilding, *Records of the Borough of Reading & Notable Events*. p270

11   Mortimer, *The Time Traveller's Guide to Elizabethan England, 2013* p 61

12   Darter, *Reminiscences of Reading*.

13   Summers, *History of Greyfriars Church, Reading*. p31

14   *The said House of Correction was made a court of guards by the soldiers who did ruin and pull down a great part of the said house* BRO ref; R/Z 8/4/2.

15   Man, *A Stranger in Reading*

16   Summers, *ibid* p 52

17   RL 1206455

18   B Ford et al. *Under the Oracle*,

19   RL 1323858

Part 2 Chapter 3. The Forbury County Gaol, 1786–1842 Pages 42–46

1   Man, *A Stranger in Reading*

NOTES

2   Reading Mercury, Monday 18th March 1833. The report noted that 'at least two thirds were women'.

3   Southerton, *Reading Gaol by Reading Town*, Appendix II.

Part 2 Chapter 4 Reading Gaol, 1844 –2014 Pages 47-62

1   Reading Mercury 30th July 1842

2   RL 1266030

3   RL 1266034

4   RL 1266022

5   RL 1266017

6   RL 1266018

7   The author is in possession of this written account as passed on to him by an acquaintance of the lady concerned.

8   RL 1266030

9   RL 1266034

10   RL 1266022

11   RL 1307773

Part 2 Chapter 5 St James' Church and School Pages 63-76

1   *The Cowslade Manuscript* edited by L. Mullaney, 2013

2   For a full account of the founding of St James' Church see Mullaney & Mullaney, *Reformation, Revolution and Rebirth*. For Wheble's own account of the finding of the Reading Stone see Appendix C.

3   Reading Mercury, 16 Dec 1837

4   Hill, R. *God's Architect.* 2007

5   This letter is reproduced in full in *Reformation, Revolution and Rebirth*. The original is in the Catholic Westminster Diocesan archives.

6   RL 1250621

7   Cowslade, Marianna F. *Views in Caversham , Whiteknights, Woodley and Reading*, . Reading Library.

8   The full article is reproduced in *Reformation, Revolution and Rebirth*. For a full description of the windows see J Mullaney *The Stained Glass of St James Church, Reading*, 2014.

9   St James' Church archives.

10   *The Cowslade Manuscript*

11   Slater's Berkshire Directory 1850 p36. lists: *Roman Catholic School (boys' & girls'), Vastern Street.*

Francis Dearlove, master Mary Dearlove, mistress. The Dearloves' gravestones are to be found in the churchyard behind St James' Church. Also see Mullaney *St James's Catholic Church and School*, 1987.

12 RL 1290904

13 Gold. *Biographical Dictionary of Architects of Reading*, p120

14 RL 1235796

15 RL 1285405. Canon Alexander Scoles came from a distinguished family of Victorian architects. Among many other works, Alexander Scoles designed St Anne's church in Caversham, St William of York in Reading and helped complete the Catholic Cathedral in Portsmouth. (See Gold p163)

16 Sowan. *All Change at Reading*. 2013

17 RL 1167210. Tomkin's book is dated 1791. This is five years after the first Forbury prison was built, yet there is no sign of this in the drawing, possibly because it was just out of sight to the east or because the original sketch was executed before the prison was built.

18 See *Reformation, Revolution and Rebirth*.

19 St James' Church archives

Part 2 Chapter 6. Abbots Walk, The Inner Gateway, The Abbey Mill   Pages 77-96

1 RL 1162652

2 RL 1205198   See Part 1 Chapter 2 note 5

3 RL 1162636

4 RL 1162628

5 RL 1162624

6 RL 1162630

7 RL 1162643

8 RL 1162632

9 RL 1162639

10 RL 1210514

11 RL 1339720

12 RL 1331614

13 RL 1162634

14 RL 1162641

15 RL 1290908

16 RL 1162635

NOTES

17 RL 1209967

18 The Corporation, particularly the Finance Committee, led by some Councillors such as Alderman Brown, had been pressing for its restoration. There had been at least one public meeting in August 1859 calling for a knowledgeable and reputable architect to be consulted. (Berkshire Chronicle 27 August 1859).

19 Gilbert Scott report to Reading Corporation, March 30, 1860.

20 It is difficult to make conversion between historic amounts and modern values. If one considers that a teacher would be paid about £50 pa in the mid 19th century one might say that the restoration cost was about £600,000 in today's money, using the average earnings index, or £75,000 using the retail price index. These figures show just how difficult it is to reach an accurate estimate of equivalent money values.

21 Slade ibid p 68.

22 Reading Mercury - Saturday 24 August 1861. This describes the opening of the Forbury's new recreation grounds and its fountain. It is worth reading the whole report to understand the background and divisions within the town which resulted in the restoration work.

23 RL 1162642

24 *Under the Oracle*, Oxford Archaeology, 2013. This gives a fascinating detailed account of the excavations around the Oracle.

25 Slade, in *The Town of Reading and its Abbey*, makes the comment that although the Parliamentary forces had ordered the construction of these two forts under the direction of Jacob Culemburg, subsequent to the Royalist withdrawal from the town, that these were never in fact completed. Slade, p33-34.

26 RL 1257056

27 RL 1257057

28 RL 1257076

29 The Berkshire Archaeological Journal volume 66, 1971-72, © Berkshire Archaeological Society.

30 J Kenneth Major's drawing of the 1860s mill Berkshire Archaeology Journal, vol 66 1971-72 © Berkshire Archaeological Society.

31 Langdon, John. *Mills in the Medieval Economy: England 1300-1540*

32 Berkshire Archaeology Journal, vol 66 1971-72, © Berkshire Archaeological Society.

PART 3   THE SOUTH SIDE OF THE FORBURY   Pages 99-114

Chapter 1   The Assize Courts, the 19th Century Central Police Station and the Shire Hall. Pages 99-102

1 RL 1279969

2 Berkshire Chronicle - Saturday 21 September 1861. This report gives a full description of the building process.

3   RL 1210601

4   RL 1209606

5   RL 1209612

6   RL 1210605

7   RL 1332141

8   RL 1332140

Part 3   Chapter 2. Between Shire Hall and St Lawrence's Church   Pages 103–114

1   Roger Amyce; see Appendix D

2   Map of Amyce's *Survey of Reading 1552*, transcribed by M Clark. Reading Library

3   RL 1162639 NB. This illustration shows both the Inner Gateway and in the distance the Compter Gate

4   RL 1210544

5   Hurry. *Reading Abbey* 1901

6   Anderson, A H. *Reading and its Surroundings… Handbook for Reading 1906.*

7   RL 1210605

8   RL 1327642

9   RL 1327635

10   RL 1310774

11   RL 1210607

12   RL 1210603

13   RL 1210617

14   RL 1210565

15   The style persisted and was especially popular during the reign of Queen Anne, 1702–1714.

16   RL 1210616

PART 4   THE WESTERN EDGE OF THE ABBEY QUARTER   Pages 115–141

Chapter 1   St Lawrence's Church and The Compter Gate   Pages 115–123

1   Dr Stevens, Berkshire Archaeological Society 1881–2, p45.

2   Kerry. *A History of the Municipal Church of St. Lawrence, Reading.*

3   St James' Church archives. However Reading Museum is doubtful about this, believing that the remains were unlikely to be of early Saxon origin.

4   Gold.. *Biographical Dictionary of Architects of Reading* and Corpus of Romanesque Sculpture website

NOTES

5   Hurry. *Reading Abbey.* 1901

6   RL 1162639

7   RL 1147142 and 1147146. In 1820 the Reading Mercury reported on William Cubbit's work on the tower and that stated he was erecting *a curious bell frame at St Lawrence church.* The Mercury also commented on his design for *a tower for the better supplying this town with water.* On page 44 we saw that Cubbit was responsible for the Gaol treadmill. Reading Mercury 1820 June 5th and 1822 Nov 25th

8   RL 1147191

9   Berkshire Chronicle - Saturday 28 July 1860. *The fountain is from a very tasteful and handsome design by Messrs. Poulton and Woodman, architects, which includes some very beautiful carving, and has been carried out with great skill by Messrs. Wheeler, stonemasons, Reading… The inscription on the fountain is;—" Erected July, 1860, Reading Thomas Rogers, Esquire," and under this is the following text The fear of the Lord is a fountain of life." On the gable of the fountain there is a crest.* See also Gold *Biographical Dictionary…,* entries for Poulton and Woodman.

10   Berkshire Chronicle - Saturday 30 March 1867. This was part of a much wider development of the whole area around St Lawrence's Church, the east end of Friar St and the then existing Vastern Lane, which was replaced by Blagrave St and Valpy St.

11   http://www.crsbi.ac.uk/ (Corpus of Romanesque Sculpture).

12   RL 1147160

13   Reading Mercury - Saturday 30 July 1887

14   RL 1212057

15   RL 1234398

16   RL 1332025

17   RL 1210544

18   RL 1210565

19   RL 1328499 Enlarged detail.

20   RL 1224121 Enlarged detail

Part 4   Chapter 2   The Hospitium and the Municipal Buildings   Pages 124-141

1   Foundation Charter 1125. Henry I states that he has *endowed it* (Reading Abbey) *with Reading, Cholsey and Leominster with their appurtenances, woods ….* At the Dissolution the accounts show that Leominster contributed £480 to Reading Abbey. Ministers Accounts 30-31 Henry VIII No 85

2   The difficulty of making monetary comparisons has already been alluded to. See Part 2, Chapter 6, Note 20. This figure is based upon the National Census of 2011 which put Reading's population at 155,700. .If we take •5% of this as 780 people and allocate an annual expenditure of £10,000 per person, this gives a figure of £7.8 million. One might argue that complete food, clothing and lodging would entail a much higher figure.

READING'S ABBEY QUARTER

3   RL 1156295

4   Leland *Itinerary Vol ii, fol 4* – (Hurry p19). It should be noted that there were two abbots in succession named John Thorne. The first was from 1446 to 1486 and the second from 1486 to 1519.

5   Naxton, M. *Floreat Redingensis ; the History of Reading School.* 1986.

6   RL 1147142

7   RL 1138932

8   RL 1138951. This photograph, by Taunt, is dated c.1875 by Reading Library.

9   RL 1249391. Opening of the Reading Industrial Exhibition. Illustration from the London Illustrated News, Towards the end of the Exhibition The Reading Mercury reported that more than 70000 people had attended this event.

10   RL 1287318

11   RL 1325082

12   RL 1269804

13   Mullaney, *Reformation, Revolution and Rebirth.*

14   Sowan, A *All Change at Reading* 2013

15   RL 1246556

16   RL 1246555

17   Darter, *Reminiscences of Reading.* 1888. p19

18   Naxton. ibid. Ch 4. The consequence of this was the Corporation, as the School's trustees, set up in 1862, petitioned Parliament and was granted a new Act, the Reading School Act of 1867, which allowed for the creation of a modern grammar school. This was finally built and opened on a different site in September 1871 to a design by Alfred Waterhouse.

19   RL 1196431

20   RL 1236358 and 1194619

21   Berkshire Chronicle – Saturday 30 March 1867. This gives a detailed listing of the houses, properties and streets which are to be demolished in the vicinity of St Lawrence's, Friar St and Vastern Lane.

22   RL 1196371

23   Reading Mercury – Saturday 24 September 1892. It is worthwhile reproducing sections of this article here.

On the invitation of Mr. Slingsby Stallwood ... members of the Corporation and others on Thursday afternoon inspected the works of re-construction at the Hospitium in St. Lawrence's Churchyard (which has been adapted for the use of the Extension College and School of Science), ...(and) assembled in the Lecture Hall, Mr. Stallwood sketched the history of the buildings, which originally formed part of a

NOTES

dormitory attached to St. John's Hospital, erected by Abbot Hugh in 1192. He remarked that when Mr. Blagrave was about to sell the property as they all remembered, Alderman Hill, with great public spirit, purchased it to prevent it being demolished, and thereby did a great public service. As a Science School simply the buildings would probably have been found rather too large. Now they had been attached to the University Extension College he hoped they would be found too small. The buildings were then inspected. They consist of a fine lecture hall and a class room, two sets of lavatories and cloak rooms, on the lower floor, with communication from the Churchyard and from Valpy Street; on the next floor a good room used as a council room by the college authorities (where the party were received by Mr. H.J. Mackinder, the Principal, Mr. F. H Wright secretary and Mr. Ernest Wright assistant secretary);' and on the top floor a laboratory with bench accommodation for 32 students, a room for the science master, a balance room, and a capital little theatre.

24 RL 1285650

25 RL 1156302

26 Childs, *Making a University* . Chapter 1.

27 RL 1224591

28 RL 1224589

29 Berkshire Chronicle, June 1898

30 Smith and Bott, *One Hundred Years of University Education in Reading*. 1992

31 RL 1332042

32 RL 1210565

PART 5   THE FORBURY GARDENS   Pages 142-174

Chapter 1   The War Years 1793 –1815   Pages 142-146

1 Slade. *The Town of Reading and Its Abbey.* p47

2 Dictionary of National Biography Vol. XIV . Viscount Duncan.

3 Reading Mercury – Monday 23 October 1797

4 Darter. *Reminiscences of Reading.* 1888. p18

5 L. Mullaney, *Francois Longuet.* Unpublished booklet in St James' archives and Reading Library

6 This refers to Louis XVIII. If, as it seems, the letter was written whilst the exiled French King was in England then it must be between 1809 and 1814.

7 For the full text and discussion about this see Mullaney *Reformation, Revolution and Rebirth* .

Chapter 2   The Forbury: 1815 to 1840   Pages 147-155

1 RL 1205201

2 RL 1210565

3 cf pages128, 149 and 152.

READING'S ABBEY QUARTER

4   Reading Mercury, 26 July 1824

5   The origins of the Hill are unknown and disputed. There have never been any excavations to substantiate or challenge any of the theories proposed. These include the theory that it was a burial ground for one of the Danish-Viking leaders, following the 9th century struggle between the Saxons and the Danes at this site. Another suggestion is that its origins lie in the illegal castle erected by Stephen in the 12th century and that there was no mound on the site before this date.

6   RL 1210514

7   Reading Mercury - Monday 08 April 1833. *How Mr. V. could be persuaded to think that these trees, particularly oak, would be further improvement is not for me to decipher* (sic)… *On the other hand, a superficial observer may, with difficulty, trace the injury and deterioration that must ensue, should they be permitted to remain. In its present state, the invalid, the timid and young children, need not confine themselves to the gravel walk, but, in fine dry weather, equally enjoy the soft verdant sward with which the hill is so richly clothed. To young children especially, even from the moment they commence 'toddling' on their feet, it is now become, both to parent and child, an invaluable resort. Here they may play about without fear or restraint, and exercise, to healthy weariness, their infantine limbs in all the varieties of merry and instinctive freaks. Independent of these attractions, the present landscape scenery opening to view between the two noble clumps of elms, and increasing in beauty to the eye of the spectator as he advances on the southern footpath, will, in the course of a few years, if these obstructions are allowed remain, be completely shut out and exchanged, — and for what? A dead, unmeaning blank, bringing with it inevitable destruction to the open, airy, and health giving pasture now much enjoyed and so deservedly appreciated.*

8   RL 1246556

9   Kerry. *A History of the Municipal Church of St. Lawrence.*

10   The Plymouth Herald and Devonshire Freeholder, Plymouth, May 24th 1828.

11   Reading Mercury - Monday 28 September 1829

12   Darter. *Reminiscences of Reading.* Paper XII

13   Reading Mercury - Saturday 30 June 1838

14   Reading Mercury - Saturday 25th May 1839 and the Berkshire Chronicle - Saturday 25 May 1839.

Part 5   Chapter 3   The Creation of the Forbury Gardens 1840 — 1860   Pages 156-165

1   Mullaney, *Reformation, Revolution and Rebirth.*

2   This engraving, probably made by one of the priests, also appears on the so called *French priests' box* held by Reading Museum. The flower beds are laid out in a formal fashion with various inscriptions, including *God Save the King*… The left foreground one reads *Rooted by gratitude*. Most probably this refers to the cedar of Lebanon we can see today, as seen in the modern photograph on the previous page.

3   In all fairness to the editors of the Chronicle, they did also present the advantages of the railway as in a lengthy article in September 1833.

4   RL 1246555

5   Sowan. Ibid p10

NOTES

6   RL 1246556

7   RL 1242774

8   Berkshire Chronicle – Saturday 11 November 1854. *The Corporation expressed its thanks to Mr. Wheble for the liberality he has displayed (applause). They might congratulate themselves upon having such a gentleman in the neighbourhood.*

9   RL 1328499

10 1858 original deed of gift from J. J. Wheble which was used to convey the land for the underground passage and access land to the Ruins to the Board of Health, marked in red in the original and as a heavier line in this reproduction.

11 RL 1210563

12 Reading Mercury – Saturday 25 November 1854. Pages 5 and 8.

13 Reading Mercury – Saturday 26 May 1860

Part 5   Chapter 4   The Creation of the Forbury Gardens 1860—1919   Pages 166-174

1   Slade. *The Town of Reading and its Abbey*, p62

2   RL 1162652

3   RL 1235796

4   RL 1235767

5   RL 1236795

6   RL 1285374

7   RL 1285411

8   RL 1286444

9   Reading Standard 18th June 1909. Reading Corporation Order of Proceedings June 18 1909.

10 RL 1332934

11 RL 1167185

PART 6   PLANS AND DEVELOPMENTS 1919 — 2000   Pages 175-185

Chapter 1 Plans and Developments 1919 –1939   Pages 175-178

1   RL 1135528

2   RL 1389647

3   RL 1271269 and the Reading Standard, 10 November 1928.

4   Slade. *The Town of Reading* p. 112

5   RL 1209591

READING'S ABBEY QUARTER

Part 6   Chapter 2   The War Years 1939 –1945   Page 179

1   http://en.wikipedia.org/wiki/Air_Raid_Precautions

Part 6   Chapter 3   Plans and Developments 1945-2000   Pages 180-185

1   A detailed account of this survey is in the Berkshire Archaeological Journal Vol 66   *Excavation at Reading Abbey 1964 –67.* Slade. C.

2   RL 1323241 Photograph by Gareth Thomas

3   RL 1224071 Photograph by David Cliffe

4   RL 1224072 Photograph by David Cliffe

5   Berks. Archaeological Journal Vol 68. *1971 –1973 Excavation of Reading Abbey,* Slade

6   RL 1322460

7   RL 1257077

8   RL 1257076

9   RL 1265182

Postscript   Pages 186-187

1   *Potts' regimental number was 1300. Research indicates that he enlisted in 1907. The Regimental Museum records show he was serving from at least 22nd June, 1908.* Captain Andrew French, Assistant Curator The Berkshire Yeomanry Museum, Windsor.

2   Citation from the Gazette – *For most conspicuous bravery and devotion to a wounded comrade in the Gallipoli Peninsula. Although himself severely wounded in the thigh in the attack on Hill 70 on 21st August, 1915, he remained out over 48 hours under the Turkish trenches with a private of his Regiment who was severely wounded and unable to move, although he could himself have returned to safety. Finally he fixed a shovel to the equipment of his wounded comrade, and, using this as a sledge, he dragged him back over 600 yards to our lines, though fired at by the Turks on the way. He reached our trenches at about 9.30 p.m. on 23rd August.*
At the time of writing the memorial to Trooper Potts has yet to be erected.

3   Photographs courtesy of the *Trooper Potts VC Memorial Trust.* Photograph of the Certificate by Robert Binham

Conclusion Page 188

Photograph of Reading Abbey Ruins and the Blade by David Merret
http://commons.wikimedia.org/wiki/ File:The_Blade_from_Reading_Abbey.jpg

INDEX

The Abbey Buildings

    Abbey Almshouse: 116, 125, 127

    Abbey Chapter House: 15, 16, 18, 21, 23, 25, 27, 28, 29, 31, 64, 116, 165, 173, 174

    Abbey Cloisters: 10, 11, 15, 16, 18, 20-23, 26, 28, 31, 64, 66, 68, 77, 79, 84, 94, 162, 180

    Abbey Monks' Dormitory: 18, 23, 26, 91, 179

    Abbey Inner Gateway: 1-4, 15, 18, 20, 28, 31, 77, 79, 80, 81, 82-89, 97, 99, 100, 101, 104, 105, 106, 116, 117, 147, 148, 151, 162, 164, 167, 168, 177, 179, 182

    Abbey Compter Gateway: see Compter Gate

    Abbey Hospitium Dormitory: 1, 5, 126, 127, 128, 131

    Abbey Hospitium Refectory: 1, 116, 124-128, 130

    Abbey Lady Chapel: 18, 28, 29, 31, 32, 34, 35, 42, 61

    Abbey Mill: 12, 20, 89, 91, 93 - 96, 180, 182, 184

    Abbey Nave: 10, 11, 18, 25, 27, 28, 29, 31, 32, 68, 115, 173, 190

    Abbey Necessarium or Reredorter: 26, 89, 91

    Abbey Refectory: 16, 18, 21-23, 26, 63, 64, 91, 177, 178, 180, 196

    Abbey Transepts: 11, 16, 18, 21, 23, 25, 27-29, 32, 63, 68, 72, 73

    Abbey Treasury: 23, 25

Abbey Reading: 1-33, 35, 36, 42, 49, 56, 58, 60-63, 65-68, 71, 73, 75, 77-79, 81-84, 86, 88-95, 97-99, 101, 103-105, 109, 111, 115, 116, 120, 124-127, 134, 139, 142, 147, 148, 151, 156, 157, 160-162, 164, 165, 167-170, 172, 173, 176-178, 180-185, 188, 190-192

Abbey Seal: 5, 29

Abbey Stone (The Reading Abbey Stone): 22, *66*, 109, 192, 193

Albury, W: 121

Amyce, Roger: 103, 104, 189

Annesley (Francis and Martin): 142, 143,

Armed Association: see Berkshire Militia

Aston, Sir Arthur: 9-12, 30, 39

Bands and the Bandstand: 64, 142, 143, 153, 161, 167, 172, 176

Benyon, J H: 175

READING'S ABBEY QUARTER

Berkshire Chronicle: 28, 63, 140, 158, 196, 199, 201, 202, 203, 204, 205

Berkshire Militia and Militia: 45, 48, 52, 142-144, 146

Ball, George: 46

Billings, Richard: 46

Blagrave: 7, 14, 15, 84, 104, 116, 119, 132-134, 136, 142, 152, 164, 185

Blake, Robert. (also Blake's Bridge): 116, 157, 165

Blandy: 117, 119, 121, 122, 124, 134

Board of Health (Reading): 72, 76, 84, 85, 86, 118, 119, 133, 160, 162, 164, 165, 166. 206

Borstal: *51*, 57, 58

Booth, General Evangeline: 167

Boswell Henry: 16, 22, 27, 32

Boswell, Abraham: 53

Bowland, The Rev Mr. Francis: 65, 66, 132

Brettingham, Robert Furze: 35, 43

British Dairy Institute: 139

Canal: 26, 89, 147, 157

Chapel of the Resurrection: 17, 65, 72, 132

Cheney, J: 116. See also St Lawrence's Church, 117-118

Childs, William: 137, 138

Civil War: 1, 9-10, 18, 29-32, 39, 61, 75, 82, 83, 91, 92, 105, 107, 128, 151, 183
    Bodleian map, 10

Clacy, John Berry: 48,100

Clarges, Sir Thomas: 13, 14

Commonwealth Survey of 1650: 12-15

Compter Gate, Prison and House: 1, 7, 40, 41, 45, 99, 104, 106, 115, 116, 117, 182

Conway, General: 15

County Gaol: (See Gaol)

Court of Augmentation: 6,128

Cowslade family see also Smart.

Cowslade Manuscript: 66

Cowslade, Marianna Frederica; 69

Cromwell, Thomas: 2, 5, 103, 189

INDEX

Cubitt, William: 44, 46

Dalby, John: 14

Darter, William: 151, 154

Davis (Head Gardener of the Forbury): 161-163, 169

Dissolution of the Monasteries: 1, 2, 5, 20, 23, 29, 32, 37, 38, 79, 92, 103, 116, 127, 134, 147, 152, 156, 166, 168, 183, 189, 201

Earley Charity: 17, 196

Eastaff, Thomas: 42, 45

Edward the Confessor: 93

Edward IV: 127, 189, 196

Edward VI: 5, 6, 103, 195, 196

Elizabeth I: 1, 3, 6, 7, 195

Englefield, Sir Francis: 6,17

Englefield, Sir Henry: 17-19, 22, 25, 27-31

Execution and the Death Penalty: 2-4, 6, 28, 43, 52, 54, 55, 58, 66

Extension College: see University.

Eynon, John: 2, 3

'Father' Willis organ: 130, 135,

Fairs: 5-7, 13, 14, 147, 148, 152-155, 164, 165, 167

Ferrey, Benjamin: 118

Field, The Rev John: 47, 54,

Finch's Buildings: 17

Forbury Hill: 10, 11, 28, 31, 73, 82, 83, 105, 106, 142, 147, 148, 150-153, 155, 159-164, 167, 168, 172, 177, 205

Forbury, The: 1, 3-11, 13-15, 18, 19, 25, 28, 35, 40, 43, 45, 50, 64, 66, 73, 75, 77, 79, 81, 82-85, 87, 97, 99, 101, 104-113, 115, 116, 118, 121, 128, 132-134, 139, 141-144, 146-157, 159-162, 164, *166*-169, 171-174, 176, 177, 180-182, 186, 191, 192, 196, 198, 199, 210

Frink, Elizabeth: 22

Gaol: Bridewell; 34, 35, 37, 39, 40, 43, 45, 46, 48, 127

Gaol, County: 34, 35, 37, 39, 40, 42, 43, 45, 60, 150.

Great Ditch: 9, 10, 13, 30, 31

Godfrey, R: 16

Grammar School: 79, 83, 118, 121, 127, 130, 133, 134, 136, 138, 147, 148, 153, 203

Grey, William: 103, 104

The Green: 105-107, 113, 149, 150, 152, 153, 155

Greyfriars: 35, 37-40, 45, 46, 48, 66, 127, 128, 155, 195, 197

Gunston, Lelsey: 175

Hackett, Edward: 44, 53

Havell: *16, 131*

Henry I: 19, 29, 58, 63, 64, 115, 173, 174, 190, 196, 203

    Forbury Memorial Cross: 19, 173

    Commemorative Tablets: 173, 174

Henry VIII: 1, 2, 5, 6, 37, 139, 188, 192, 203

Hill, Sir Arthur: 136

Hole, The: 40, 41, 117

Holy Brook: 10, 12, 26, 89, 91-93, 95, 104, 147, 151, 182, 184, 185

Hore, John: 157

Hospitium: see Abbey Hospitium

House of Correction: see County Gaol above

Howard, John: 34, 39, 43

Hugh Faringdon, (Abbot Hugh Cook): 2-5,

Hurry, Dr Jamieson: 91, 107, 108, 116, 128, 173, 174, 188, 195, 196

Hynde, George: 6

IDR (Inner Distribution Road): 110-112, 180, 181

Irish: 52, 56, 57, 143

Kennet (River/Canal): 10, 11, 16, 26, 35, 46, 49, 64, 89, 91, 92, 104, 110, 115, 127, 147, 157,159, 165, 206

Kenneth Major, J: 95, 200

Kerry, J: 115, 151, 202

Knight. George: 35, 43

Knollys, Richard and John, 12, 168

Lainson, Thomas: 135

Leguay, Rev: 145

Loader, Mr: 176

INDEX

Longuet, François: 65, 132, 144, 145, 205

MEPC (Metropolitan Estates & Property Corporation); 180, 181

Mackinder, Halford: 137, 138, 204

Maiwand and Maiwand Lion: 110, 121, 170, 171, 175, 177

Man, John: 39, 43, 61, 92, 105, 106, 149

Marten, Henry: 9, 39

Mary Tudor: 5, 6, 103, 115,

May, William Charles: 135

Memorial Cross: see Henry I

Mill: see Abbey Mill

Militia: see Berkshire Militia

Moffat, William Bonython: 48

Morris, Joseph: 73, 119

Municipal Buildings: 119, 121, 124, 132, 135, 136, 138, 177, 180, 185, 186, See also Museum (Reading), School of Art, Reading Extension College

Museum (Reading): 66, 137, 138, 180, 181, 196, 202, 206

Pageant House: 112, 113

Palmer, William: 167

Paving Act: 128, 149, 152

Penison, William: 5

Pentonville Prison: 47, 52

People's Pantry: 119

Phippen: 169, 176

Pimker, Charles: 135

Plummery: 1, 79, 147, 152, 181

Potts, Trooper Alfred William Owen: 186-188

Poulton, Charles; 129, 130, 135

Prison: see Gaol above

Prudential (The): 110-112, 185

Pugin, AWN: 52, 67-72, 76

Queen Victoria: see Victoria

211

READING'S ABBEY QUARTER

Railway: 66, 69, 75, 77, 108, 110, 118, 132, 133, 134, 147, 149, 151, 152, 155, 156, 158, 159, 161, 163, 164, 206

Ravenscroft, FWB: 120, 173

Reading Abbey Stone: see Abbey Stone.

Reading Library: 69, 73, 74, 80, 81, 83, 88, 93, 118, 122, 138, 167, 171, 182-186, 195

Reading Civic Society: 180

Reading Extension College: see University

Reading University: see University

Reading Gaol: see Gaol above

Reading Mercury: 35, 66, 67, 128, 149, 158, 159, 177

Reading Grammar School: See Grammar School

Reading School of Art: 135, 136, 138

Reading Volunteers: 142-144, 146 see also Berkshire Militia

Rennie, John: 157

Rising Sun Public House: 116, 132

Royal Berkshire Hospital: 119

Royal Charters: 5-7, 14, 124, 138, 164, 195, 203

Royal Seed Establishment: 107, 108, 152

Rugge John: 2, 3

Russian (Sebastopol) Gun: 163, 167

Sarcophagus: 28, 190

Saxon: 113, 115, 151, 183, 191, 202

Schuts, Augustus: 46

Scott, Sir George Gilbert: 48, 49, 51-53, 59, 61, 86, 87, 88, 200

Seymour, Edward, Duke of Somerset: 5-7, 103

Shades, The: 41

Shire Hall: 99, 101-103, 109, 111, 180, 186

Siege of Reading: 9, 30, (see also Civil War)

Simonds: 107, 121, 132 153, 171,

Slade, Cecil: 12, 13, 18, 19, 30, 31, 36, 37, 81-83, 91, 94, 99, 128, 166, 179, 183, 196, 197, 207

Smart - Cowslade Family: 66, 69, 70, 72, 77, 128, 158, 198

INDEX

Solitary, Silent and Separate Systems: 35, 47 52, 54

Soundy: 95, 182 see also Abbey Mill

Speed, John: 7, 8, 29, 105, 183, 195

Spicer, John: 134

St Giles' Church: 3, 4, 159

St. James' Church: 11, 17-19, 21, 22, 27, 30, 32, 36, 43, 51, 62, 63-70, 72, 74, 75, 77, 115, 118, 132, 147, 159, 160, 162, 172, 179, 188, 190, 191, 196

St Lawrence's Church and grounds: 1, 3, 6, 7, 12, *16,* 32, 38, *40,* 41, 54, 97, 99, 101, 104, 106, 110, 111, 115-120, *124,* 126, 127, 129, 132, *133,* 134, 136, 141, 142, 147, 150, 151, 159, 177, 202

St Mary's Minster: 3, 34, 80, 145, 146, 159, 171

Stables: 5, 8, 13, 93, 105, 116, 128, 182-184

Stallwood, Slingsby: 73, 137-139, 204

Stanshaw, Robert: 37

Stukeley, William: 15, 22, 23

Surveys:

    Board of Health: 72, 76, 84-86, 118, 119, 133, 160, 162, 164-166, 207

    Commonwealth Survey 1850: 12, 105, 107

    Englefield, Sir Henry; 18, 19, 22, 25, 27, 28, 30, also see Sir Henry Englefield

    Ordnance Survey 1879: 166

Sutton: 101, 107-109, 112, 132, 136, 147, 152, 161

Tablet, The: 67, 71

Taunt, Henry: 74, 121, 169

Thomas, John Harvard: 175

Tomkins, Charles: 16, 21, 23, 25, 29, 75, 79-81

Tyrie, David: 54

University (Extension College): 136-141, 186, 205

Vachell, Sir Thomas: 5, 190

Valpy, Dr. Richard: 79, 130, 131, 134, 136, 138, 147, 152, 153

Vansittart: 14, 15, 28, 84, 142

Vastern Lane or Street: 65, 72, 118, 132, 136, 159, 200, 203, 205

Victoria (Queen): 108, 121, 155, 174

READING'S ABBEY QUARTER

Victoria Gate: 174, 175

Victoria Hall: 135

Villeneuve, Admiral: 145

Vines, Joshua: 150

War Memorials:

    Afghan War see Maiwand: 173

    1914 -1918 War Memorial: 175

    Trooper Potts: 186, 187, 209

Waterhouse, Alfred: 121, 122, 125, 130, 135, 136, 204

Wheble, James (and Wheble family): 22, 63-70, 77, 84, 142, 160, 162, 163, 207

Wilde, Oscar: 34, 56

Woodman, W H: 119, 135, 203

Yeomanry: 146, 186, 187 see also Berkshire Militia

ACKNOWLEDGMENTS

First of all I should like to thank the staff of Reading Library, most especially Ann Smith, who have kindly allowed me to use their resources and been so patient with some of my more obscure enquiries over the last three years. I hope the book will encourage readers to use the Library and its website to find out more about Reading's rich and varied history.

Special recognition should be given to David Cliffe, whose expertise and unstinting work, over so many years in the Library, have resulted in the extensive catalogue of material now available to the public.

I should also like to thank my wife, Lindsay Mullaney, who not only checked, read and corrected the proofs but who has been an integral part of the research over the years taken to produce this work.

My son John R Mullaney, a Fellow of the Society of Architectural Illustration, very kindly drew the detailed illustration of the Abbey. This appears, either in part or in whole, throughout the book.* We spent many hours finding similar Norman Romanesque religious houses built to the Cluniac formula. We decided to offer the reader a view, as an alternative to those found in other works, of what the Abbey may have looked like, especially if there were no towers at its western end. Until further archaeology is carried out there is no way of creating a definitive picture of what was, for many centuries, one of the most glorious buildings in England.

John R Mullaney's illustration appears, in whole or in part, on pages 20, 24, 62, 78, 90, 97, 178, and 182. The map on page 4 is also by him.

Scallop Shell Press

Ever since the Middle Ages the scallop shell has been the symbol of those going on pilgrimage to the shrine of St James in Compostela, Spain.

The shell became a metaphor for the journey, the grooves representing the many ways of arriving at one's destination. At a practical level the shell was also useful for scooping up water to drink or food to eat.

Today the pilgrimage is even more popular than ever as people of all faiths, and none, seek a meaning for their journey through life.

Scallop Shell Press aims to publish works which, like the grooves of the shell, will offer the modern pilgrim stories of our shared humanity and help readers arrive at their own meaningful interpretations of life. We hope that our books will be shells within whose covers readers will find an intellectual and spiritual source of sustenance for their own personal pilgrimages.

Other published titles

Reformation, Revolution and Rebirth,	John Mullaney and Lindsay Mullaney
Catholic Reading, A Pilgrimage Trail,	edited by J and L Mullaney
Battle Lines,	Lya Tuner
The Cowslade Manuscript,	edited by Lindsay Mullaney
Watercolours and Weevils,	Mary Colbeck
The Stained Glass of St James' Church Reading,	John Mullaney
The Timms Family of Reading and London,	Katie Amos

If you would like to find out more about Scallop Shell Press visit our website

www.Scallopshellpress.co.uk